Inheritance in Public Policy

Inheritance in Public Policy:
Change without Choice in Britain

Richard Rose and Phillip L. Davies

Yale University Press   New Haven and London

Published with assistance from the foundation
established in memory of Philip Hamilton
McMillan of the Class of 1894, Yale College.

Set in Times Roman type by Keystone Typesetting,
Inc., Orwigsburg, Pennsylvania.
Printed in the United States of America by
Vail-Ballou Press, Binghamton, New York.

Rose, Richard, 1933–
    Inheritance in public policy : change without
choice in Britain / Richard Rose and
Phillip L. Davies.
        p.   cm.
    Includes bibliographical references and index.
    ISBN 0–300–05877–2
    1. Great Britain—Politics and government—
1945–   . 2. Policy sciences.   I. Davies,
Phillip L.   II. Title.
JN309 IN PROCESS
320.941—dc20   93-49088
                                          CIP

A catalogue record for this book is available from
the British Library.
The paper in this book meets the guidelines for
permanence and durability of the Committee on
Production Guidelines for Book Longevity of the
Council on Library Resources.

10   9   8   7   6   5   4   3   2   1

Dedicated to Aaron Wildavsky,
1930–1993
Scholar. Friend. Mensch.

Contents

Tables and Figures

Tables

Figures

Acknowledgments

Tracing the origins of a book about inheritance in public policy is as difficult as researching a family tree. For the senior author, the original impetus was a humanistic education at Johns Hopkins University. The significance of inheritance and of time have been major themes from the writings of Aeschylus to Proust. Whereas they emphasized the importance of ideas, this book concerns material phenomena, the inherited commitments of government. Quantitative data is necessary but not sufficient to understand these commitments. Understanding requires a theoretical framework that connects past and present.

The stimulus for this book came from a five-year program on the growth of government, sponsored by the British Economic and Social Research Council (ESRC). It showed the dangers of the reductionist practice of thinking about government in aggregate and the need to examine specific programs of government. To test whether changes in organizations affected changes in expenditure, we did an intensive study of two British government departments, published in the *European Journal of Political Research* (Davies and Rose, 1988).

The present book is the result of a subsequent ESRC-financed investigation of continuity, innovation, and termination in public policy (EOO 23 2247), in which the second-named author served for two years as a research officer. We compiled a comprehensive data base identifying and costing the hundreds of programs of British government for nearly half a century since 1945, the most long-term detailed data about continuity and change in public policy available for any advanced industrial nation.

In developing the themes of this book, seminar papers were presented at the Wissenschaftszentrum Berlin, the University of Toronto, the University of Wisconsin–Madison, and at the founding meeting of the Society for the Advancement of Socio-Economics at the Harvard Business School. The ideas that are the core of this book were first set out in an article in the *Journal of Theoretical Politics* (Rose, 1990).

We particularly appreciate the patient work of Ms. Anne Shaw, who entered a vast quantity of data into a computer while working from extremely bulky and awkward volumes of many years of Appropriation Accounts of Her Majesty's Stationery Office.

Richard Rose   Phillip L. Davies

No decade in the history of politics, religion, technology, painting, poetry and what not ever contains its own explanation. In order to understand the religious events from 1520 to 1530 or the political events from 1790 to 1800, or the developments in painting from 1900 to 1910, you must survey a period of much wider span. Not to do so is the hallmark of dilettantism.

Joseph A. Schumpeter

1 Rooted in Time

In the long run we are all dead, said J. M. Keynes.

No, Maynard, in the long run each of us is dead, replied his fellow Cambridge economist, Joan Robinson.

Policymakers are heirs before they are choosers. Upon taking office in government, an individual must take an oath to uphold the laws of the land. The statute book consists of laws made by past generations yet binding upon each new incumbent. For the moment, at least, a policymaker must accept the legacy of past administrations—and all the constraints that go with it. Policymakers are thus rooted in time.

An inheritance is not chosen; it is given by history. Past events and past choices create the situation to which policymakers are heirs. Offered a choice between governing an oil-rich nation or a country without natural resources, every policymaker would choose a rich country; however, nature does not offer politicians such a fortuitous choice. Nor would a politician choose to be responsible for a situation like the enduring conflict between Protestants and Catholics in Northern Ireland. Yet every British prime minister must accept as part of his or her inheritance an unresolved armed conflict in Northern Ireland that began in 1912 and is in lineal descent from wars of the seventeenth century.

The familiar maxim *to govern is to choose* is reductionist in the extreme. It implies that government is carried out by individual decisionmakers who have as much freedom of choice as an individual in a shopping mall trying to decide whether to have a pizza or an ice cream cone, and then free to decide what kind of pizza or ice cream to have. The statutory commitments of a newly installed official are not a menu specifying what an individual might choose but a description of what a policymaker is committed to do. Like it or not, each new arrival in office must recognize that *to govern is to inherit*.

Inheritors do not choose; they accept. Even though the legacy of the past may not be desirable, it must be accepted because it is impossible to do otherwise. As Michael Oakeshott (1951: 10) has noted, "To try to do something which is inherently impossible is always a corrupting enterprise." The inheritance of the past is imposed upon the present by institutions that maintain policies from one administration to another. Laws remain on the statute book indefinitely. During their time in office, policymakers do not have the time to read, let alone react to, all the laws that they have inherited; nor is it necessary to do so, for public institutions and public employees are at hand to mobilize the money and resources needed to deliver inherited programs. Large bureaucratic organizations do not wait on the choices of the government of the day. Laws, institutions, and public employees propel inherited programs forward with the force of political inertia.

The commitments of government are not the choices of a single decisionmaker, as in highly abstract economic models of behavior, nor are they the sum of the ephemeral preferences of the leaders of the party that has emerged victorious at the last election, or of voters on the winning side. Government is a complex of hundreds of departments, bureaus, and agencies, each with a legacy of commitments that started to accumulate long before the term of office of a transient political head.

The exchange between two intellectual giants in a Cambridge seminar sixty years ago encapsulates the contrast between inheritance and choice. As a hedonist, John Maynard Keynes believed in the pursuit of pleasure in the present and wanted economics to promote current material wellbeing. When one of his proposals for improving short-term conditions was challenged as having harmful consequences in the long run, he dismissed this with the familiar epigram, "In the long run we are all dead." The retort by a fellow Cambridge economist, Joan Robinson, is often forgotten. She stressed that although Keynes's remark was true of individuals, it was not true of society as a whole, nor was it true of continuing collective organizations such as government.

Just because each of us dies, it does not follow that present actions are without consequences for the future. Although each individual passes from the scene—and four years is a long time in office for a policymaker—choices made today become part of the inheritance of future governments and society.

The Priority of Inheritance

"First things first" is an ambiguous maxim, for it begs the question: What comes first? An individual decisionmaker is likely to give priority to those matters that he or she can influence through current choices. But a social scientist seeking to understand the causes of current problems should give priority to what comes first in time, and the past always comes before the present.

Inheritance is a concept with relevance in many fields of study. In biology, it is central to genetics. Plants do not make choices; they are the result of a genetic process in which characteristics—whether strengthening, debilitating, or neutral—are transmitted from one generation to the next through inheritance. In literature, inheritance can be a boon, if an unexpected legacy resolves the problems of a novel's protagonist. Or it can mean doom, as in Greek tragedies. Lawyers deal with inheritance as part of the law of probate, which concerns the transmission of a deceased individual's assets to survivors and future posterity. The author of a will makes choices about the disposal of his or her estate. A will is also the means by which these choices are enforced on others after a person is no longer alive and, in the case of trusts, for decades after death. Prospective heirs cannot choose how much of an estate they are to receive; this choice is made by the deceased. Nor can recipients choose the amount of wealth in an estate or its liabilities. An individual's estate normally has a positive cash value; a newly elected government, however, invariably inherits a substantial debt from past public expenditure.

Historians study the importance of the past, but few historians today argue that the past determines what happens in the present. One reason is that many historians concentrate upon centuries and civilizations remote from contemporary events. Another is that historians are skeptical about formulating "laws" predicting what must happen. They usually deal with a particular configuration of events, emphasizing the contingency or uniqueness of causation. When history is seen as an evolutionary process, the emphasis is on change, and this implies the possibility of change occurring as a consequence of choice.

Inheritance is a process that links the past with the present. As Joseph Schumpeter (1946: 3f) has succinctly observed, the present cannot contain its own explanation; what has happened in the less or more distant past is necessary for understanding the present. Furthermore, what has happened in the past constrains current choices. Policymakers are not confronted with a blank sheet of paper on which to inscribe their preferences; choice is always constrained. The "bounded rationality" of which Herbert Simon (1957) writes is principally bounded by what is inherited from the past. In a situation constrained by inheritance, an action is rational if it is explicable: "Rationality makes sense of what has been, not what will be" (Weick, qtd. Majone, 1989: 33).

Policymakers spend far more time living with the consequences of inherited commitments than with making choices that reflect their own initiatives. Much of a policymaker's time in office is spent learning to understand programs and problems left by their predecessors. A study of federal bureau chiefs found that they spent very little time making decisions. "Even the youngest of the bureaus has a history with which the administrator has to come to terms. The slate not only was not clean; in all cases it was already quite full when the chief came to office" (Kaufman, 1981: 91). Confronted with an issue, a policymaker needs to ask: "What's the story; how did we get in the mess we are in?" Once this is understood, the question is: "What do we do next?" Understanding the past causes of present concerns is necessary to identify weaknesses in existing programs and to guard against facile assumptions about policies. It also "provides the person at the top some protection against being sold a solution designed for a different problem" (Neustadt and May, 1986: 38).

Whereas an inheritance is a given that policymakers must accept, a *choice* is a conscious decision of an individual in favor of one alternative rather than others. A choice differs from routine behavior in that alternatives are at hand to which conscious consideration is given. Since politics is about the articulation of conflicting views about what government ought to do, there is inevitably controversy about the choices of policymakers.

Inheritance does not preclude choice. Initially, the legacy that a new administration receives constitutes the totality of the programs for which it is responsible. However, during its term of office an administration has some scope for choice. It can introduce new programs and make fresh choices in response to unexpected or unprecedented situations; it can amend or repeal inherited programs; and make marginal adjustments in spending during the annual budget cycle. Because political choices are the object of visible conflicts, the political spotlight focuses upon the choices of the government of the day, however small they may be in comparison with commitments inherited from the past.

Choices reflect present political pressures and calculations. The inheritance from the past is taken as a given. Concern with the future is usually limited too. Harold Wilson, a long-serving British prime minister, had as his motto, "A week is a long time in politics." The farthest ahead that a politician may calculate is next week, next month, or the date of the next election, which is always psychologically near. Non-elected civil servants may have a longer time horizon, but the more closely they are involved in policymaking with politicians, the more likely the time horizon of civil servants is to be foreshortened.

Choice is a central concept in many social sciences, from mathematical decision theory to experimental psychology and business management. Max Weber's (1922) classic analysis of social action identified four motives for choice: an instrumental calculation of expected benefits; pursuit of an ultimate value independent of rational calculation; emotions; and traditional habits. An interdisciplinary guide to the theory of choice starts with the statement, "We experience life as a series of choices, large and small" (Heap et al., 1992: vii). Ringen's (1987) study of the growth of welfare state policies declares, "In one sense, politics are necessarily under perfect control. Political decisions do not make themselves but are always the result of choices that politicians make" (70).

An often cited definition of politics by David Easton is framed in terms of choice: "the authoritative allocation of values for a society" (1965a: 50). Decisionmaking studies of political scientists define choice as "an identifiable political act that resolves a conflict about what to do in a given context" (Parry and Morriss, 1974: 324; see also Dahl, 1961). Incrementalist theories of budgeting focus on marginal choices in the annual budget cycle. Studies of Congress examine the choices made by individual members voting in subcommittees, committees, or in the full House or Senate. A choice between competing parties is a defining attribute of democracy; the first survey study of voting behavior was called *The People's Choice* (Lazarsfeld et al., 1944).

Economics analyzes the choices of individuals when confronted with the problem of "the allocation of scarce resources which have alternative uses" (Robbins, 1935). This approach is increasingly applied to social activities remote from the marketplace (e.g., Becker, 1976). Public choice is defined as "the economic study of nonmarket decisionmaking. . . . The basic behavioral postulate of public choice, as for economics, is that man is an egoistic, rational utility maximizer" (Mueller, 1989: 1f). Even when critics of this paradigm attempt to introduce another dimension, attention is still focused upon individual choice, for example, between egoistic and non-egoistic behavior (cf. Sen, 1977; Etzioni, 1988).

Choice focuses upon concrete events from a "decisionist" perspective; the object of analysis is "a limited number of political actors engaged in making calculated choices among clearly conceived alternatives" (Shklar, 1964: 13f). The group can be members of the White House staff, a congressional committee, or the members of a British Cabinet. From such a perspective, the important assumptions are that everyone influencing a choice is active at the time a decision is made, they have real alternatives, consequences can be and are calculated, and the group has the authority to commit government. As these conditions are often not met, "decision theory does not apply to decisionmaking in general but only to choice situations of a rather special type." Since policymaking is a dialectical process involving many participants pursuing conflicting goals, some social scientists write about programs emerging more or less accidentally from a "garbage can" (Cohen et al., 1972).

Theories of choice tend to confuse the preferences of individual politicians with the actions of a formal organization. Even when the issue addressed is a collective choice, the problem is often defined simply as that of summing individual preferences through procedures that may or may not produce consistent results (see, e.g., Arrow, 1951; Black, 1958). But to ignore the fact that government is a set of collective institutions rather than an aggregate of individuals is to commit the "individualist fallacy," projecting assumptions and inferences about individuals to a larger collective unit of analysis, formal organizations (Scheuch, 1968: 158–64; see also Kirman, 1989: 126ff). The fallacy is compounded if choices taken by individuals at one point in time, such as at an election, are confused with the consequences of collective choices taken across many decades or generations.

Strictly speaking, it is impossible to have a behavioral theory of *government,* for government is an impersonal organization. The statement of intentions of an individual politician, whether a president or prime minister, or a single member of a legislature, cannot be put into effect in the same way that each individual in a supermarket can immediately act on his or her preferences. The preferences of individuals or political parties only become effective if they are made legally binding and implemented by government. As M. Morishima (1984) notes, even if choices of governors could identify an optimal equilibrium, "should it lack the institutional backing to realize it, then that solution will amount to no more than a utopian state of affairs."

Public policy is an institutional commitment. Commitments of office exist before individuals are elected. Office confers authority upon the actions of an individual who is its temporary incumbent, but office also imposes the constraints of inherited obligations. Changes in public programs cannot be made by an exercise of individual will, as in Dahl's (1957) classic formulation of power as the capacity of individual A to make individual B do what B would not otherwise do. Because policies are commitments of government, influence must be exercised within and between organizations, with all this implies in terms of complexity, making the exercise of influence doubly remote from individuals.

Whereas individuals die, government continues. In English, the word *government* confuses what is permanent with what is transient. By contrast, in most European countries there is a clear distinction between the durable commitments of the state, as against the views of the government of the day, consisting of the party and politicians victorious at the last election. The state is a permanent body; it pays social security benefits, maintains military defense, and builds highways. Such policies are part of the legacy received by each new set of officeholders. In British constitutional usage, the idea of the state is usually represented by the Crown; it is the duty of Her Majesty's Government to see that the Crown's business is carried on. By contrast, the government of the day has a limited term of office, and individuals appointed to decisionmaking positions can reckon to hold a particular office for only about two years. Here, the distinction between the permanent state and transient policymakers will be paralleled by calling the former the government, and the latter the government of the day or the administration.

Historical Time before Logical Time

Public policy is rooted in historical time, a fact that is critical for understanding the inheritance of public policy. Joan Robinson (1979: 286) has described thus the difference between historical time and time in the abstract: "Logical time can be traced from left to right on the surface of a blackboard. Historical time moves from the dark past behind it into the unknown future in front."

Time in the Abstract

Logical time specifies a sequence of events. Causes precede effects; the present is caused by past events; and the future exists as the consequences of present choices become manifest. In a dynamic model, time does not have a number but a letter: t. From time t one can trace determinants of present circumstances by moving leftwards on the blackboard to time $t - x$, or one can move to the right to time $t + y$ in order to demonstrate the future consequence of present circumstances. The result is coherent, integrating determinants in a single, concise cause-and-effect model.

Since dynamic models of cause and effect can be projected into the future, they can be used to simulate future events or possible alternative consequences of different choices in time $t + y$. For example, a model can show the effects of different choices for economic growth. Analytically, the procedure is simple. Given a model of the determinants of economic growth, logical calculations can be made to indicate the positive or negative effect upon growth of making different policy choices. However, a logical model of change achieves clarity at the expense of omitting information about historical context. At the extreme, calculations in the logic of neoclassical economics are undertaken without regard to whether they are consistent with empirical observations, or even whether axiomatic theorems about choice should be rejected if their predictions are falsified (cf. Kaldor, 1972: 1237f).

Historians intentionally leave loose ends in a discussion of the causes; uncertainties reflect the indeterminacies of the process of historical change, which is conceived as a process of collective action rather than as a consequence of individual choice. Political science has its roots in studying institutions in historical time, but economics is concerned with logical time, that is, time in the abstract. This accounts for Alfred Marshall's comment that time is at "the centre of the chief difficulty of almost every economic problem" (qtd. Currie and Steedman, 1990: 1), for most major changes in macroeconomic structure and microeconomic behavior cannot be understood outside their historical context.

There is a fundamental difficulty in the use of logical models to evaluate choice: *time $t + y$ never arrives, because it is outside historical time*. The generality achieved by abstraction is purchased by a loss in specificity. When Schumpeter said that to understand the French Revolution we needed to examine the period before 1790 and to understand cubism we had to understand developments in late nineteenth-century painting, he was emphasizing a historical as well as a logical point: causes are not only logically antecedent but also specific to a particular period. A model that treated 1790, 1900, and 1990 as equivalent because each could be labeled time t would be abstract and academic in the pejorative sense.

There is inevitably a tradeoff between theoretical generality and realism in studies of society. Logical theories are often clear and consistent in explaining a sequence of hypothesized events or stylized facts, but they achieve clarity and coherence at a high cost, for they cannot be applied to concrete historical situations. It is fair to note that they are not intended to apply to the world as it actually is. But a science of policymaking that is so pure that it lacks applicability is not a science as that term is understood in engineering, which uses science as a foundation for deriving measures that can be applied in the everyday world (Simon, 1969). In reflecting on the theme of "history versus equilibrium," Joan Robinson (1979: 58) goes further: "The lack of a comprehensible treatment of historical time . . . makes the theoretical apparatus offered in neo-classical textbooks useless for the analysis of contemporary problems."

Real Time in Real Societies

Anyone concerned with studying societies rather than logic has reason to ground analysis in historical time. To reject thinking in abstract time does not mean the rejection of logic but testing abstract models by applicability to concrete phenomena. As the Nobel laureate Robert Solow (1985: 328) has argued, the "true function of analytical economics . . . is likely to be a collection of models contingent on society's circumstances—on the historical context, you might say."

An empirically meaningful theory of public policy must recognize real time as well as time in the abstract. History imposes a hard constraint on choice. The starting point for a decisionmaker is the past; it is known, and its consequences in the present are inescapable. As G. L. S. Shackle (1966: ix) emphasizes, "Among what, then, are men free to choose? Not among situations or events which exist or occur in some objective reality, for when something is actual the time is too late for choosing something else." To study the logic of choice without regard to historical context is to ignore the inheritance that constrains choice.

In public policy the argument for thinking in terms of historical time is overwhelming, for a specific inheritance is the starting point for each policymaker. Past commitments cannot be avoided by the government of the day, for they are embedded in public laws and public institutions, and carried out by public employees. The budget is the most familiar summary statement of the legacy of the past. A newly elected administration does not ask how much it would like to spend on public policies. Instead, it is confronted with a budget identifying how much it is already spending on inherited commitments and how much it must spend next year to meet its legacy of obligations.

The path of a public program depends upon what previous governments have done. A newly installed administration may be able to influence current events, but it cannot undo what previous administrations have willed it. The particular path reflects the choice or choices of past policymakers. In a historical sense, there was once scope for choice; choices could be made casually or after prolonged and careful calculation. Even if past choices once appeared optimal, the circumstances that led to them gradually alter. Unforeseen consequences of unanticipated changes can make past choices unacceptable. Yet the inheritance remains in effect insofar as policymakers are, in Brian Arthur's (1989: 116) phrase, "locked in by historical events." The past is irreversible; even the act of rejecting the past is a recognition of its present significance. Present choices may alter what happens in future but what has gone before is, for the moment, inescapable.

The commitments that a new administration inherits are not without cause; they are the consequence of past choices. Every commitment can be traced for generations through the statute book, legislative debates, and administrative histories. To learn why two leaders who professed to be against the welfare state—Ronald Reagan and Margaret Thatcher—presided over administrations spending hundreds of billions on social programs one must look to history, not choice. Both the Reagan administration and the Thatcher government were committed by choices made by predecessors that institutionalized social benefits.

Whereas choices are actions of the present, summing up past influences and expectations of the future in a single moment of decision, inheritance is the work of generations. The transformation of an inheritance cannot occur instantly, or predictably. Because inheritance comes before choice, the historical process is more important than a single moment of choice.

Political Advantages and Disadvantages of Inheritance

The consequences of inheritance are in themselves neither good nor bad; they are merely inescapable. An incoming administration will approve much that it inherits. It is convenient, both managerially and politically, to claim credit for choices inherited from predecessors. For example, the Conservative government of John Major may associate itself with Winston Churchill, even though Major was only two years old at the end of World War II. The British Labour party claims credit for the national health service introduced by the 1945–51 Labour government even though its leader, John Smith, was only ten years old when it was enacted. The politician who appears on television opening a new highway will not be the person who initially approved the highway plan. "Credit-claiming" (or, as the historian might say, "credit-stealing") is a painless and congenial way for politicians to court voters (cf. Mayhew, 1974).

Voters and pressure groups satisfied with the status quo will welcome a government's lack of room for maneuver, for this assures a continuance of benefits, whether a program is assured an annually recurrent appropriation of public funds, or the absence of government action shows that the forces that have prevented predecessors from acting remain in place. Political inertia guarantees a high degree of predictability and continuity in such fields as social security and health programs, independent of the party in office (cf. Rose, 1984: chapter 7).

During its term of office, the government of the day does have some scope for choice. Altering public expenditure by a few billion allows it to claim that it is doing something, even though alterations may be only a few percent of the budget that it inherited. A politician introducing a new law can claim credit for it, even though it is only one law among thousands on the statute book. Inherited programs that run by routine can be dismissed as of no political consequence. Reducing political attention to the choices of the government of the day makes its concerns, however limited, the primary object of political debate.

Every administration is able to make some choices that it leaves as a legacy to its successors. The extent of its impact reflects many influences, including the length of time that it is in office. The 1980s was unusual in that both Britain and the United States had political leaders with strong ideological goals and long periods in office to put their views into effect. Ronald Reagan was the first president in a generation to serve two full terms, and Margaret Thatcher was the longest-serving British prime minister of the century. Such durability, however, is atypical. Since World War II, presidents have served an average of five years in office, and in the twentieth century British prime ministers have on average served less than four consecutive years in office.

The bad news for politicians is that a new administration also inherits some things that it dislikes but is powerless to reject. Technically, the calculation of inherited spending commitments is not difficult; however politically, inheritance creates difficulties for policymakers because it leaves them with little scope for choice. For example, when George Bush entered the White House in 1989 he did not inherit the same economy as had Ronald Reagan eight years earlier. Instead, he inherited a rising budget deficit. Four years later Bill Clinton replaced George Bush and, because of the compounding of inherited commitments, inherited an even bigger deficit.

Building Bridges between the Past and Future

The inheritance of the past is not a dead hand; it is the starting point for action by the current administration. The more deeply rooted present commitments are in the past, the greater the constraints on present choice. To recognize the persistence of the past is not, however, to espouse historical determinism. The proper question to ask is: Under what circumstances and to what extent do programs persist? Identifying the extent of persistence also identifies the boundaries of present choice.

The choices of the government of the day are added to the bequest that it leaves to future governments. As its choices become constraints inherited by successive administrations, the government of the day may influence the future more than it influences the present. Thus, the process of inheritance constitutes a bridge between the past and the future. Just as the past constrains the present, so present choice can influence future events. The consequences of choice do not disappear when those responsible leave office; they continue with the force of political inertia until stopped by an equal and opposite force. However, the longer a program endures in the legacy of public policy, the more unpredictable are its effects. For example, when Members of Parliament voted for a bill introducing old age pensions for the elderly in 1908, they could not have foreseen the consequences it would have in 1948, let alone 1998. Similarly, when the Roosevelt administration introduced social security in the United States in 1937, the program was intended to help the elderly poor. Half a century later, it pays benefits to older people who usually are not poor and provides public revenue used for short-term financing of the federal deficit.

Historians rarely link past and present events systematically. A biographer will write about the life and times of a Lincoln or Churchill, concentrating upon their choices while in office. A historian of institutions will examine the problems confronting an organization at a critical period of time which is now in the more or less distant past. A historical study may conclude with reference to the "lessons" or "relevance" of past events for the present. A historical study normally leaves a discontinuity between the past and the present.

Political scientists, by contrast, are much more concerned with the present than the past. The distant past is often ignored, and anything prior to the latest election or the current administration can be regarded as remote. Alternatively, different decades can be treated as if they all belonged to the present. Events from the 1960s, 1970s, and 1980s may be indiscriminately used as "current" illustrations of generalizations about public policy in the 1990s. For example, scholars of the presidency may jumble together examples from the Truman and the Bush administrations, or compare Franklin Roosevelt and Reagan, even though their periods in office were separated by half a century. British scholars can cite precedents of Cabinet or parliamentary practice from a century ago.

Purpose of the Book

The goal is to show how public policies inherited from the past influence the present and the future. To achieve this purpose first requires an analytic model of inheritance as a process joining past choices to the present and future. Chapter 2 presents such a model, showing how we can distinguish at any given point in time the policies inherited from the past and the choices of the government of the day. It also shows how to calculate the future impact of a policy after the administration that has chosen it has left office. The model thus makes it possible to divide the totality of public policies into three categories—those inherited from predecessors; choices made by a particular administration and bequeathed to its successors; and changes made by successor administrations. The model of inheritance does not deny choice but discriminates between choices in the past and those of the government of the day.

Secondly, the model must be applicable to a specific historical process in order to demonstrate the extent to which inheritance or choice is more significant empirically. Chapter 3 sets out the requirements for applying the model. Since inheritance is continuing, the period of time examined must be measured in generations, not just a single administration or even a single decade. The analysis must focus upon specific programs of government, such as dental care or military pensions, and not upon generic and therefore continuing functions of government, such as health or defense. In order to weigh programs, distinguishing between those that cost billions and those that cost very little, accurate public expenditure data is needed for each program in each year under review.

Since at least one program can be cited as an example for every type of policy change, the myriad activities of government should be examined systematically and comprehensively. Comprehensive coverage is necessary in order to test whether inheritance or choice is the exception to the rule. By definition, a case study is an unrepresentative sample of the manifold of public policy and cannot be a valid basis for generalization. The conclusions from a case study of a military crisis are likely to differ from those of a study of unemployment measures (cf. Allison, 1971; Heclo, 1974). A case study can only represent a limited area of public policy; it cannot give a sense of the relative importance of inheritance or choice. Given that there are distinctive and different responsibilities at the national and local levels of government, a comprehensive analysis should cover public policy at all levels of government.

Public policy in Britain since 1945 here provides the evidence for testing the importance of inheritance before choice. Changes in society, economy, and politics over nearly half a century give ample reason to expect that many programs will not have persisted throughout the postwar era. Even if only a few choices are made in any one year, the cumulative effect of more than four decades of choice can be substantial. British government is unitary, centralizing choice in Whitehall and reducing local authorities' scope for choice. Party government means that the leaders of the party winning an election are in a strong position to turn their choices into commitments binding both the executive in Whitehall and Parliament. British government is also a good record-keeper, annually reporting the audit of expenditure on hundreds of programs in effect each year since 1945. The addition and subtraction of programs from the annual appropriation accounts registers choices of the government of the day.

The third step is to determine whether inheritance or choice has been more important for public policy in Britain since 1945. Chapter 4 sets out conflicting hypotheses about the persistence or obsolescence of old programs. Testing the hypotheses requires the identification of all the programs in effect at the end of World War II, new programs introduced in the decades since, and programs terminated. Altogether, 360 different programs have been in effect at some point in the postwar era. The evidence shows the extreme durability of inherited programs. Notwithstanding many changes in politics and society, five-sixths of programs in effect at the start of the postwar era remain in effect nearly half a century later.

The legacy that each successive administration leaves is not identical to the one it inherits. The government of the day can modify its inheritance by adding new programs, thus leading to the long-term growth of government, or cut back activities by terminating programs. If each administration starts more programs than it stops, the process of inheritance gradually leads to a great increase in public policy.

Insofar as new programs result from careful deliberation about choices prior to adopting a program, then they should be a lasting addition to the legacy that each successive administration leaves behind. An alternative theory is that choices tend to be trial-and-error responses to unexpected events, and thus will often be terminated because many new measures turn out to be mistakes. Chapter 5 shows some support for each hypothesis. More than one hundred programs introduced since 1945 have become incorporated into the inheritance of public policy, and more than one hundred have been terminated.

Although inheritance is of primary importance, there is also evidence of some scope for choice. Hence, the book's fourth object is to test three alternative explanations of circumstances in which choice occurs: parties matter, the economic climate matters, and programs matter. By defining choices in terms of the introduction or termination of programs and changes in program expenditure, it is possible to determine which theory best accounts for the choice of new measures or their termination, and to compare different influences upon choice with the effects of inheritance.

Normative theories of representative government hypothesize that party control of government makes a difference in the choice of public policies. The adversary theory of party competition predicts that the choices of one government will be repealed by its ideological opponents. However, if trial and error predominates, then a party will be as likely to repeal its own programs as measures introduced by its opponents. What is more, if there are ideological differences in the disposition to take initiatives, then the party of the left will add new programs to the manifold of public policy, whereas a party of the right will simply conserve what it has inherited. The evidence in chapter 6 rejects the adversary and ideological theories, and supports a moving consensus about the inheritance of public policy.

Because new programs cost money, the state of the economy may determine the scope for choice. A booming economy offers the government of the day a fiscal dividend, as public revenue increases without any increase in tax rates, whereas recession cuts tax revenue and makes it difficult to fund established programs or think about introducing new ones. Since politicians are usually in a hurry to anticipate benefits, instead of waiting until after the fiscal dividend is in hand, the government of the day's choices can be shaped by its expectation of economic growth. Insofar as spending on inherited programs grows faster than the economy, then inherited programs will "crowd out" new programs, preempting available fiscal resources and making it harder for each successive administration to introduce new measures. Chapter 7 shows that it is the economic expectations of policymakers, whether or not justified by subsequent economic performance, that create more scope for new programs.

Because programs are the basic unit in the inheritance of public policy, a third theory is that differences between types of programs determine which persist in the legacy and which stop and start. Whereas most theories of public policy treat all programs as if they were identical, chapter 8 outlines differences in program attributes likely to affect their durability. Some policy environments are relatively predictable and stable, whereas others are turbulent and unpredictable. Programs also differ in their goals, for some are finite, such as relieving the damage of a particular flood, while others have persisting objectives, such as flood control programs intended to prevent the occurrence of disasters.

A theory that programs matter assumes that persistence depends upon the "problem cycle," that is, whether programs address long-term, predictable concerns of individuals or of the state or address problems caused by turbulence in a particular policy environment. Three different types of programs are identified. Those that concern the defining *sine qua non* activities of government, such as defense and the administration of justice, are likely to remain part of the continuing inheritance. Social programs addressing education, health care, and social security in old age address needs of the individuals throughout their lifetime; once adopted, they are difficult to terminate without disrupting the long-term security of families. By contrast, economic programs address market conditions that change rapidly. In a single term of office, an administration will experience both ups and downs in the economy; each reversal in the economic cycle creates pressures to introduce new programs and abandon others.

Differences between programs provide the best explanation of why some programs remain part of the inheritance of government, while others both start and stop. Chapter 9 shows that social programs affecting lifelong concerns of individuals are most likely to persist in the legacy of successive administrations. By contrast, in an economy continuously in flux, programs are often stopped a few years after they have been introduced, as part of a continuing trial-and-error search for ways of cushioning recessions and stimulating growth.

Inheritance does not deny change; it is possible to have change without choice. The concluding chapter shows how much the manifold of public policy is altered by the cumulative effect of adding programs to the legacy for nearly half a century. However, the greater part of increased expenditure is due to increases on programs inherited from the pre-1945 era. The cumulative effect of growth in inherited programs is not intended when the program is originally chosen; unintended consequences cumulatively produce change without choice. The importance of inheritance before choice is not unique to Britain. A look at public policy in Washington demonstrates the importance of inheritance there too. The Clinton administration inherited the problem of controlling "uncontrollable" commitments in the federal budget. The extent to which choice is limited is bad news for proponents of public choice theories. However, ordinary people, who make plans for their future on the assumption that government will continue to educate their children and provide social security and health care in times of need and old age, may prefer the continuity of inheritance to the discontinuities of frequent choice.

2   The Legacy of the Past

Asking "What's the story?", tracing the time-line from the story's
start and asking journalist's questions about trends or change
points in the issue's history, can profitably illuminate current
concerns.—Richard E. Neustadt and E. R. May, Thinking in Time

A new government needs to look backward before it can look forward. As Richard Neustadt and Ernest May argue (1986: 108), the first question to ask is not "What's the problem?" but "What's the story?" "That way," they explain, "one finds out what the problem *really* is." Very few of the problems facing the government of the day originated during its term of office; they are inherited as a cumulative consequence of past decisions of many administrations. The starting point for incubating a new program is inherited policy. The policy question is usually not "Where do we go?" but "Where do we go from here?" (cf. Heclo, 1974: 16f).

Entry into office is a shock to most politicians, for what they find differs fundamentally from the slogans and visions raised in an election campaign. Since the primary objective of an out-of-office politician is winning office, little thought is devoted to what can be done once there. In the United States three of the last four presidents—Clinton, Reagan, and Carter—had no experience of Congress or even of Washington when they entered the White House. In Britain the opposition party normally takes office within hours of the election result being known, and many freshly appointed heads of government departments will be new to the job of Cabinet minister. A new administration regards the defeat of the incumbents as proof that they made the wrong choices, and that the victors can make the right ones.

New entrants to office invariably overestimate their scope for choice and underestimate the scale of inherited commitments.

The inheritance of a new administration is a mixture of assets and liabilities. One part consists of problems that have ripened through the decades and cannot be removed overnight, like the federal deficit in Washington or the low level of investment in British industry. Other parts of the legacy are popular, such as social security or education programs; the new administration will take credit for them even though they were the choices of departed and often long-dead officeholders. Some popular programs—and some problems too—will be the legacy of the incumbent party's previous terms of office. For a prime minister such as John Major, the inheritance of Thatcherism is more immediately visible than the legacy of past Labour governments.

Whereas a trust company can treat an individual's legacy as a portfolio of fungible assets that can be reallocated at will to obtain an optimal return, a portfolio of inherited policies is not easily altered. *Programs are not saleable assets; they are obligations.* A newly installed administration is committed by law to maintain the programs that it inherits. It must accept its legacy as a condition of office. On inauguration a president takes an oath to uphold the Constitution, which lists as one of his duties to "take care that the laws be faithfully executed." The immediate task of a newly installed official is learning to live with inherited commitments carried forward by the force of political inertia. If a choice had been available, the Bush administration would not have chosen to inherit an annual deficit of $153 billion, nor would a Clinton administration have chosen to inherit a budget deficit of upwards of $400 billion. Nor would an incoming British government want to find the "mess" that it campaigned against at election time to be even worse than it had claimed.

Inheritance precludes a new administration from making many choices. A newly elected president or prime minister is not given a blank sheet of paper on which to inscribe what he or she would like government to do. An accumulation of programs from many different administrations is already there. This accumulation is the consequence of a process of amendment, revision, addition, and subtraction by previous administrations. A program for which the government of the day takes responsibility can be an amalgam of commitments made over a century. In Britain, for example, each new secretary of state for education inherits responsibility for compulsory education. It was introduced in 1870, with a minimum school-leaving age of 11. By 1918 the age was raised to 14. In 1944 the school-leaving age was raised to 15 and free secondary education made available to all. The present school-leaving age of 16 was set in 1973, more than nine ministers prior to the present incumbent of the office. Changes in the policy environment can also alter the significance of programs. The initial pensions act chose to pay pensions to persons who were without any other source of income support and over the age of 70. Since average life expectancy in 1908 was then 58, the claim on public funds was very small. The great increase in longevity since has exploded the significance of the pension commitment.

Paradoxically, the government of the day may exert more influence after it has left office than while there. Choices of transient officeholders become part of the legacy left to successors. When an administration vacates office, it bequeaths its chosen programs as commitments that constrain its successors. In that way, what was once new becomes incorporated into the continuing inheritance of public policy.

To understand the process of inheritance, we must understand two complementary processes—how programs endure, and under what circumstances they change. The first section sets out a formula showing the cumulative effect of past choices upon the inheritance of a new administration, and explains how political inertia results in the persistence of incremental additions to the manifold of public policy. It also shows that the cumulative effect is very different from conventional theories of incrementalism. The government of the day may alter its legacy in real, albeit limited, ways, so that what it bequeaths to its successor is different from what it has inherited. This is the subject of the second section. As one administration's bequest becomes its successor's legacy, choices made in the past cast an extended shadow ahead. Calculating the impact of an administration's legacy long after it leaves office is explained in the third section. The chapter's conclusion describes the logic of comprehending both the whole and the parts of public policy.

A Persisting Inheritance

An incoming administration inherits a collection of programs that aggregate the choices of different administrations in varied circumstances. The choices of the government of the day do not lose effect when it leaves office; they become part of the legacy that its successor inherits, along with all the programs that the outgoing administration had received as part of its own inheritance and which have persisted through political inertia.

The Force of Political Inertia

By definition, the policies that a new administration inherits are not of its choice; they are given by actions of many different predecessors at many different points in time. The inheritance of policy (InP) when a new administration enters office (time t) can be described by a simple identity:

$$InP = TPP\ t-1$$

where TPP stands for the totality of public policies. Assuming persistence, this identity justifies the following hypothesis:

*2.1 (*Inheritance*) If a program is part of the legacy of one administration, it is likely to remain part of the legacy of the next.

Routine is the mechanism that carries programs forward from year to year. Millions of civil servants administer thousands of laws and hundreds of programs without intervention by elected politicians. A teacher does not ask a mayor how to teach arithmetic, a nurse does not ask a state health administrator how to administer injections, and a naval officer does not ask a defense secretary how to submerge a submarine. Laws and expert values provide clear signals for the routine direction of public programs (Rose, 1989a: chapter 4).

"Routines are simplifying devices that officials use to avoid lengthy processes of rational decision-making" (Sharkansky, 1970: 5). The object of bureaucratic rules is to give public officials no choice about what they do in order that programs can be delivered with more or less mechanical predictability. A social security clerk does not ask what a politician wants an elderly person to receive but what a claimant of a benefit is entitled to receive. To determine an entitlement the clerk turns to laws and regulations, not election returns. Rules, regulations, and standard operating procedures constitute the routines that enable a government agency to carry on its day-to-day activities.

The goal of many policymakers is "satisficing" (Simon, 1957). The word is derived from the Latin *satis,* enough. The proof of satisfaction is the absence of dissatisfaction. As long as the outputs of programs meet public expectations then programs can run by routine. No choice is required; as the old adage has it: "If it ain't broke, don't fix it." In order for politicians to have the time and resources to make some choices on matters of high priority, most programs must run by routine.

Inherited programs vary greatly in their longevity; a few will be recent, some will be a few decades old, and others have persisted for many generations or even centuries. The laws authorizing programs are impersonal; they do not have a natural life span. Unlike

Table 2.1 Sources of Laws Inherited by the Thatcher Administration

	Number (1979)	In force (%)	Cumulative (%)
Enacted before 1761	132	4.0	4.0
1761–1836	215	6.4	10.4
1837–1901	866	26.0	36.4
1902–1918	192	5.8	42.2
1919–1945	479	14.4	56.6
1945–1951	200	6.0	62.6
1951–1964	438	13.2	75.8
1964–1970	284	8.5	84.3
1970–1974	195	5.9	90.2
1974–1979	328	9.8	100.0
Totals	3,329	100	100

Source: Van Mechelen and Rose (1986), table 10.5. Up to 1945, calendar years. From the return of the Labour government, 1945, sessions of Parliament. Note that in Britain, unlike Washington, a session normally combines parts of two calendar years. Hence, years will normally appear twice from 1945.

automobiles, laws are not routinely inspected for obsolescence and scrapped. Programs concerning such traditional functions of government as defense and the administration of justice can antedate by a century measures regulating television.

Britain is an extreme example of the persistence of laws from the distant past. Parliament's authority to enact laws has been continuous for more than six centuries. A newly elected government inherits many programs adopted before its most senior member entered Parliament or was even born. When Margaret Thatcher's administration entered office in 1979 it promised a fresh, radical approach, but it could not ignore more than three thousand laws inherited from the past (table 2.1). More than a tenth of laws in its legacy dated from before the accession of Queen Victoria in 1837, and more than one-third were on the statute book before Queen Victoria died in 1901. Altogether, two-thirds of laws in force in 1979 had been enacted before Thatcher entered the House of Commons in 1959, and all the laws that her administration initially administered were choices of administrations that the prime minister rhetorically scorned.

In fact, the longevity of laws authorizing programs is actually greater even than these figures indicate, for many laws are composed of clauses and sections far older than the date of their latest re-enactment. Consolidation acts combine in a single omnibus statute measures enacted at different times about a given program, so as to bring together related measures enacted at different points in time and to remove gaps and inconsistencies. Consolidation means that older acts are formally repealed and their contents reenacted as part of a new act, thus giving a much later date to a program based on earlier statutes. For example, although elementary education was made compulsory in England in 1870, the original Education Act and generations of subsequent additions have been consolidated in post-1945 legislation (Statutory Publications Office, 1982: 1:637; Page, 1985).

Since the persistence of past programs produces a slow but steady growth in the legacy of public policy, it matters whether time $t-1$ is 1870, 1950, or 1979. An administration entering office in the pre-1914 days of laissez faire inherited far fewer commitments than, say, the Heath or Wilson governments of the 1960s, for many programs of the welfare state were then running on only a small scale or had not yet been adopted. An administration entering office in the 1990s, whatever its ideological inclination, will find it impossible to return government to the low level of commitments that prevailed at the beginning of the century.

The connection between the past and the present is the result of political inertia. Political inertia is a persisting force: once adopted, programs continue. Momentum comes from laws that authorize programs and remain in effect from one administration to the next. Laws are usually not forbidding commandments. In an era of big government the most significant laws are those that tell citizens what they are entitled to claim from government, such as social security payments. Laws also authorize public employees to deliver a host of benefits, such as education and health care. Unless a government decides to repeal a law, every measure that it inherits must routinely be carried out.

Organizations also sustain the momentum of inertia, for they institutionalize the means of financing and delivering programs. Each program is an established line in the budget. In the annual review of public expenditure, the great bulk of money for the great majority of programs is approved routinely. Moreover, the organization responsible for a program can ask for more money for established measures. Each public agency has officials skilled and committed to administering particular programs, and organized to deliver benefits nationwide.

Public employees are an important link between government organizations and recipients of public policies. The great majority of employees are specialists, trained to deliver particular programs such as health care, police protection, or factory inspection. They derive job satisfaction from using their skills to deliver a service. Because they are paid to do so, public employees also have a material interest in maintaining programs. Given their strategic location within government, officials can resist proposals to stop a program. Together, recipients, producers, and interest groups can make any popularly elected government think very hard before repealing a measure that it has inherited.

The expectations of recipients of benefits are important too, whether they are poor people, business firms, or a cross-section of the population. An established program has a cluster of beneficiaries, and everyone who benefits expects that the program will continue regardless of the outcome of an election. These expectations are reinforced by pressure groups articulating demands to maintain and expand programs.

Inertia and Incrementalism

There is substantial common ground between the incrementalist model of policymaking (Braybrooke and Lindblom, 1963) and inheritance through political inertia. Both reject the idea that policymakers carry out a comprehensive review of alternatives; they lack the time and the cognitive capacity to comprehend everything that might in principle be considered. Both recognize that there are political incentives to concentrate upon immediate pressures. The emphasis of incrementalism upon a stable base of commitments and relatively small rates of change at the margin is consistent with the gradualism of political inertia. However, differences between the two models result in very contrasting consequences (table 2.2).

1. The *span of time* of an incrementalist decisionmaker is short: the significant time periods are now (today or this week), soon (next week or later in the current year), or soon enough (before the next budget or the next election). By contrast, political inertia operates over decades or generations. What was done in the distant past can have consequences extending far into the future.

A long time horizon is particularly important in understanding the growth of government. The massive commitments of contemporary government are cumulative; they were not decided in a single budget or by a single administration. In Europe, the origins of the welfare state extend back more than a century (Flora and Heidenheimer, 1981). In the United States, developments can be traced back more than half a century to the New Deal or to protest movements from the Progressive Era at the turn of the century (cf. Skocpol, 1987). None of today's policymakers was in office when big-spending programs were

Table 2.2 Differences between Inertia and Incremental Policymaking

	Inertia	Incrementalism
1. Span of time	Long duration	Year-to-year
2. Unit of analysis	Organizational commitments	Individual choices
3. Linkage	Cumulative	Disjointed
4. Reversibility	Difficult, impossible	Easy
5. Consequences	Unforeseeable in long term	Short term only
6. Compounding	Important	Ignored
7. Scale of change	Large, potentially destabilizing	Small, regular

Source: Adapted from Rose and Karran (1987: 100ff).

first adopted. President Clinton, for example, was not born until after the New Deal, and was too young to vote when War on Poverty programs were enacted.

The inertia of taxation illustrates the extent to which old laws cast a long shadow into the present. The oldest taxes in use today in Britain, customs and excise duties, were introduced more than six hundred years ago (Dowell, 1884: esp. vol. 1). Income tax was initially introduced in 1799. About half the revenue of the British Treasury today is accounted for by taxes first introduced before 1800. A relatively "modern" tax such as social security was first levied in 1911, and license taxes for automobiles in 1910. Taxes that date from very different eras of the distant past today account for more than four-fifths of public revenue in Britain (Rose and Karran, 1987: 102ff).

2. The two theories differ in their *unit of analysis*. Inertia focuses upon the commitments of organizations, whereas incrementalism concentrates upon the choices of individual policymakers. Because organizations are persisting and durable, their activities do not require positive choices to be made by individuals. Once a law commits an organization to deliver a given program, the organization ensures that

the program continues in effect until it is acted upon by a stronger force.

Incrementalism perceives government as a set of individual policy-makers who want to be free to change their minds with each alteration in policy fashion. The media give great attention to politicians who deliver instant opinions and who change their minds quickly. An individual's preference of the moment, however, is not the same as the collective choice of government. Public agencies can only be committed by the slow and difficult-to-modify process of enacting statutes, recruiting personnel, and authorizing an annual budget.

3. The *linkage of choices* differs, for political inertia is about the accumulation of many commitments, whereas incrementalism is about disjointed and serial choices. Incrementalist decisionmaking prescribes that problems be dealt with one step at a time. Only after the consequences of one choice are evident is it deemed appropriate to decide what to do next, confirming successes and rejecting failures in a step-by-step process in which the next choice is what matters, and is determined on an ad hoc basis. The readiness of incrementalists to uncouple present actions from past and future commitments is illustrated by Braybrooke and Lindblom (1963: 99–100), who describe social security as a program "amended every few years to increase incrementally the level of benefits"—as if each increment were not piled on top of commitments inherited from predecessors.

Political inertia accepts that particular decisions are likely to be piecemeal and disjointed, but regards this as less significant than the cumulative impact that discrete choices have upon the inheritance of public policy. No major public policy reflects a single decision taken by an individual or a particular administration; instead, it is the composite of a succession of decisions taken through the years. A model of government as a set of individual choices is counterfactual as description because it ignores the substantial weight of inherited commitments.

4. *Reversibility* is a necessary condition of incrementalism; any decision that is deemed unsatisfactory can be abandoned and another put in its place in a self-correcting trial-and-error process. For example, a rise in interest rates to reduce inflation may be followed by a cut in order to stimulate the economy. As long as policies are reversible, patterns of change can be cyclical and the long-term consequences will tend toward a more or less stable equilibrium.

However, many programs are based upon choices from which there is no going back, for example, a decision about war and peace or, less dramatically, about running a highway through the countryside or razing old houses for a new urban development. As presidents Johnson and Nixon learned, inheriting a military commitment such as the war in Vietnam is very different from making a choice to deploy troops where none are yet committed. When programs are irreversible, the process of inertia will make them persist without any choices being made. Even when a policy can be reversed, its effect may not be constant. For example, a prolonged period of inflation may so raise interest rates that even once inflation is reversed, the new, higher standard for a "low" interest rate remains in force.

Altering the momentum of programs driven by the force of inertia is much easier than reversing them. Reducing or increasing the amount spent on a program, a typical incrementalist choice, will affect it at the margin but does not alter the substance of a program. Even terminating a program may not dispose of long-term consequences. For example, a major cut in urban renewal programs does not mean that the buildings razed are restored or those newly constructed removed. The government's obligation to meet the costs of financing past developments continues for half a century or more.

5. When the *consequences* of choices are viewed from the perspective of decades or generations, then the cumulative effect of many linked actions becomes unforeseeable. This point is accepted in both inertia and incrementalist theories.

An incrementalist policymaker confronted with the opportunity of making a choice will focus on immediate political pressures. The groups supporting and opposing alternatives can be identified, and immediate political repercussions anticipated. Uncertainties can be coped with by making small incremental changes that can readily be reversed. If the consequences are popular, a program can be continued; if not, it can be abandoned. Even if policymakers wanted to focus on long-term consequences, this would not be possible. Lindblom (1965: 145f) emphasizes, "As decisionmaking is in fact practiced, important consequences of policies under analysis are simply disregarded. Forthright neglect of important consequences is a noteworthy problem-solving tactic. What kind of important consequences are neglected? The answer is: any kind."

Even though long-term consequences are difficult or impossible to anticipate, they nonetheless exist, and since the past cannot be undone, they must be accepted by the government of the day as part of its inherited responsibilities. When difficulties are the consequence of actions taken over many years, the time required to overcome them may be longer than a party's term of office.

The importance of unforeseeable consequences is illustrated in the history of the income tax. In Britain, the income tax was first introduced as an emergency measure in 1799 to finance the Napoleonic Wars; it was not meant to be permanent. In 1901 the standard rate of income tax was 5 percent, but the threshold of taxation was so high that few families had a large enough income to be required to pay. The rate and coverage has gradually risen. When the income tax was introduced as a peacetime measure in the United States in 1913, only 2 percent of the working population had a sufficiently high income to pay any tax, and the highest tax rate was 7 percent. Today, income tax is paid by the great majority of wage earners in both countries, and the maximum rate has multiplied five to eight times.

6. *Compounding* is another critical distinction between theories of

political inertia and incrementalism. Compounding occurs by adding each year's change to the accumulated commitments of previous years, so that a seemingly small annual change gradually produces a big effect, a procedure familiar in savings and pension policies. Political inertia takes account of compounding because it links the consequences of actions over many years.

The incrementalist model regards inherited commitments as given. In any one year the issue at stake is a matter of "decisions affecting small changes" (Braybrooke and Lindblom, 1963: 62ff). As long as the rate of change is predictable and regular, it can be considered incremental. Dempster and Wildavsky (1979: 375) argue, "There is no magic size for an increment. . . . It is the regularity or irregularity of the changes in size that matters, not the absolute amount of change."

However, once concern with regularity is introduced, programs must be viewed over a longer time perspective than an annual budget. A program registering growth at the rate of 5 or 10 percent each year over a decade may be described as changing incrementally, for the annual rate is steady. But the base is not constant. In the course of a decade or more, compounding can produce radical alterations in the base. Compounding a 5 percent annual budget increase for ten years produces a 70 percent increase in ten years, and in two decades it trebles expenditure on a program. If the rate of growth is 10 percent, then expenditure will double in eight years and treble in eleven years.

Compounding does not contradict the logic of incrementalism; it completes it. Comparative surveys of major welfare state policies have found that the age of a program is a significant determinant of expenditure growth (Wilensky, 1975; cf. OECD, 1985). The long-term result is a structural change in public policy that no policymaker has chosen.

7. The *scale of change* in incrementalist theory is small, because attention is focused on an immediate and bounded problem affecting current actions; long-term and second-order consequences are ig-

nored. The limited scope for choice at any particular moment is regarded as offering a secure floor for policymakers as well as imposing a ceiling upon change. Incremental theories also concentrate upon specific programs within the control of a given decisionmaker or agency. The collective effect of a large number of small-scale decisions is not considered. The perspective is that of a lower-echelon official or an individual member of Congress rather than the Office of Management and Budget or the White House.

By contrast, political inertia can create a "camel's nose" effect, that is, a program can appear small at the beginning, like a camel's nose protruding into a tent, and gradually get larger as the whole of the "camel" becomes evident. It is also concerned with linking the parts to the whole. The conjoint effects of individual programs compounding at different rates over the years can collectively be large, like the impact of a herd of camels upon a tentful of policymakers. Insofar as the effects are not chosen and are not even foreseeable, they can be destabilizing for public policy. Destabilizing changes are not inherently good or bad. Some can be desirable, such as the compounding of economic growth, whereas others are unwanted, for example, compounding government debt. The large and unpredictable variability of outcomes in the long run is a significant feature of political inertia, introducing a high degree of uncertainty about the inheritance of public policy.

Adding Choices to a Legacy

The logic of political inertia emphasizes that starting and stopping programs are both difficult. To introduce a new program requires overcoming the inertia of public agencies, and not all bureaucrats are empire builders seeking to expand their programs. Bureaucrats administering established programs according to familiar rules can resist proposals to change in the belief that "whatever is, is right" or at least preferable to anything else, and that introducing a new program threatens new risks and burdens (cf. Holden, 1966; Blais and Dion, 1991). Once introduced, a program is carried forward by inertia; to terminate it requires building a coalition that constitutes a greater force than the coalition of beneficiaries, officials, and routines supporting it. Yet the persistence of programs does not deny the possibility of choice. To describe inherited programs as past choices is to adopt a retrospective view; at one time, these programs were part of the present.

Forces Opposing Persistence

If there were no forces to resist inertia, then, once chosen every program would persist in perpetuity. However, satisfaction is contingent and the frequency with which dissatisfaction occurs makes the job of policymakers anything but routine. Each outburst of dissatisfaction calls into question the existence of an inherited program and stimulates a search for a new measure.

Choice-oriented theories of governance emphasize the incentives for out-of-office politicians to create dissatisfaction with the status quo in order to gain competitive electoral advantage. A program may be attacked as unsatisfactory because critics dislike its goal. The rise of the new right in Britain and the United States broke a longstanding consensus about the goals of government. Margaret Thatcher often challenged the assumptions and goals of public programs, and Ronald Reagan delivered anecdotes that stressed that government programs were a "waste" of resources. New right theories are, however, ambiguous in their empirical predictions: they prescribe that programs ought to be terminated but also pay tribute to powerful forces maintaining them. Even if ends are consensual, a program may be attacked as an unsatisfactory means to an agreed end. For example, a youth unemployment measure can be criticized if it does not lead to the reduction of youth unemployment.

Since the choice of a program is made in a specific historical context, in the course of time changes in the political and social environment in which the policy operates can cause a program to lose effectiveness or even become counterproductive. Decay is a process, not a specific event. When a program shows signs of obsolescence, the question is when rather than whether a choice must be made to terminate it and introduce a new program. Even if the great majority of programs persist from one administration to the next, this is definitely not an indication that they persist ad infinitum.

When changes in the policy environment reduce the effectiveness of an inherited program, a decision to do nothing has consequences as significant as the choice of a new measure. It becomes risky to allow a program to continue routinely in the belief that what has been desirable and effective in the past will remain satisfactory for another decade. If policymakers do nothing a program may *not* continue as before, instead becoming ineffective due to changes in its policy environment. If policymakers stick to an inherited program in the face of rising dissatisfaction, then they must find new ways of justifying doing so. For example, dissatisfaction with a youth employment program may be countered by policymakers arguing that, in difficult economic circumstances, the original goal was overly ambitious and whatever the program is currently achieving is the best that can be done in the circumstances. However, such an argument concedes that there is something wrong in the present and gives an opening for critics to propose fresh choices.

Choices about Means and Ends

Newly elected politicians do not want to be hamstrung by a legacy from the past; they want to make an impact, and that means introducing new programs or repealing established programs. At the beginning of a new administration, the president is not thinking about maintaining laws inherited from predecessors but about introducing new measures as quickly as possible, while public support is high (Light, 1982; Pfiffner, 1988). But a politician's desire to make choices does not guarantee that a new administration can choose to do anything and everything. What kind of choices can politicians in a hurry add to the inheritance of public policy?

To become part of the persisting inheritance of government, the preferences of policymakers must go beyond statements of intentions. Unfortunately, the word *policy* is often used indiscriminately, referring to intentions of governors as well as to programs of government. Statements of intention are easy to make during an election campaign, and in office an administration can change its intentions frequently in efforts to put a popular gloss on its record. However, statements of intent are not binding, and can disappear when the government of the day leaves office. While intentions come and go, programs embodied in laws, institutions and expectations of beneficiaries can be carried forward indefinitely by the force of political inertia.

If the government of the day wants to alter the legacy it has received, it must make choices that change the means and/or ends of public policy. Often a party entering office accepts the goals of its predecessors; it campaigns with the claim that it can be more effective than its opponents in achieving a widely shared goal (cf. Stokes, 1963). If it rejects an inherited goal in favor of a new objective, then it must introduce a new program to achieve its fresh end. Four different types of choice are available to an administration, depending upon whether it wants to alter the ends or the means of policy, do both, or leave things unchanged (figure 2.1).

1. *Maintainence of a routine.* When a government is satisfied with a program that it has inherited, both goals and means can be kept as they are. An administration does not normally expect to introduce new

Figure 2.1. Alternative choices about policy

Intended Goals

		No change	Change
	No change	MAINTAIN ROUTINE	SYMBOLIC GESTURES
Program			
Means			
	Change	INSTRUMENTAL ADAPTATION	INNOVATION

goals in such fields as social policy: its intention is to maintain social security, health care, and education. As long as there is widespread satisfaction with the means in place to attain these goals, then instead of introducing fresh choices, an administration can simply claim credit for programs chosen by its predecessors (cf. Mayhew, 1974).

In a buoyant economy, a program can even expand by routine. An education program can remain the same in law, yet changes can occur as teachers are paid more, new schools are built, and more pupils are taught. The program does not alter its goal; it expands the number of people and institutions delivering and receiving an inherited program. Much of the growth of government occurs through "pluralization," that is, increasing the number of standard service delivery units, such as schools or post offices to increase the volume of standardized services. Pluralization has been particularly important in the United States, given an increase of more than 100 million in the population in the past half century (Rose, 1988).

2. *Symbolic gestures.* When dissatisfaction becomes strong, a government is under pressure to do or say something in response. Since words are the politician's stock in trade, it is often easier for a harassed minister to say something instead of doing something. Even though words may not materially alter conditions, they can change how people feel about a problem, or at least how people feel about the

politicians responsible for it. Symbolic gestures show the public that the government of the day cares about their anxieties (Edelman, 1964).

However, a symbolic gesture does not commit government to do anything in particular. For that reason, it adds nothing to the legacy that the administration bequeaths to its successor. With luck, dissatisfaction may disappear without any intervention by the government of the day. If a problem continues, the most that a symbolic gesture can do is buy time while the administration searches for measures to remove the cause of dissatisfaction. If there is widespread dissatisfaction, for example, rising unemployment or inflation, doing nothing risks loss of office, in which case the problem will be left behind as part of the legacy to its successor.

3. *Instrumental adaptation*. When government acts instrumentally, a new program is chosen to attain an established end. Insofar as the major goals of government are broadly popular—for example, promoting economic growth or health care—the government of the day cannot repudiate such goals without risking electoral defeat. It can seek to win additional favor by introducing new programs that show it more competent than its opponents in achieving consensus goals. This alters the repertoire of programs that an administration leaves as a legacy to its successor while keeping goals the same.

New programs can come from many different sources. An incoming government can derive programs from its partisan principles and from the cluster of interests that it represents. Pressure groups and public officials will urge it to adopt programs that have not found favor with a predecessor. Whereas any change contemplated by the White House is always subject to congressional constraint, a British Cabinet has a much freer hand in choosing new programs, because party discipline normally guarantees that its choices will be endorsed by Parliament.

4. *Innovation*. Commitment to a new goal as well as a new program

distinguishes policy innovation from instrumental adaptation. Innovation is doubly difficult because it involves two linked choices. Policymakers must wage a political battle to gain support for a new goal to replace what they inherited. In addition, they must identify new means to achieve this goal. If policy advisers are to know how to draw up a measure to achieve what elected politicians want done, a new goal must be much more concrete than such abstractions as maximizing welfare, promoting prosperity, or winning re-election, and sufficiently realistic so that effective measures can be devised to attain it.

The government of the day simultaneously faces demands to leave some programs alone, make symbolic gestures about others, find new programs to achieve established goals, and adopt new programs for new goals. An administration could pass through all four phases during a term of office. Initially, it may find everything proceeding routinely. If it does not, it can respond with symbolic gestures while trying to figure out what new programs to introduce to achieve established goals. Subsequently, it can innovate by introducing a new goal and new programs. If the results of the innovation appear satisfactory, it can then operate by routine.

Alternative Strategies for Implementing Choice

Once policymakers understand what they would like to do with inherited commitments, the next step is to adopt a strategy to implement their choice. The alternatives include altering the personnel in charge of programs, introducing new programs, repealing inherited laws, amending programs, or altering budgets.

"To govern is to appoint." The choice of personnel in the hands of a newly elected president or prime minister is not constrained by the distant past. Immediately after an election dozens of positions fall vacant, and more vacancies arise during an administration's term of office due to retirements, resignations, and death. The use of patronage can signal policy priorities. Especially able politicians can be appointed to head departments where fresh choices are meant to be made, and lightweights named to head departments that can be run by routine. The power of appointment is about political patronage as well as policy. The patronage that a prime minister dispenses is specially important in maintaining the party unity upon which he or she depends for continuance in office. In the United States, many presidential appointees are given office for representational reasons; racial, ethnic and gender characteristics of appointees are carefully scrutinized, and this was especially notable at the beginning of the Clinton administration.

A second strategy is to enact new laws. In the United States, however, the great majority of bills proposed by the president and by members of Congress are not enacted into law. About half of a president's legislative proposals are endorsed by Congress, and about 5 percent of bills introduced by individual members of Congress (Stanley and Niemi, 1988: 175). The introduction of new bills is often a symbolic attempt by the president to get political advantage or by members of Congress to claim credit for intentions, not legislation. When control of government is divided between a Republican White House and a Democratic Congress, substantial cross-party cooperation is necessary in order to secure passage of a bill. Nor can cooperation between members of the governing party be taken for granted (Powell, 1991; Mayhew, 1991). The centralization of legislative and executive authority in the British Cabinet virtually assures ministers that the 60 bills it puts to Parliament each year will be enacted into law. But this total is less than 2 percent of the acts that it inherits from its predecessors (Van Mechelen and Rose, 1986: tables 2.3, 10.1).

Repealing laws inherited from predecessors is a third method of carrying out choices. In practice, however, repealing programs is politically difficult because of the cluster of interests and expectations that accumulate around established programs. The government of the day accepts the great bulk of its inheritance of legislation, willingly or *faute de mieux*. In Britain, even if the opposition votes against the principle of a bill when it is introduced, once it gains a majority in Parliament it rarely repeals an act (Rose, 1984: 87ff). One reason for the infrequency of repeal is that many programs are not so much the choice of the government of the day as they are the product of continuing negotiations between a Whitehall department and extra-governmental interests. Three-quarters of the measures that the Cabinet chooses to put to Parliament are noncontroversial bills that the opposition does not vote against in principle.

Amending existing laws is a fourth way of institutionalizing a choice, and it is much more likely to be desirable inasmuch as an amendment is incorporated in a program already part of the inheritance of public policy. Existing legislation can be amended by expanding or contracting the coverage of a program, increasing or decreasing the level of benefits that it provides, or altering institutions or procedures for delivering it. Because amendments are added to legislation already in effect, such changes are easy to implement. But the impact of the change is usually small in relation to a particular program. For example, the average amount of money affected by alterations in British tax laws in a year is only 2 percent of total tax revenue (Rose and Karran, 1987: table 7.2).

Budgets are a fifth method of altering choices, albeit at the margin. However, modifying the margin should not be confused with modifying the base, that is, commitments inherited from the past. As Webber and Wildavsky (1986: 31) emphasize, "The base is non-discretionary"; it reflects "social agreement on essentials." In France, this procedure is fully institutionalized; all past spending is considered a continuing commitment of government (Wildavsky, 1975: 217ff). The French Parliament is not expected to make choices about the whole of the budget; it only votes to add or subtract sums from the inherited base. The politics of the annual budget cycle is such that a change of a few percentage points in expenditure is magnified by controversy into a matter of great importance. Yet while controversy rages in Washington about billions or tens of billions of dollars, the force of political inertia carries forward more than a trillion dollars of expenditure on inherited commitments (see chapter 10). Moreover, changes in the amount of money spent on a program do not alter its substance but only the volume of benefits that it confers.

From Legacy to Bequest

The totality of public policy is not the same from year to year, as would be the case if the inheritance of public policy were static. The base is always changing as a consequence of conscious choices of the government of the day and the unintended consequence of past choices. Whereas incrementalism emphasizes that changes are likely to be limited in scale, inertia emphasizes that new programs can become a durable part of the legacy that each outgoing administration leaves to its successors. Its legacy (L) is the sum of inherited programs (InP) plus new programs (NP) and amendments to inherited programs (aInP) that it introduces, less the repeal of inherited programs (rInP).

$$L = InP + NP + aInP - rInP$$

Theories of political will as the basis of public policy assume that the choices of the government of the day are of primary importance. What is willed is more important than what is inherited. This implies the hypothesis:

*2.2 (*Will to choose*). Most of the programs in an administration's legacy will be measures that it has chosen itself.

However, theories of inheritance before choice hypothesize the opposite:

*2.3 (*Dominance of inertia*). Most of the programs in an administration's legacy will be measures that it has inherited.

Impact of a Legacy

Paradoxically, an administration has more time to exert influence *after* it has left office than while it is in government. A president or prime minister cannot be sure of a tenure of more than four or five years, before an election intervenes. Departure from office, by election defeat or other cause, ends a politician's opportunity to make fresh choices. However, the choices made during a relatively brief tenure of office become part of the legacy inherited by each successor.

Just as a new administration is constrained by the programs it inherits from its predecessors, so its legacy can constrain the choice of successors. Although every member of the New Deal administration of the 1930s or of the 1945–51 Labour government of Clement Attlee long ago retired from politics, major programs launched by those administrations remain on the statute books.

Persistence offers a contemporary politician a chance to leave a durable monument. President Reagan's departure from office has not meant the end of his influence, for the major tax changes enacted in 1981 and 1986 are greatly constraining the revenue available to both Republican and Democratic successors; the massive federal deficit is part of Reagan's legacy to the 1990s too. During the 1980s Margaret Thatcher's program of privatization transferred ownership of major industries such as telephones, gas, electricity, and water from public to private hands. Her successors, whether Labour or Conservative, cannot easily return such industries to state ownership, for the proceeds from privatization sales have already been spent.

Impact on the Future

An administration that brings in a new program that is administratively viable, politically popular, and addresses a continuing concern of society can expect it to persist in the inheritance of successor administrations for decades after it has left office. The durability of a program introduced by a given administration can be measured by the number of years it has been in effect *after as well as during* its term of office. If an administration introduces five new programs a year, then in a four-year term it will adopt 20 new programs. By the end of its term, the first five will have been in effect for four years each, a total of 20 program years; the second cohort will have been in effect for three years, a total of 15 program years; and the third and fourth groups for two years and one year each respectively. Altogether, by the time it leaves office, an administration's choices will have been in effect for 50 program years.

Even though the choices that a departing administration leaves may be only a small part of its total legacy, if all 20 programs remain in effect during a four-year term of its immediate successor, they gain an additional 80 years of program impact. This is actually more than their impact while the administration introducing them was in office. In a decade after leaving office, the choices of a given administration can be in operation for 200 program years.

Although statutes can limit the time individuals hold office, there is no statute of limitations on the time that the programs they introduce remain in effect. If it makes a small number of durable choices, a government that has been out of office for a quarter century can cumulatively have an impact on public policy of up to 500 program years. By the 1990s the impact of a major reforming administration such as Roosevelt's New Deal or the 1945 Labour Government can total well over a thousand program years.

The impact of a particular administration (ImpA) at any given point in time is the sum of the years in effect since each new program was added during its tenure of office:

$$\text{ImpA} = {}^{n}\Sigma_{i=1} (YE)_{i}$$

where n = the total number of new programs (NP), and YE the number of years that the ith program was in effect. Even if the number of programs that a particular administration adds to the legacy of public policy is limited, the longer each program endures, the greater its cumulative impact.

In addition to calculating the number of years a program remains in effect, it is also possible to weigh the impact of inherited programs by calculating the amount of money an inherited program claims. For example, the 1945 Labour government's national health service included programs for free or subsidized prescriptions and for ophthalmic services. By 1989 expenditure on both programs had grown greatly, but the two had not grown an equal amount. The prescriptions program cost £2,482,000,000, more than 20 times the £116,000,000 spent on ophthalmic services.

Insofar as programs tend to be durable, then the total impact of a given administration's choices is a function not only of how many new programs it adopts but also of how long ago it was in office. At this point in time, the cumulative impact of the 1945–51 Labour government is greater than that of the 1979–90 Thatcher administration. But the identity predicts that insofar as programs chosen in the 1980s remain in effect for decades thereafter, the Thatcher administration's choices will cumulatively have a greater impact in the twenty-first century than in the decade when they were introduced.

Comprehending the Whole and the Parts

The persistence of routines without explicit decisions by policy-makers does not deny the existence of choice; it highlights the importance of past rather than present choices. The inheritance of public policy is like a great cathedral; its late-twentieth-century form is the consequence of a large number of additions and renovations since its foundations were dug about eight hundred years ago. Just as no one of its hundred bishops could claim to have chosen its present appearance, so no one administration can claim to have chosen the whole of public policy. Studying a cathedral emphasizes the contribution of architects and archbishops living in different centuries, and sometimes with different religions too. An analysis of public programs can likewise identify the contribution of administrations distant from each other in time and ideology. Although no one administration can claim credit for the whole, each can claim credit for some parts.

The manifold of public policy is the sum of hundreds of discrete choices. If we want to know what effect the choices of the government of the day have upon the current manifold, it can be subdivided into two categories: choices that a given administration inherits from the past and choices that it makes itself. If we want to evaluate the contribution of a past administration to the manifold of programs in effect today, then we must divide the current totality into two different categories: programs inherited from a given past administration and all other programs.

No administration's term of office can be treated as self-contained; each is an amalgam of many inherited programs and some that it adds itself. Current choices are important in setting the agenda for current political controversies, but the rhetoric of debate is not as substantial as the inheritance of programs operating by routine. To divide historical time into discrete eras, such as the Reagan Revolution or a Thatcher Revolution, is to misunderstand the cumulative process of inheritance. The Reagan Revolution inherited major New Deal and Great Society programs, and the Thatcher administration inherited programs from the 1945–51 Labour government. If their choices had been all-important, then these programs would have been repealed wholesale; insofar as inheritance comes before choice, inherited programs are not repealed but persist. The legacy of each "revolutionary" administration contains hundreds of programs that it inherited from its predecessors. And this is even more true of their successors, whether of the same party or a different party.

This book places inheritance before choice because the persistence of a legacy provides a better explanation of public policy than do theories of choice. Whereas the program choices of any one administration will be measured in the dozens, the totality of public policy consists of hundreds of programs chosen by many administrations. In the last decade of the twentieth century the government of the day administers an inheritance of programs accumulated since World War II or before.

The priority of inheritance before choice does not prevent change, but it places limits on what the government of the day can immediately alter. In the short run, the choices of the government of the day are restricted by inherited programs and by a limited time in office. Yet gradually some programs are likely to be terminated, others added. Even more important, measures that were once considered new become established as a time-honored part of the inheritance of successive administrations. In the fullness of time, an inheritance that appears overwhelming to a new administration can be seen to have altered with the accumulation of choices made by its numerous successors.

The force of inertia does not mean that the "dead hand" of the past makes public policy static. The compounding of past choices can lead to change—qualitative as well as quantitative—without choice. Although some social programs may persist from early in the century, the totality of contemporary welfare state programs is qualitatively different from that of a pre-1914 government. Analytically, we may say that a tipping point is the year in which programs adopted thereafter outnumber those adopted earlier. Similar, the tipping point for public expenditure is the year in which total expenditure on programs adopted since exceeds that on earlier programs.

Even though plausible reasons can be given to support each of the three hypotheses outlined in this chapter—inheritance, the will to choose, and dominance of inertia—they cannot all be true, nor is each likely to be of equal significance. To test the extent to which the government of the day administers an inheritance rather than making choices, we need empirical data about the commitments of governments over many decades, even generations.

3 Programs as Building Blocks

Q. What grows when government grows?
A. Programs.

Abstraction is necessary to create theories, but a concept as broad as public policy risks describing everything and therefore nothing. In order to identify the specifics of public policy, the activities of government need to be differentiated. Government (or in European parlance, the state) cannot be reduced to a single attribute; it is a label for a family of concepts. Even though in constitutional form a government may be unitary, in public policy it is not a single actor using a single resource to produce a single undifferentiated output. Instead, government is a conglomerate of institutions producing heterogeneous outputs. As Simon (1969: 73f and 99ff) observes, the careful decomposition of such large-scale aggregates is a crucial step in analysis.

In this book government is not viewed in terms of what it is, a set of formal institutions, but in terms of what it does, deliver programs that constitute the goods and services of government (Rose, 1985a). The chief institutions that each administration inherits are constitutionally prescribed and change very slowly. But the programs inherited by a new administration are not constitutionally prescribed. Whereas amendments of a constitution are infrequent and often require special procedures to enact, a new program can readily be adopted in an ordinary legislative vote.

The familiar term *policy* has at least three different uses (cf. Heidenheimer, 1985). In its most general sense, the word is synonymous with problems of government concern, as in the references to economic policy. Secondly, a policy can be a statement of political intentions, identifying a goal that politicians would like to achieve.

However, intentions can be vague rhetorical expressions of preferences, as in a declared intention to reduce inflation. The record of every administration is full of good (and, sometimes, bad) intentions that never come to pass.

To move from a statement of intentions to action requires a program that is the instrumental means of realizing an intended goal. In this book the term *policy* is used to refer to the concerns and intentions of policymakers, and the term *program* is used to refer to a specific combination of laws, appropriations, agencies, and personnel directed toward a more or less clearly identified set of goals. Because programs are tangible commitments of the state and not just the best intentions of the government of the day, they can be transmitted by inheritance without choice.

Whereas all government officials may intend their actions to promote the nation's welfare, the programs for doing so differ greatly between departments of defense, education, and agriculture. Programs to develop new weapons systems are very different from programs for teaching handicapped children or programs paying subsidies to farmers. Differences in ends and means make it impossible to generalize about policymaking from a single case study, However, general hypotheses can be tested against evidence from the hundreds of programs that constitute the stuff of public policy.

A satisfactory test of inheritance as against choice makes substantial demands on both concepts and data. We must distinguish programs from high-order abstractions and measure programs empirically. The first section deals with these points. Secondly, it is necessary to observe programs over a lengthy period of time, for the longer programs remain in place, the greater the impact of inheritance. To test the robustness of programs when different parties control government and in variable economic circumstances, it is necessary to examine programs over more than a quarter century. In order to include the whole range of government commitments, it is desirable to cover programs delivered by local as well as national government. The third section relates general criteria to the choice of a country and span of time for analysis; Britain since 1945 meets all these stringent requirements.

Conceptualization before Quantification

Before we can examine quantified evidence of public policy, we must have an idea of what we want to measure; otherwise, any set of numbers may be invoked without regard to their appropriateness for the theoretical task at hand. A necessary requirement for testing the relative importance of inheritance and choice in public policy is to define the dependent variable, public policy (Sartori, 1984).

Many familiar methods of discussing public policy use very high-level abstractions, such functional universals as the maintenance of order, or else categories so broad, such as education or social security, that the programmatic details are obscured. A *program* focuses on activities within the structure of government. For example, officials in a department of education do not deal with the subject in general but with specific programs for preschool children, secondary schools, teacher training, and so forth. Programs are also central in budgeting, for money is allocated to particular programs authorized by particular statutes. Thus, public expenditure data can be used to weigh the significance of different programs. A program that accounts for a billion in public funds is likely to be more important than a program that accounts for a few millions.

What Does Government Do?

Many different answers are given to this seemingly simple question, each justifiable within a particular theoretical context but not appropriate for use in testing the importance of inheritance.

A common assumption is that since government allocates money, public expenditure as a proportion of the national product can be used as a measure of public policy. The higher the percentage, the bigger the government and the more policy there is. By this measure, a country such as Sweden has two-thirds more public policy than the United States, for public expenditure there is about 60 percent of the national product, as against 35 percent in the United States.

Although public expenditure is significant, a summary total of public expenditure reveals nothing about the content of public policies. The total aggregates expenditure on discrete programs, lumping together spending in areas as different as debt interest payments, health care, and transportation. Doing so ignores the fact that governments differ greatly in the composition of public expenditure. For example, the United States federal government spends more than twice as much of its national product on defense as does the average advanced industrial nation, and much less on health care and other social policies (Rose, 1991a: table 7.3). Figures of total expenditure obscure such differences. The aggregation of spending for many different purposes makes it impossible to know whether an increase in the total is due to all programs expanding slightly, a few new and expensive programs being introduced, or changes in only a few programs. Moreover, it is possible for total public expenditure to remain constant, while some new measures are chosen and others are terminated.

Philosophical discussions often focus on a global abstraction, the state. From this perspective, change is the metamorphosis from one type of state to another, for example, from a premodern to a modern state or from a capitalist to a postcapitalist state. Such shifts tend to occur very infrequently; the modern state has been in existence for well over a century (Poggi, 1978; Dyson, 1980). The concept is thus incapable of identifying changes in public policy from one decade to the next, or from the start of the first world war in 1914 to the end of the second in 1945, or since the growth of the welfare state. This study accepts that institutions of the state are needed to authorize and deliver programs, but it is more concerned with substantive outputs, the programs that institutions deliver, than with structures per se.

In reaction against legalistic theories of the state, political scientists have propounded systems theories. The literature poses a fundamental functional question: How can the political system persist? (cf. Easton, 1965a). The answers given emphasize a variety of formal and informal functional requirements, such as political socialization, recruitment, interest articulation, rulemaking, implementation, and so forth (see e.g. Almond, 1960: 2ff). But persistence of the political system, like persistence of the modern state, tells us nothing in particular about the programs and choices of government.

Decisionmaking studies are relevant for understanding the choice of programs, because they address immediate questions of how government is stimulated to act and why one program is chosen in preference to another. Decisionmaking sees public policy as a series of collective choices within a structure of conflicting interests, institutions, and values. The standard critique of decisionmaking studies is that they ignore nondecisionmaking, that is, the exclusion of some alternatives from the agenda of collective choice because dominant values make them politically impossible for the moment (cf. the classic studies by Dahl, 1960; Bachrach and Baratz, 1962; and the agenda-setting literature, e.g., Cobb and Elder, 1972; Kingdon, 1984). A similar criticism is relevant here: decisionmaking studies focus upon what is happening now and tend to ignore the significance of choices inherited from the distant past as means of imposing commitments on today's nominal decisionmakers.

Case studies often focus on issues, for example, adopting a new health program, stressing the importance of bargaining. Often the same case, depending on the bias of the researcher, can be used to demonstrate the importance of inherited constraints or the making of a choice. Because a case study is about a single event, it cannot consider which types of programs are most likely to be dominated by inheritance and which allow scope for choice. Even a case study cast in a generic conceptual framework, such as Allison's (1971) study of the Cuban missile crisis, can only be suggestive of general propositions. We cannot conclude that generalizations derived from the study of the 1962 Cuban missile crisis would be true of all problems and programs of government (cf. Bendor and Hammond, 1992).

A developmental typology of the priorities of government is particularly relevant for the examination of inheritance, because it recognizes that government not only grows in aggregate but also alters its priorities. An analysis of the departmental structure of more than two dozen European and North American governments from the mid-nineteenth century to the present (Rose, 1976) has identified three stages of development. In the first, programs maintained the authority of the state; they primarily address military defense, diplomacy, the courts, and police, and financing these necessary but limited goals. In the nineteenth-century "nightwatchman" state, such programs constituted nearly the whole of the inheritance of public policy. Once these choices were made and remained effective, there was no need for further action.

With industrialization, governments faced new problems and gave priority to developing programs to mobilize economic resources. This arose from conviction in countries such as France and Germany, where the state was seen as necessarily having a positive role to play in economic development. In England, even when laissez-faire ideology was dominant, necessity forced the British government to introduce programs that provided a legal framework within which the market could operate. In the United States, programs were required to foster the economic development of territories for pioneer settlement, and then to regulate new industrial powers.

In the past half century, social welfare has become the spending priority of government. Social programs have expanded in number and expense as government has undertaken responsibility for the welfare of individuals and families in childhood, ill health, and periods of income insecurity. At the extreme, writings about social welfare are reductionist; all programs are assumed to be part of a general goal of abolishing poverty or promoting economic equality. The whole of government is reduced to social policy, as in the term *welfare state*.

The developmental approach to public policy implies that an administration entering office in 1990 will inherit many more programs than an administration taking office in 1890 or 1940. Moreover, the mixture of programs inherited will be different, because of the emergence of new policy priorities. However, the strength of viewing development over more than a century is also a weakness. It does not identify how much or how little scope for choice is open to policymakers who have inherited the responsibility for administering a government that has been growing for more than a century.

Defining a Program

The outputs of government are programs authorized by laws, produced by public employees, financed by public revenues, and supervised or delivered by public agencies (Rose, 1985a). Each program has its own statutory authorization and budget line and is the responsibility of a particular agency. Whereas systems and functions tend to be abstract concepts, programs can be identified in statute books, budget documents, personnel classifications, and organization charts.

Programs constitute the goods and services that government produces for individuals, families, communities, and collective institutions of society. The institutions of government are not static but continuously engaged in mobilizing resources. These resources are not hoarded within the black box of government but dispensed to produce a heterogeneous range of program outputs. The mix of resources varies from program to program; all require some statutory authority, money, and personnel.

Public programs bring nearly everyone into contact with government in ways that are important to ordinary people. Education, health care, and social security benefits are usually conceived as "good" goods that people rely upon for major parts of their life. Although programs are called public, in economic terms they are private benefits, that is, the recipients are individuals rather than society as a whole. Whereas less than one-quarter of public expenditure was devoted to individual benefits in the mid-nineteenth century, today more than three-quarters is allocated to programs that immediately and visibly benefit tens of millions of individuals and families (Rose, 1989a: chapter 1).

Programs are important to public officials too, for the job of virtually everyone in government, from a Cabinet minister to a hospital attendant, is to deal with a specific program or set of programs. A defense official is not concerned with agriculture or labor legislation, or even with defense in general. A Ministry of Defense official will be involved with specific problems within this policy area, for example, weapons procurement for the air force or military pensions. An agriculture department official is not concerned with farming in general but with administering programs that address crops, animals, soil, or farmers. Each year's budget is not only a document of macro-economic significance but also a statement detailing expenditure on hundreds of programs.

Programs cannot be examined at the level of total expenditure by department, because spending in broad areas of public policy such as health, education, and social security may remain relatively steady while there is continuous choice about programs within a departmental budget, as some are repealed and new ones introduced. For that reason, OECD (Organisation for Economic Co-Operation and

Development) statistics that aggregate expenditure on all income-maintenance programs under a single social security heading cannot be used to test theories of inheritance before choice. The same limitation applies to organization-focused studies of policy change (cf. Dunsire and Hood, 1989). The persistence of an organization or its total expenditure is not proof of persistence at the program level, and many changes in organizational structure create new departments while leaving the substance of their programs unaffected (Davies and Rose, 1988).

Unlike relatively abstract functional goals, programs are discrete units. A function such as public order is a general heading that can refer to programs involving the police, prisons, probation, compensation for victims of crime, and so forth. Similarly, social security is a goal that can be achieved through programs providing cash benefits or benefits in kind, and may address the unemployed, single-parent mothers, or individuals with chronic illnesses.

Because programs are formal commitments and governments are good bureaucratic recordkeepers, there is a long paper trail in the statute books and in annual publications of government detailing program expenditure, personnel, and activities. Tracing the genealogy of legislation and appropriations through mountains of official documents is difficult and often tedious work, but it can be done. By contrast, attempts to identify the intentions of policymakers who initially chose a program and those subsequently responsible for its administration are handicapped by a shortage of written records and by the fundamental problem of inferring what politicians "really" intended when they talked about a measure or acted.

Because programs differ greatly from policy area to policy area, the records examined should be comprehensive. Concentrating solely upon local government or state government would be insufficient for generalization, since lower levels of government are excluded from responsibility for many important areas of government. Education bulks large at the local level, but not social security; parks and recreation are significant locally, but a city or a state has no department of defense. Furthermore, the scope for choice of local government is often constrained by decisions taken at the state and national level or subject to preemption from above.

National government is the most appropriate level for analyzing programs. It has the most scope for choice because its authority is broadest and its resources of law and money greatest. This is especially true of unitary systems of government, such as Britain and France. The centralization of authority in a unitary state means that national government can choose what programs local and regional authorities carry out, and stipulate detailed regulations for education, police powers, and other locally delivered services. A unitary state is also more likely to centralize revenue and to have clear methods of accounting for spending on its programs. By contrast, in federal systems, the top tier of government often can only act with the concurring consent of state and local authorities. In federal systems the transfer of revenue between federal, state, and local authorities creates difficulties in knowing how much money is spent on specific programs and at which level of government choices were made.

To concentrate on programs is to put the purposes of government first. Government does not raise taxes in order to hoard money or to employ officials as retainers; it mobilizes resources in order to deliver goods and services to individuals and families. Government is not only about winning votes or gaining resources; it is also about actions taken to some purpose. Programs are the means by which policymakers can promote their goals and values. An administration that does not make any alterations in the manifold of programs that it inherits from its predecessors will add little to the legacy that it leaves behind. To be effective, an administration must make choices about programs.

Money and Programs Give Meaning to Each Other

When examining programs, we not only want to know how many there are but also how much they cost. Once a choice enters the legacy of successive administrations, we want to know the extent to which spending on it increases. Are the cumulative cash claims of new choices large or small in comparison with programs inherited from the distant past? By weighing the amount of money spent on programs as well as counting the number of programs newly chosen, we can assess the relative importance of inheritance and choice in the manifold of public policy. Statistics can thus be used in the original sense of the word, facts and figures describing activities of the state.

To discuss public expenditure without reference to programs is to indulge in vague generalization. A proposal to cut public spending by 10 or 25 per cent is meaningless without identification of the specific programs that would be abolished or severely curbed as a necessary condition of achieving such huge savings. Similarly, a proposal for a major new program is empty without an indication of its cost, and how it can be financed.

Money is the most commonly employed measure of the scale of public programs. Each year the budget cycle concentrates the attention of public officials on a line-by-line analysis of programs for which it is responsible. How much is spending on inherited programs to be increased or decreased? Inherited budget commitments are a constraint upon the introduction of new spending measures. In an attempt to contain public spending, policymakers sometimes agree that the introduction of new measures requires an offsetting cut in established spending commitments (see Tarschys, 1985).

The annual budget process reveals political priorities in a broad sense. An administration never has enough money to do everything it may desire. Even a small increase in a major spending program such as health care or social security will run into billions. A significant tax cut will also require a significant cut in program expenditure. Budgeting involves a balance of competing claims for public funds. Aaron Wildavsky (1988: vii) declares, "The State of the Union and the state of the budget have become essentially equivalent."

The budget process is a test of political wills. Every program has advocates, and every administration is subject to pressure from groups with an interest in promoting programs for its clients. Within a single government department there is competition for funds between already established programs. Within education, for example, policymakers face competing claims for more spending on preschool, primary, secondary, and higher education—and for new programs too.

Most quantitative analyses of public policy unhesitatingly use expenditure data, for it is easy to quantify expenditure and changes in expenditure. But organizations, a familiar unit of political science analysis, cannot be treated quantitatively. They vary greatly in the size and significance of their activities (Rose, 1988). For example, every country has only one foreign affairs ministry and one ministry of defense, but thousands or tens of thousands of units of local government. Such differences in the number of organizations does not make local government thousands of times more important than defense.

The number of public employees involved in a program is a second indicator of its scale (Rose 1985b), since many programs, as in education and health care, are labor-intensive. The services delivered are not a sum of money but the skills of a teacher or a doctor. Money is an input, not a final output, of such programs; it is used to pay salaries of teachers and doctors and maintain schools and hospitals. However, there are also programs that are money-intensive but not labor-intensive, such as social security and the payment of interest on the national debt. Relatively few public employees are required to administer cash transfers that can be paid by computer.

Laws are a necessary condition of public expenditure, for a law must authorize a program before money can be appropriated and spent. Laws are important in establishing entitlements to benefits, such as free and compulsory education, health care, and social security benefits. Laws also determine how much money people are entitled to receive in cash benefit programs such as social security (Rose, 1986a; Katzmann, 1989).

Laws and money can be used in complementary ways. Laws tell us what the government at some point in time chose to authorize. However, this is insufficient, since as long as programs are identified only by their unique names, they are literally incomparable. Public expenditure, however, gives weight to statutory programs and makes it possible to compare how much money government spends on different programs, discriminating between large- and small-scale programs.

The Test of Time Is Long

The media's concentration upon political controversies about current choices radically foreshortens public policy, because only a small number of measures can be crowded onto the agenda of political debate at any one time. In order to understand the legacy of programs of the current administration, a much longer time perspective is needed than a session of Congress or Parliament. To understand the process of inheritance requires a span of time long enough to allow programs to be conceived, implemented, become part of an administration's legacy, and demonstrate durability or obsolescence through a series of administrations.

Measuring Political Lifetimes

Unlike the biological lifespan of individuals, political time is not limited. A constitution can last indefinitely; the American Constitution has been in effect for more than two hundred years, and the

English Constitution's origins are dated from Magna Carta in 1215. By contrast, a budget covers a 12-month period, a legislative session has a life of a year, the life of a Congress is two years, and a Parliament or a president's term of office lasts about four years.

To observe the process of inheritance we must study at least three "generations" in government. Just as we would not consider an object a family heirloom if it had not been in the family for at least three generations, so we would not consider a program to be part of the continuing inheritance of government if it were only in place for one generation. The first generation is the one that makes an initial choice and adds something to the legacy left its successor; the second receives the legacy and transmits it; and the third generation rejects or confirms programs as part of the inheritance of public policy.

A generation in government is not measured simply by the passage of time; it also requires a change in the direction of government, whether determined by governors or by turbulence in the policy environment. A change in the holder of the office of head of the government of the day is insufficient to achieve this. The succession of Ronald Reagan by George Bush or of Major by Thatcher does not of itself represent a change in direction. In coalition governments of Europe, the office of prime minister can rotate almost annually without this implying a significant change in policy.

Insofar as different parties stand for different political values and policies, then the shift from Democratic to Republican or from Conservative to Labour or vice versa should lead to program change. Alternatively, if the legacy remained unchanged when party control of government switched, this would demonstrate the importance of inheritance before choice. If party control of the White House is taken as marking a political generation in Washington, then a span of three generations will cover a quarter century or more, e.g., from the start of the Eisenhower administration in 1952 through the Kennedy and Johnson administration to a long period of Republican dominance since, followed by a Democratic victory in 1992. In Britain, a quarter century is also a normal span of time for party control to shift at least twice. Since 1945 control of British government has changed hands between parties six times, and partisan control of British government has only shifted twice since a Conservative administration took office in 1970.

A generation can be defined by a dominant political problem, mood, or zeitgeist. A period in which many new programs are chosen and old ones abandoned can be followed by exhaustion and consolidation without choice. Scholars of the American presidency have sought to identify cycles of innovation and consolidation in the behavior of White House incumbents (cf. Skowronek, 1988). David Mayhew (1991) has shown that the enactment of major legislation in Congress is not so much a function of which party is in control of the White House but whether or not the political climate provides a stimulus to action. Thus, much of the activism of the Kennedy-Johnson administration was carried over to the administration of Richard Nixon. Equally, inactivity can continue from one administration to the next—if that is the temper of the times.

In Britain, too, periods of movement and consolidation can be identified. The decade of the 1940s was a time of great changes in British political life, under the Churchill-led wartime coalition government and its successor Labour government. By contrast, the period from 1951 to 1964 appears a time of consolidation. The enthusiasm of the 1964 Labour government for change was matched by the enthusiasm for activity of the Conservative administration entering office under Edward Heath in 1970. The Thatcher administration reflected a desire for movement—but in a different direction.

Whereas some political climates offer a window of opportunity for introducing new programs, others do not. Hence, the importance of inheritance and choice will vary with the climate of opinion. To test whether this is the case, it is necessary to observe government over a minimum of a quarter of a century, and a longer period is better still. A span of several decades, while not long comparable to successive generations of a family, is sufficient to allow choices of one decade to be repudiated by a successor generation or incorporated into a legacy that persists without choice.

When and Where to Start

The length of time for monitoring programs is only one consideration in testing the inheritance of public policy. It is equally important to take care about when to start, for as Solow (1985: 331) advises, "The validity of an economic model may depend on the social context." It would be wrong to test a model of inheritance when there was little to inherit, and so much scope for choice, because laissez faire values dominated the political climate, resulting in policymakers not being expected to make many choices. An administration today inherits spending commitments accumulated throughout the twentieth century; this is very different from the position of an administration entering office in a century of laissez faire. The contemporary demand for government activity creates pressure for policymakers to exercise choice, notwithstanding (or because of) an accumulated inheritance of programs from the past.

Periods of equal duration can be unequal in activity. A few years of war can involve bigger choices and greater change than decades of peace (cf. Peacock and Wiseman, 1961). Analysis can be disrupted for technical reasons, such as a change in conventions of accounting for public expenditure. Disruptions can also reflect a substantive political problem. In the extreme case of Germany, a pioneer in welfare state programs, there have been four distinct regimes since 1870, two democratic and two authoritarian. In addition, the boundaries of the German state have been very greatly altered by three wars and by reunification in 1990. In the United States, territorial expansion has transformed the expanse of the country in less than a century, and immigration has transformed the population in receipt of public programs.

Major studies of the growth of government often start in the nineteenth century to give a picture of the transformation of government from a nightwatchman state to a welfare state (see, e.g., Flora and Heidenheimer, 1981; Baldwin, 1990). The approach can be microscopic, concentrating on case studies of a few programs (see, e.g., Heclo, 1974; Alber, 1982). It is more usual for breadth of coverage to be achieved by aggregating individual programs into broad policy areas (see, e.g., Flora, 1983: chapter 8). Instead of dealing with separate programs of income maintenance for older people, the unemployed, the sick, and others, data is lumped under the single heading of transfer payments, a heading too gross to be useful in determining what happens at the program level. Although analysis of the growth of government is not explicitly teleological, the present often appears as the culmination of a century-long process, leaving little scope for further choice, whether rolling back or further expanding public programs.

The *present* is an elastic term. It may refer to the year in which the author finished a book, to the latest year for which data is available, or to some more or less appropriate "end" date in a narrative. Some leading studies of the postwar growth in the welfare state since 1945 stop in the early 1970s; they do not treat the challenges since the world recession of the mid-1970s and subsequent growth of market-oriented ideologies. Other studies address the period of "cutbacks" or "rolling back the state" since then. In principle, theories of continuity and change in public policy ought to be robust enough to deal with different political climates and circumstances (cf. Hood, 1991).

The period of almost half a century since the end of World War II is particularly appropriate for testing inheritance before choice. By 1945 governments of major nations already had a range of social and economic programs in their ongoing legacy. The attention given new programs in the immediate postwar era, and again in the 1960s, implies wide scope for choice. Since 1945 there has also been consistency in the structure of states and regimes, and expenditure data about programs is much more detailed than for earlier eras.

The postwar era has witnessed sustained periods of economic prosperity and economic growth that have provided a buoyant tax base for expanding public programs through the massive fiscal dividend of growth. Without raising tax rates policymakers could collect additional revenue to finance new choices, expand inherited programs, cut taxes, or do all three in combination.

Within the postwar era there have been changes in the climate of political opinion as well as in party control of government. The immediate postwar years were a time of military demobilization and reconstruction. In the 1950s there was a widespread expectation of stability, implying few choices. The following decade saw a self-conscious political emphasis on active government, implying the introduction of many new programs. The world recession of 1975 ushered in a period of fiscal austerity, questioning the maintenance of inherited levels of expenditure and discouraging plans for expansion. Shifts in the climate of opinion can test whether inheritance or choice is continuously dominant, or whether the prevalence of each alternates according to changes in the political climate, the state of the economy, and party control of government.

Britain as a Test of Inheritance before Choice

The continuity of government in Britain makes it extremely well suited to test a theory of inheritance before choice. Along with Germany, it is one of the progenitors of the welfare state. Although

Germany has a stronger claim to be first in developing the programs identified with the welfare state (cf. Flora and Heidenheimer, 1981; Mommsen, 1981), any attempt to analyze German program choices over a long period of time is bedeviled by its frequent changes in regimes.

Because Britain is a unitary state, choices about public programs are not complicated by the constitutional and political constraints of federalism (as in the United States and Canada), which can rule some policy areas out of bounds for the national government. In Europe, Germany, Belgium, and Switzerland are subject to substantial federal constraints in policymaking, and regionalism or federalism complicates policymaking in countries such as Austria, Italy, and Spain.

Swedish public policy is often the subject of analysis, but that is because it is atypical. Among advanced industrial nations Sweden has been in the vanguard in promoting public programs; it consistently ranks first among OECD nations in the percentage of its national product allocated through public expenditure. The hegemony of the Social Democratic party there for more than fifty years greatly limited the prospect of choice through the alternation of parties in government. The occasional nonsocialist Swedish administration, as in the period since 1991, has had its political agenda defined by an inheritance of two generations of social democratic programs.

Britain is more representative of public policy in advanced industrial nations than Sweden or the United States, because its level of public expenditure is near the average rather than at an extreme (Rose, 1991a: table 7.2). During the postwar era Britain has been part of major trends, as in the surge of social democracy after 1945 and the revival of the right in the 1980s. Public expenditure as a percentage of national product is close to the OECD average. British government also meets practical requirements for testing the importance of inheritance before choice: power for choice is concentrated at the center of central government, there is comprehensive and accurate data about programs and program expenditure, and the data cover all programs since 1945.

Concentrating the Power for Choice

British government is an extreme example of centralization, for there are very few constraints upon the choices of the government of the day. Whereas other countries have a written constitution limiting what government can do and mandating procedures that inhibit the adoption of new programs or the repeal of old measures, these are absent in Westminster. The British Constitution is an unwritten document, a confusing and often disputed jumble of ordinary laws, customs, and conventions. Given the importance of laws as a constraint upon choice, it is important to note that English courts do not restrict the executive as in the United States or European democracies, which have much more legalistic cultures (Ehrmann, 1977). They will not challenge a government decision to start or stop a program, as long as there is authorization by an act of Parliament.

The British first-past-the-post electoral system manufactures a parliamentary majority for a party that has the largest share of the popular vote, whereas in most European countries proportional representation makes coalition government the norm, because it divides seats in Parliament among a multiplicity of parties. It is much easier to arrive at decisions within a single-party government than when bargains must take place within a coalition in which several parties can exercise a veto on choice (cf. Laver and Schofield, 1990; Rose, 1991b).

The combination of single-party control of the House of Commons and the fusion of legislative and executive authority gives great potential freedom of choice to the government of the day. When deliberating about programs, the prime minister and Cabinet ministers need only consider opinion within the majority party. Members of Parliament are expected to vote in accord with the party whip. Although the government of the day must pay some attention to the opinion of its supporters in Parliament, in a showdown party discipline almost invariably delivers the government a majority in favor of any program that it chooses. Hence, virtually every proposal contained in the annual statement of the government's program, the Queen's Speech to Parliament, is subsequently enacted into law.

In Britain the powers of choice rest with a handful of politicians at the center of central government, with the prime minister occupying a unique place. Whereas the literature of the American presidency tends to emphasize constraints, the literature about the prime minister complains about the lack of checks on his or her administration's scope for choice. Complaints about "elective dictatorship," which escalated in response to actions of the Thatcher administration, are a recurring feature of British politics (cf. Hewart, 1929; Holme and Elliott, 1988).

The British Treasury is in an exceptionally strong position to control expenditure on established programs and authorize expenditure on new programs. No minister can put a new spending program to Parliament without the Treasury certifying that the additional cost is accurately estimated and acceptable. The annual negotiation of the next year's budget is a perennial test of the relative strength of spending departments, whose ministers have a political interest in promoting new programs, and the Treasury, which has an institutional commitment to limit expenditure (see Heclo and Wildavsky, 1981; Barnett, 1982). The Treasury's head, the chancellor of the exchequer, works closely with the prime minister in determining overall macroeconomic policies that establish constraints within which expenditure for new programs is allocated. The Treasury's powers are not unlimited; for example, spending on inherited programs can escalate through an increase in the number eligible to claim an entitlement, for example, health care. Nonetheless, the Treasury can act as a gatekeeper, making it difficult for politicians to slip a new program into the statute book against its view of the limits of public expenditure.

The unitary character of the state, including central control of local government, expands the scope for choice by British government. Acts of Parliament delimit what local government can and cannot do; there is restricted scope for local initiatives, especially if a significant sum of money is involved. Westminster is constitutionally able to control all spending and taxing powers at all levels of government. Expenditure of noncentral agencies on programs for education and health is subject to close control by central government. Even when programs are locally delivered, British government is about central choices.

Comprehensive and Accurate Program Data

In principle, governments are good recordkeepers, for public agencies need legal authorization for each penny spent and must account in detail for their use of public funds. In practice, the records of public expenditure are often difficult to draw together in a systematic way. One obstacle, the decentralization of taxing and spending authority, is not a problem in Britain, for central government levies nine-tenths of taxation and strictly controls the remaining tenth levied by local authorities. Secondly, public agencies may keep records according to different historical practices, leading to inconsistencies that make comparison between policy areas difficult or impossible. Thirdly, major programs may be administered off budget, as part of a numbers game to reduce the government's reported level of public expenditure.

In Britain, Treasury control has made comprehensive budgeting normal. Acts of Parliament authorize each program, and the annual budget's Finance Act details exactly how much money can be spent for a particular program. Expenditure is not authorized in total or in departmental aggregates but in budget lines linked to programs. Total expenditure is arrived at by adding up thousands of lines of expenditure authorized under hundreds of different acts.

The most widely publicized statement of program expenditure is the white paper proposals for expenditure in the forthcoming financial year. The statements in the public expenditure white paper are translated into appropriation bills, listing expenditure authorization in great detail. The bills are debated in the House of Commons, not on points of detail but on matters of principle. Participants in the debate know that their words will not affect the actions of government. Thanks to party discipline, in Britain the government's budget is assured of approval without alteration by the House of Commons. By contrast, in Washington, the president's budget proposals are only the start of a lengthy political bargaining process between the White House and Congress, so much so that the president's proposals are often pronounced dead-on-arrival.

An annual statement, *The Government's Expenditure Plans,* first published in 1962, is issued after the conclusion of prolonged interdepartmental negotiations between the Treasury and spending departments. It identifies expenditure approved for the coming year, with nonbinding indications of planning targets for three years further into the future. Data are also reported for the several preceding years. The form of the white paper, which now runs into many volumes, is dictated by the Treasury's concern with controlling public expenditure (see Mackenzie, 1976; Likierman, 1988). In 1993, subsequent to the period covered by this research, procedures were altered to link taxing and expenditure data more closely. The intent of the reform is to increase the comprehensiveness with which choices are made about program expenditure.

However, this politically important statement of spending intentions is "deficient" as a record of program expenditure past or present (cf. Heald, 1991). The first weakness is that prospective figures are only estimates of expenditure. In an era of inflation, any estimate will be altered by fluctuations up or down in price levels. There are also unexpected fluctuations in the demand for services such as unemployment benefits, in the cost of interest payments and arising from unanticipated events such as the Gulf War.

A second weakness of white paper projections is that they fail to take into account changes in political judgments. Statements of intent about expenditure two or three years ahead are subject to change before the date arrives to put them into effect. Alterations may reflect shifting political calculations or party control of government. There is a saying in public expenditure negotiations, "Year 3 never comes," that is, notional commitments three years ahead are not kept because of intervening events.

Thirdly, successive administrations have made long-term comparisons impossible because of radical shifts in the way in which public expenditure figures are calculated and published. In an attempt to control for the effect of inflation, in the 1960s and 1970s figures were published in inflation-adjusted "constant" or "real" pounds sterling. The annual recalculation of past and future figures to bring them into alignment with the "constant" value of the pound at the given moment resulted, paradoxically, in inconstancy, as each year's white paper rewrote the past, reporting a new set of numbers for spending in past years, as previous figures were adjusted upwards to take into account subsequent inflation. Future spending was similarly adjusted. The size of the adjustment was variable because the annual rate of inflation has varied substantially and reversed at irregular intervals. Short-term comparisons between the previous, current, and next year were possible under this system, and this was the primary concern of public expenditure officials in the Treasury and ministries. However, no long-term analysis was possible, and the system assumed that spending on public programs would be indexed, that is, increased in line with inflation (cf. Heclo and Wildavsky, 1981:

preface). As part of its anti-inflationary strategy, the Thatcher administration returned to budgeting in actual cash in 1982, thus creating a discontinuity with the annually revised "real" figures reported in the past.

Fourthly, public expenditure reports aggregate spending on a number of programs under a single heading. For more than a decade after introduction, information was published about expenditure only at the level of the department or major divisions within a department. Annual reports are now more detailed, but this creates greater inconsistencies with the past, as in the central government's attempt to "distance" itself from the cost of local government expenditure by treating it as if it were not its responsibility.

Before rejecting this familiar document of the current cycle of public expenditure, the authors solicited the view of the then chief secretary of the Treasury, John MacGregor. It took a three-page letter for him to explain why the Treasury found it operationally desirable to use different measures of expenditure in a given year and to change methods every few years. The chief secretary advised that the Treasury's own published sources could *not* be used to provide a comprehensive picture of program expenditure, especially for the period before the mid-1970s, and suggested that we use the appropriation accounts, which contain the audited figures of public expenditure. The chief secretary added, "As you will appreciate, to do this for some 180 votes and 40 odd years' data is not a task to be undertaken lightly" (MacGregor, 1986: 3). These are the accounts used in this book.

The definitive statement of programs and expenditure must be *retrospective,* the audited record of what government actually did in a given year. This information is reported on a program-by-program and pound-by-pound basis in the annual appropriation accounts of the Comptroller and Auditor General, whose National Audit Office has a staff of hundreds scrutinizing expenditure of all government departments at the program level. Its work is augmented by finance officers of spending departments, who are directly involved in disbursement on a program-by-program basis. Unique among the major agencies of British government, the National Audit Office is an agency of Parliament rather than the executive. It is supervised by the Public Accounts Committee of the House of Commons, which is chaired by a leading member of Parliament of the opposition party, and is charged with protecting the audited accounts from partisan influence or undue influence by spending ministries.

Accuracy and probity are the first concerns of the audit. Unlike the budget estimates, the purpose of audit is to identify sums actually spent and to verify that they were spent for specific programs in ways authorized. In the absence of statutory authorization, auditors can rule that expenditure is illegal. This very rarely happens, for in anticipation of audit civil servants normally carry out program expenditure consistent with authorization by acts of Parliament.

Specificity is a second fundamental feature of audited accounts. Audit requires a verifiable link between particular items of expenditure and legislation. Actions taken, such as payment of a social security benefit or the salary of a factory inspector, must be authorized by a particular act of Parliament. Auditors tend to interpret their terms of reference narrowly; they do not think in terms of such nonverifiable and nonauditable functions as welfare, health, or defense but about specific programs.

Continuity is a third characteristic of auditing. Whereas Treasury officials can switch between the use of actual or inflation-adjusted sums in keeping with changing intellectual fashions or political priorities, auditors are as inflexible as acts of Parliament. Their duty is to verify actual sums of money spent, and not to be distracted by figures that represent hypothetical costs or savings. Because auditors rely upon statutes as the basis for analyzing programs, they are resistant to reshuffling headings in response to political fashions. Only when the government of the day makes a firm and binding choice, expressed in an act of Parliament, will auditors accept that new programs have been introduced or established programs terminated.

The Comptroller and Auditor General annually reports data in a dozen volumes under upwards of 20 different headings. Each major heading corresponds approximately to the name of a Whitehall department. Since the program rather than the department is the unit of analysis, the many symbolic changes in departmental names in the postwar era do not affect analysis here (cf. Pollitt, 1984). In chapters that follow, department names are sometimes used to illustrate points and (chapters 8 and 9) to test hypotheses. In each case the data reported are based on the analysis of programs.

For technical reasons, social security and some local government measures are not fully reported in the appropriation accounts. Details of these programs can be extracted from annual official publications on social security programs financed by contributory benefits. Where necessary, rate support grant programs have been disaggregated to match relevant substantive programs (see Davies, 1989: 5ff for details).

Although spending is separately reported for territorial ministries in Scotland, Wales, and Northern Ireland, normally the figures refer to programs that parallel measures already reported under the name of the appropriate functional ministry, such as education or health (see Rose, 1982: chapters 5–6). Furthermore, for a large part of the postwar era many programs were administered on a Great Britain basis by the functional department now primarily responsible for England, and some, such as those in the field of defense and trade and industry, still are. The Welsh Office was not created until 1964, and its program responsibilities and those of the Scottish Office only gained momentum in the 1970s. The Northern Ireland Office was not created until 1971, and the accounting of its programs is anomalous. Given that nearly all programs of territorial ministries parallel measures in effect in England, to record them separately would be misleading, for it might double, treble, or even quadruple activities. They are therefore excluded. This marginally reduces expenditure on some programs, but since England constitutes five-sixths of the population of the United Kingdom, and important programs such as social security and defense are accounted for on a United Kingdom or Great Britain basis, these exclusions have no substantial effect.

Very small programs that have never accounted for at least 0.0007 per cent of public expenditure in a year (that is, £1mn at 1989 prices) are aggregated under the most appropriate heading to avoid trivial distractions. The small number of programs appearing under more than one departmental heading in the appropriation accounts, such as civil defense, are added together and reported as a single program. The relabeling of a persisting program or its transfer from one department or appropriation account is not treated as a substantive change of program.

Inflation has greatly eroded the effective value of money in the decades since 1946. A pound spent by government in 1946 was worth less than 6p by 1990. Hence, to report expenditure data according to the sums published in the appropriation accounts each year would grossly exaggerate real change. To keep purchasing power constant between 1946 and the beginning of 1990, spending would need to increase by more than 1,500 percent.

To control for the effects of inflation, it is necessary to convert all figures for annual expenditure into constant sums. Since current money values are more meaningful to the reader than money values at the end of World War II, the retail price index of inflation has been used to recalculate expenditure on programs in earlier years in terms of the value of the pound in 1989, and all figures in this book are given in terms of the pound's value then.

Time to Start

The initial legacy is here defined as programs in place at the end of World War II; analysis commences in 1946, the first full financial year after the end of World War II. The British government's financial year is not a calendar year. For reasons that predate the transition from the Julian to the Gregorian calendar in 1752, it starts 1 April and ends 31 March in the following year. Since three-quarters of spending is in the first of two overlapping calendar years, each financial year is here referred to by the calendar year in which it begins. For example, the year beginning on 1 April 1946 and continuing through the following March is described as 1946. Since the programs inherited in spring 1946 were in operation the year before, these programs are inherited from the end of World War II and virtually all civilian programs from before World War II.

In theory it would be possible to go back far longer, since audit has existed for centuries, and the Comptroller and Auditor General has been responsible for the annual accounts since 1866. Yet this would cross the watersheds of world war and make everything since 1938 or 1913 or 1866 falsely appear as "newly chosen."

Nearly half a century is a sufficient span of time to test the importance of inheritance, for any program that has lasted since 1946 cannot be considered the choice of today's government. Equally important, a period of nearly half a century is sufficient for choices of different administrations to become cumulatively numerous as they are added to the legacy of successive administrations. Within this long timespan, it is possible for old programs to be terminated and for some programs to stop as well as start.

The year 1946 is a politically apt starting point, too, for at the end of the war a Labour government under Clement Attlee entered office with a mandate for a major expansion of public policy. In the decades since, many political generations have passed through Westminster, and fashions in public policy have waxed and waned. The period examined extends to March 1990, the latest year for which data was available at the time this book began to be written. The final decade thus encompasses the administration of Margaret Thatcher, a prime minister ideologically committed to imposing choices on public policy—albeit choices that were controversial because they rejected program commitments inherited from predecessors. In the period under review there were 12 general elections and 10 changes in prime minister, and control of government changed hands six times between Labour and Conservatives, with each party in office for an almost equal amount of time.

On all counts, Britain meets the requirements for testing the relative importance of inheritance as against choice. Detailed and comprehensive data about programs avoid the problems of case studies or of sampling; it is possible to analyze *all* the programs of British government. Once this is done, we can address the critical analytic question: Under what circumstances and to what extent do some programs persist through inheritance, while others are the subject of choice?

4   The Persistence of a Legacy

There is a bit of the eighteenth century, a bit of the nineteenth century, and a bit of the twentieth century about Winston [Churchill].
The trouble is that one never knows which will be on top.
—former Prime Minister Clement Attlee

Inheritance is inevitable, but it is not necessarily durable. A legacy can be dissipated or transformed rather than merely conserved by those who receive it. Attlee's description of Winston Churchill emphasizes the ambiguity of inheritance; within an individual, elements from different eras or even different centuries can coexist. The same is true in the manifold of public policy, especially in England, with a continuity of political history extending over many centuries.

The legacy of the past is an important theme of studies of modern British government. Contemporary policies can be traced to predemocratic origins. The programmatic foundations of the welfare state can be traced at least to 1870, when free primary education was made compulsory, and some writers would trace them back to a preindustrial era (cf. Rose, 1965; Beer, 1982). The persistence of the past is underlined by radicals who rail against what they see as the dead hand of tradition, as well as by those who welcome continuity.

Theories of political inertia are conservative in the literal sense, postulating that inherited programs persist whether introduced by parties of the right or the left. A variety of theories support the idea that inherited programs persist (see, e.g., Tarschys, 1975; Larkey et al., 1981). From the demand side, programs can be said to persist because they are what the electorate wants. A supply-side theory holds that programs are popular with producers; public employees have a material and ideological interest in maintaining or expanding their professional activities.

*4.1 (*Persistence*). Once a program becomes part of the legacy of public policy, it persists indefinitely.

However, obsolescence is an alternative consequence of longevity; the older an inherited program becomes, the less suited it may be to current circumstances precisely because of its age. Although a program is current when it is first added to an administration's legacy, as the time since it was introduced lengthens, the more it becomes vulnerable to obsolescence, and thus termination, due to changes in the policy environment.

*4.2 (*Obsolescence*). The older a program is, the more likely it is to be terminated.

In contrast to theories of the irreversibility of government commitments, obsolescence assumes that the persistence of a program from one administration to the next is part of a process of decay rather than permanence. Even if one cannot be precise about when an established program becomes too old, the term *indefinitely* in hypothesis 4.1 is not to be interpreted as persistence ad infinitum.

In the course of five decades both hypotheses can be supported. For example, if the average program remained effective and relevant for a quarter century, then it would remain part of the legacy of successive administrations for part but not all of the period under review here. As of 1964 the great majority of postwar programs would remain in place, but by 1990 there would be an almost complete turnover of programs, with very few surviving from the end of World War II. Insofar as programs are not susceptible to obsolescence, then most inherited at the end of World War II would remain in effect. War introduces a complication in testing for inheritance because of its potential displacement effect on programs. Insofar as war is disruptive of domestic policies as well as defense programs, the immediate postwar years will differ from the decades that followed. This is a common theme of historians writing about the 1945–51 Labour government (see, e.g., Hennessy, 1992). Hence, the first section of this chapter concentrates upon public programs in the immediate aftermath of war. The second section then tests whether persistence or obsolescence best characterizes the legacy of public policy in the four decades that followed.

Is There a Displacement Effect Due to War?

World War II was an unprecedented challenge to British government; for the first time in more than a century Britain faced the imminent threat of invasion. In 1940 the government declared a total mobilization of the civilian as well as the military population. The Emergency Powers Act of 1940 gave the government the authority to require everyone "to place themselves, their services and their property at the disposal of His Majesty" for the defense of the realm and the maintenance of essential services. The end of World War II introduced another challenge, demobilization for peacetime.

In a classic study of the growth of public expenditure in Britain from the nineteenth century to the middle of the twentieth century, A. Peacock and J. Wiseman sought to explain major shifts in public policy as a consequence of the differential effect of periods of war and peace. In a period of peace, "when societies are not being subjected to unusually violent pressures or disturbances," an equilibrium is achieved that leaves public programs "fairly stable." But upheavals such as total mobilization for war have the opposite consequence:

> Social disturbances destroy established conceptions and produce a displacement effect. People will accept, in a period of crisis, tax levels and methods of raising revenue that in quieter times they would have thought intolerable, and this acceptance

remains when the disturbance itself has disappeared. As a result, the revenue and expenditure statistics of the government show a displacement. (Peacock and Wiseman, 1961: 26)

Immediately following the end of a war, the state has a brief and distinctive opportunity to introduce changes:

The state may begin doing some of the things it might formerly have wanted but for which it had hitherto felt politically unable to raise the necessary revenues. At the same time, social disturbances may themselves impose new and continuing obligations upon a government, as the aftermath of the disturbance (for example, the provision by a government of war pensions), as the result of the government being obliged by the disturbances to assume functions that it cannot easily return to others (for example, the wartime provision by government of services formerly financed by private charity) and as a consequence of changed ideas induced or encouraged by the disturbance itself. (Peacock and Wiseman, 1961: 27)

Because war produces losers as well as winners, the displacement theory cannot be applied in every country. In countries that are defeated in battle and occupied by their opponents the capacity of government is reduced or destroyed. A refusal to pay taxes to the government of an occupying power can become a patriotic gesture. In Germany, Austria, Italy, and also France, World War II destroyed the regime itself. Britain, like America, was exceptional in not being occupied by an enemy at some time during World War II. War thus increased the government's capacity to mobilize resources. At least for the victors, Peacock and Wiseman's theory supports the hypothesis:

*4.3 (*Displacement*). As a consequence of the mobilization of resources in wartime, immediately afterwards many programs are stopped and started.

Changes in aggregate public expenditure are consistent with the displacement hypothesis. Between 1910 and 1920, the decade that included World War I, total public spending as a proportion of the British national product doubled. Between the two world wars, aggregate expenditure was fairly stable, averaging about one-quarter of the national product. After the end of World War II there was a big jump up in total expenditure; for a decade after 1945 it averaged two-fifths of a much larger national product, trebling per capita tax revenue in current money terms (Peacock and Wiseman, 1961: 42). In the United States, aggregate public expenditure also appears consistent with the displacement hypothesis. At the height of the New Deal in 1938, the federal government spent less than 8 percent of the national product. After a massive mobilization to finance World War II, federal spending in 1948 was half again as high, 12 percent of a much larger national product (Office of Management and Budget, 1990: A-282).

Insofar as the displacement theory is correct, it has major implications for the inheritance of public policy. The experience of the 1945–51 Labour government would be fundamentally different from that of subsequent administrations, because it had a windfall inheritance of very high wartime taxation, a standard rate of income tax of 50 percent and marginal rates of 90 percent or higher. Without raising taxes, the 1945–51 Attlee government could therefore choose to use the public revenue released by terminating wartime measures to finance a large number of new programs without raising taxes. This political boon would not be available to its successors, who would inherit a fairly stable legacy of programs, new and old, and no fiscal surplus.

Insofar as the displacement hypothesis is correct, 1945–51 would be an atypical period of choice. From 1952 onwards, when the Attlee government ceased to be in office, inheritance should dominate public policy. Aggregate figures appeared consistent with this view as of 1961, the date at which Peacock and Wiseman published their book.

Inherited Programs Survive the Displacement of War

Aggregate figures tell us nothing about the public programs that make up the total. The displacement of war could become manifest in any or all of three distinctive ways: inherited programs could be terminated, new programs chosen, and major shifts registered in public expenditure.

The Labour government elected in July 1945 inherited 115 different programs accumulated over generations of Conservative, Labour, Liberal, and coalition administrations. Postwar demobilization displaced very few; 109 were still in place when it left office six years later (figure 4.1). The six programs that it terminated concerned such wartime measures as payments to Polish troops and British former prisoners of war and wartime utility cloth. In addition, programs for Burma, India, and Pakistan ended with the grant of independence to them. Thus, the actions of the postwar Attlee government support the persistence hypothesis, for 95 percent of the programs inherited from past administrations remained in Labour's legacy to its Conservative successor in 1951.

Nor did the Labour government gain any fiscal advantage by terminating half a dozen inherited programs. The canceled programs were below average in cost, accounting in total for only 3 percent of public expenditure in 1946. This gave the Labour government little additional money to spend on measures of its own choices (figure 4.1). The displacement hypothesis is rejected.

In the unusual circumstances of the 1945–51 Labour government, choice is consistent with persistence. Even though few programs were terminated, abnormally high wartime levels of expenditure on defense programs were no longer necessary. Thus, in addition to inheriting a greatly enhanced capacity for taxation, the Labour government inherited a declining level of military expenditure, and the sums saved could be used to finance new programs.

Figure 4.1. No displacement of programs in aftermath of war

Programs in 1946:

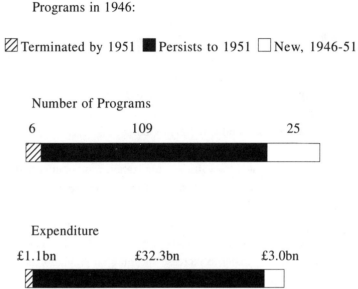

Sources: Here and subsequently, Centre for the Study of Public Policy program file, based on Comptroller & Auditor General's Appropriation Accounts; for details, see chapter 3. Expenditure adjusted to 1989 £.

Politically, the Attlee government was in a very strong position to use the fiscal dividend of peace to finance new programs. Its first advantage was that its landslide 1945 election victory gave it a 247-seat majority in the House of Commons, ample to enact any new measure it chose. Secondly, Labour's election victory was interpreted as a mandate to make big changes in the manifold of public policy and to repudiate what had been done before the war. Thirdly, Labour entered office with program commitments that it had been accumulating and waiting to put into effect since its emergence as a major party in the 1920s. Finally, since Labour's leaders had been part of the wartime coalition government under Churchill, they were very familiar with the machinery of government and confident of their ability to manage new programs (Lee, 1980: 176; Titmuss, 1950).

In its six years of office the Attlee government increased the number of government programs by 25, an average of about four a year (see figure 4.1). The new programs added to what it had inherited but did not replace it. When Labour left office in 1951, 81 percent of the programs in the legacy it left behind had been inherited from Churchill, Chamberlain, Baldwin, Lloyd George, and even nineteenth-century administrations.

The revenue created by wartime mobilization was not allocated to Labour's new choices but to programs inherited from previous administrations. Hence, 91 percent of the money spent in the final year of the 1945–51 Labour government was devoted to programs chosen decades or generations before it had entered office. This should not be surprising, for it is easier to increase spending on programs long in effect than to spend large sums on newly implemented measures.

To say that the 1945–51 Labour government created the welfare state is an overstatement; what it did was to augment and reformulate an already substantial inheritance of social programs. On entering office, Labour inherited 26 education, health, and social security programs from its predecessors. In the course of six years it added 12 to this total without terminating any.

The impact of the Attlee government was least in education, for it introduced only one new and very minor program, creating the Natural Environment Research Council in 1949. The major postwar (*sic*) education choices were actually made by the wartime coalition government under a Conservative education minister, R. A. Butler. The 1944 Butler Education Act established free secondary education for all and raised the school-leaving age by a year. Of the total spent on education in the last year of the Attlee government, 99.9 percent was allocated to programs inherited from its predecessors.

The first social security programs giving individuals a cash income were introduced by the 1906–14 Liberal administration, albeit with very narrow coverage and low levels of benefit. Social security was subsequently expanded in the interwar years. After World War II the Attlee administration introduced four new programs for sickness benefit, widows' benefit, maternity, and a death grant, but this augmented without transforming what was already being spent for social security. Of the £2.8 billion added in this policy area, two-thirds was accounted for by the expansion of programs inherited from predecessors. Overall, 85 percent of social security expenditure in 1951 was devoted to inherited programs.

Health was the field in which the Attlee government had the biggest impact. It added seven new programs to the five it inherited, and transformed what had been a hodgepodge of different programs into a comprehensive national health service providing treatment to all citizens regardless of income or employment status. Although the goal was clear, there were great political and operational problems in adding new measures to inherited programs (Eckstein, 1960). The underlying principle of a comprehensive health service free to users was new, but there was no displacement of pre-existing commitments. Of the £4.9 billion spent on health programs in 1951, 67 percent financed health programs inherited by Labour from its predecessors. New principles operated through inherited as well as new measures.

In social policy overall, the Attlee government's new programs augmented its inheritance rather than displacing it. Of the £11 billion spent on education, health, and social security programs in 1951, 82 percent was claimed by programs that the 1945–51 Labour government had inherited, not chosen. Since the number and cost of programs chosen by the 1945–51 Labour government was not large by comparison with its inheritance, 1946 can be used as the starting point for the test of inheritance before choice. Starting analysis immediately after the end of the war provides an extremely robust test of the capacity of programs to persist in the face of upheavals occurring only once in a political lifetime.

Persistence or Obsolescence?

A period of five decades is long enough for the compounding of seemingly small changes to overcome the inertia of inherited programs. Economic growth can generate additional revenue to finance new programs, and social changes can create demands for new programs and make inherited measures obsolete.

Challenging the Inertia of Inheritance

In the past five decades the environment of British public policy has undergone great changes in population and housing, in the size of the gross national product, the nominal value of money, and in public expenditure (figure 4.2). The population has altered in small ways and big. The number of people in the United Kingdom has grown by 7 million—a modest 14 percent increase. Although the total has not changed greatly, the people who constitute Britain today are very different in their life experience and expectations. In 1945 the median adult had been born about 1900; by 1990, the median adult was born in 1950. Of the population of Britain in 1990, 65 percent had been born after the end of World War II. The political values and expectations of persons raised in an era in which welfare state programs are taken for granted are likely to differ from those of individuals socialized in depression and wartime austerity. There have also been big changes in outlooks: a woman educated in the 1970s is likely to have a different outlook on life and politics than a woman educated before World War I. The creation of a multiracial society in Britain through the arrival of several million immigrants from the West Indies, Africa,

Figure 4.2. Changes in the environment of public policy since 1946

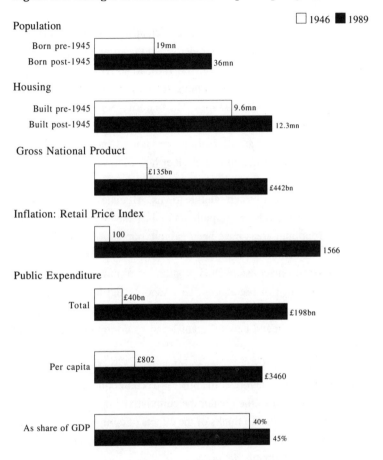

Sources: Population, housing, public expenditure, *Annual Abstract of Statistics;* gross national product, inflation, *National Income and Expenditure, UK National Accounts,* and *Economic Trends.* All publications, HMSO, London.

and the Indian subcontinent has affected white as well as nonwhite Britons.

Decades of building new houses and clearing a century-old inheritance of slums has physically transformed the communities in which people live. At the end of World War II the majority of British people resided in pre-1914 houses forming towns and neighborhoods that had developed in Victorian times. The majority were tenants in small terraced houses often lacking an indoor toilet and a fixed bath. In the postwar era more than 12 million new homes have been built to modern standards and millions of older houses have been razed.

There has been a great displacement of population from Victorian cities to newer suburbs and satellite towns. All major cities, including London, have been losing population in the postwar era, while suburban metropolitan areas have been gaining population. Building new suburbs and communities requires an enormous capital investment by government to meet established program commitments. In response to the movement of population, new schools and hospitals must be built and roads and environmental services expanded. People in new communities demand new programs, and so do immigrants in inner cities.

The size of the British economy has been transformed in almost half a century, for the longer the process of compounding annual rates of change continues, the greater the cumulative impact. Even though no individual politician thinks of the effects of compounding through a dozen Parliaments, in the course of 45 years the economy can double and then double again.

Inflation has enormously increased the nominal value of the economy, tax revenue, and public expenditure. The annual rate of inflation is rarely above 10 percent a year, but since the previous year's inflation is included in the base to which the current year's inflation rate applies, the effect of annual inflation is cumulative. Since 1946 the retail price level has risen almost 15 times.

The consequences of inflation are multiple. For technical reasons, it makes tax revenue buoyant; it rises faster than the rate of inflation. Public expenditure is buoyant, too, for the government must spend more money to buy the same amount of services from public employees and to keep cash benefits from falling below their intended levels. Inflation drives up interest rates that government must pay on its debts, but it reduces the burden of repaying debts from past borrowing. Inflation also shifts the relative amount of money required to finance particular sets of programs, since costs of health care or defense tend to rise at different rates than the overall retail price index.

Inflation has resulted in the gross national product increasing from £9 billion in the money values of 1946 to £442 billion in 1989. Concurrently, public expenditure in current money values has increased from over £2 billion to £198 billion. Inflation thus creates the money illusion of rising incomes, and also the money disillusion of increased taxes and public expenditure.

Notwithstanding complaints about Britain's low rate of economic growth, after controlling for the effects of inflation the gross national product has more than trebled in value since the end of World War II. Years of no growth or contraction in the economy have been more than offset by years of growth. Since population has been relatively constant, there has been a substantial growth in per capita national product too. If anything, the use of constant prices understates the extent of material change, for many goods and services taken for granted by consumers today, such as color television sets, freezers, cars, and foreign holidays were either not available or were the privilege of a small minority of the population at the end of World War II.

The British economy has been transformed in composition as well as value, for at the end of World War II it retained many characteristics from the period when it initiated the Industrial Revolution in the nineteenth century. The Attlee government inherited an economy based on heavy industry; coal mining, the railways, steel production, and shipbuilding were all major employers. The war increased Britain's short-term advantage as an exporter, by destroying the factories of competitors and creating shortages and pent up demand. The decades since have seen the decline of traditional industries and of traditional export markets. The difficulties of adapting old industries to produce new products for new markets are now part of the legacy that each new administration inherits.

In real terms, total public expenditure has increased almost fivefold. In per capita terms, public expenditure has risen more than four times. Since the national product has grown, too, public expenditure has increased less as a share of the national product, growing from 40 to 45 percent in the period under review. The increase of 5 percent in the share of a greatly enlarged national product actually represents an additional £158 billion of public expenditure.

The changes summarized in figure 4.2 have cumulatively had a displacement effect greater than six years of World War II. The turnover of population through death and birth has meant that only a limited minority of the population today had firsthand experience of public policies in 1946 or before. The postwar housing boom has destroyed more old houses and stimulated a far greater movement of population than bombing raids; it has also created many new suburbs and transformed many communities. The amount of money that government collects in taxes and spends on public programs has been transformed, even by comparison with World War II. In short, there have been major changes within the postwar period as well as between the prewar and postwar eras (Rose et al., 1992).

When the environment of public policy changes by such magnitudes, it is reasonable to expect many programs inherited from the distant past to become obsolete. Programs that survived the first six years after World War II could be terminated in the 1960s, 1970s, or 1980s. Changes also create new opportunities for choice. An increase in public revenue due to economic growth makes it possible to finance some new programs without raising taxes. A rising standard of private affluence can be matched by rising demands for new and better public services. Obsolescence creates problems for groups slow to benefit from change. Old programs that no longer produce satisfaction may be replaced by programs deemed more effective in the climate of the 1980s or 1990s. Case studies of once-in-a-generation changes in public policy emphasize that, sooner or later, even programs that persist for several administrations can be abandoned and replaced by choices made in the light of new circumstances.

Long-Established Programs Do Not Become Obsolete

When the Labour government entered office at the end of World War II, its leaders were politicians who had formed their political outlooks campaigning against the conditions of pre-1914 England, and the same was true of its Conservative successors. Britain did not have a prime minister born in the twentieth century until Harold Wilson entered office in 1964. Yet by the 1990s the majority of the Cabinet and the opposition had formed their political outlooks in the 1960s and 1970s.

The obsolescence hypothesis predicts that as programs grow older, they are more likely to be terminated. Just as compounding can increase the stock of the nation's wealth, so the stock of programs inherited at the end of World War II can gradually be depreciated and programs terminated because they lose effectiveness in a changed environment. Even though there is no natural life expectancy for programs, many measures in effect in 1945 would be approaching the biblical age of three score and ten years by 1990, having been adopted earlier in the twentieth century and having been subject to questioning in a dozen Parliaments.

The Attlee government terminated an average of only one program a year. If this rate were sustained up to 1990, a total of 45 programs,

Figure 4.3. Inherited programs persist for generations

Number of programs inherited in 1946
Persisting, 1989

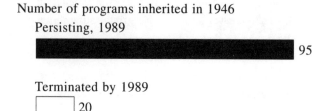

95

Terminated by 1989

20

Expenditure in 1989 pounds on programs inherited in 1946
Persisting

£105bn

Terminated

£1.5bn

Note: Here and subsequently, the value of terminated programs is the mean value in constant £ for the years the program was in effect.

nearly two-fifths of the initial postwar inheritance, would have been terminated. In fact, the rate at which these programs have been terminated averaged less than half that. Altogether, only 20 programs from before 1946 were terminated by 1990, thus rejecting the obsolescence hypothesis (figure 4.3).

Five-sixths of the programs that the 1945 Labour government inherited remained in effect in 1990. The great majority antedate one or both world wars; they have thus demonstrated the capacity to persist beyond the natural life of an individual and far beyond the life of the administration that initially chose them. Notwithstanding great changes in the polity, society, and economy, the persistence hypothesis is strongly supported.

Public programs often persist because they address concerns that are hardy perennials. This is obvious in the case of the Home Office; programs for the police and prisons may expand or contract, but they do not become obsolete. Similarly, education programs can expand as more money is spent to school more youths, but basic programs for primary education or such ancillary services as teacher training remain in place.

Terminated programs are concentrated in a few policy areas; 18 of the pre-1945 programs terminated concerned defense, trade and industry, and employment. Some defense programs ended as a consequence of the lapse of wartime commitments; subsequent terminations were the result of a once-in-a-generation rethinking of the role of military reserves at the end of the 1960s. In Trade and Industry, three of the six programs terminated were wartime measures. The six Employment programs are distinctive in being terminated in response to economic problems of the 1970s and 1980s.

When programs are weighed as well as counted, the importance of persistence is greater still. As of 1990, the 95 programs persisting from World War II claimed £105 billion in public expenditure. By comparison, the sum saved on terminated programs is trivial. Since programs terminate in different years, a straightforward way to estimate their value is to calculate the average cost for each program for the postwar years in which it was in effect. On the 1989 value of the pound, inherited programs terminated after 1946 had a total annual cost of £1.5 billion, little more than one percent of the sum spent on inherited programs (see figure 4.3).

Inherited programs not only persist but also grow greatly in their claims on the public purse. In 1946 the 95 persisting programs cost a total of £36 billion; by the end of 1989 their cost in real terms had almost trebled. The aggregate increase masks major differences in the extent to which individual programs grew in cost. Of the total increase of £69 billion, more than two-thirds was concentrated in a handful of six long-established education, hospital, and social security programs.

The concentration of expenditure growth on a very few inherited programs substantially qualifies Wilensky's (1975: 9ff) claim that as programs grow older they balloon into major claimants on the public purse. Wilensky's conclusion was drawn from analyzing expenditure under a few aggregated functional headings, principally social security. Doing this obscures differential rates of program growth. Even more, it ignores the fact that many programs grow very slowly or from a much lower base than major social security programs.

The persistence of inherited programs imposes a substantial constraint upon choice. The pre-commitment of more than £100 billion to programs inherited from the distant past means that there is less public revenue to finance new programs. Insofar as programs adopted since 1945 also persist, then a government entering office in the 1990s is further constrained, because it will inherit more than one hundred programs adopted by its postwar predecessors as well a similar number that are more than half a century old.

The termination of only 20 programs inherited from the distant past implies that the great majority will persist well into the twenty-first century. If programs launched in the first half of the twentieth century or earlier were terminated at the same rate in future as in the past, that is, less than one every two years, it would take until the year 2200 to remove from the manifold of British public policy the last of the programs inherited by the 1945 Labour government.

The most important decisions are the "*non*decisions" of each incoming government to accept programs of its predecessors. No effort and no choice is required to do this; it happens incidentally, as a consequence of a new administration assuming the obligations of past administrations.

5 Cumulative Changes in the Legacy

If things are going to stay the same, they are going to have to change.—*Giuseppe di Lampedusa,* The Leopard

Whereas government is about maintaining continuity, politics is about making choices. Politicians are much more inclined to see their role as introducing new programs than as serving as administrators of programs inherited from predecessors. There are incentives for individual politicians to be seen as active decisionmakers, for doing so can advance their personal political career. After a general election in which control of government changes hands, the new administration expects and is expected to make fresh choices.

The fact that a large number of programs persist through political inertia does not preclude the government of the day making choices. Logically, policymakers have four alternatives: to introduce programs, to terminate programs, to start and stop programs, or to make no choices. Any politician content to leave unchanged what is inherited from predecessors is not a maker but a caretaker of public policy.

Choice is a necessity if an administration is to adapt to changes in the policy environment. Without the capacity to choose new programs or terminate inherited measures, a gap will widen between the current environment of public policy and the legacy inherited from generations past. Without a capacity for choice, an administration would also be unable to respond to demands of its supporters.

Cumulative change in the manifold of public policy depends upon whether the direction of choice favors the introduction of new programs, the termination of old measures, or whether the aggregate effects cancel each other out. If the choices of policymakers are symmetrical, that is, as many programs are terminated as started, then there will be no change in aggregate.

5.1 (*Aggregate equilibrium*). If policymakers terminate as many programs as they start, then the size of a legacy remains constant.

An equilibrium hypothesis treats the current number of programs as the maximum a government can sustain on fiscal or administrative grounds. If that is the case, then an administration could only add new commitments by terminating inherited programs. Such an assumption is implicit in many normative theories of containing public expenditure in aggregate through a constitutional amendment or through government adopting a "scrap and build" rule of procedure, that is, the cost of new programs in any given year would have to be offset by savings from scrapping inherited programs (cf. Wildavsky, 1980; Tarschys, 1985). In its benign form, an aggregate equilibrium would allow the introduction of new measures. If a limitation were cast as a fixed share of a growing gross national product, then if spending on inherited programs did not grow as fast as the economy, there would even be a fiscal dividend from growth. There are also malign possibilities from aggregate equilibrium. If political pressures to launch and to terminate programs were equal in strength, then the result could be gridlock; no new programs would be adopted because no inherited programs could be terminated. Moreover, if inherited programs grow faster than the growth rate of the economy, then inherited entitlements will have to be cut or some programs terminated and no new measures adopted.

In postwar Britain, aggregate equilibrium would imply virtually no scope for introducing new programs, since only 20 programs inherited from the distant past have been terminated. This would allow an administration to introduce only two new programs in the lifetime of a typical Parliament. At that rate, it would take until the second half of the twenty-first century for the programs inherited in 1945 to be outnumbered by choices made since 1945.

In politics, addition is usually easier than subtraction, thus making choices asymmetrical. Many more programs will be added to the manifold of public policy than terminated as long as there are more incentives for politicians to confer new benefits than to take away benefits that groups have been accustomed to receive from inherited programs. A rationalistic view of politics also predicts inexorable growth. Insofar as policymaking is a process of collective learning and deliberation (cf. Heclo, 1974), then new programs are only likely to be adopted if they have a substantial amount of technical feasibility as well as political support. The low level of termination of programs before 1945 can be cited in support of this rationalistic view. Together, these reasons lead to the hypothesis:

5.2 (*Inexorable growth*). If new programs are more likely to be adopted than inherited programs terminated, growth in the number of programs is inexorable.

Although inexorable growth is often assumed to characterize public choice, the logic of most theories of government growth is reversible (Hood, 1991). For example, if public dissatisfaction with the cost of public policy outweighs satisfaction, then political incentives would encourage the termination of inherited programs rather than the choice of new measures.

Theories of inexorable growth usually assume that new choices will prove durable. In addition to being based on a calculation of current political advantage, new measures could draw upon a process of deliberation that assured continuing support and successful implementation. Once adopted, new programs can sustain support through the benefits that they produce. Insofar as this is the case, then we would expect programs chosen since 1945 to be as durable as those inherited from the distant past. Since five-sixths of programs inherited by the 1945 Labour government have persisted, we would expect five-sixths of new choices to persist too.

But there are a priori reasons why new programs may be less likely to succeed than programs that have persisted for decades. Whereas programs inherited from the past have met the test of time, by definition new programs are untried. If the choice of a new program is stimulated by a political crisis, there is no time for calm deliberation. In such circumstances pressures for action can drive policymakers to proceed by a trial-and-error process in which a program is adopted and, if it does not produce satisfaction, terminated and another tried in its stead (Simon, 1978).

Vulnerability is the obverse of obsolescence; doing anything for the first time is much more risky than maintaining by routine a program that has been part of the legacy of many administrations. Vulnerability is especially likely when dissatisfaction forces policymakers to act hurriedly, without time to diagnose the causes of a problem or to formulate a considered response. In such circumstances new programs are likely to be experimental—and many experiments fail.

5.3 (*Expansion through trial and error*). If new choices divide more or less randomly into those that succeed and those that fail, then the net increase in programs will be much less than total choices.

Trial-and-error policymaking hypothesizes that many new programs will be stopped shortly after adoption because they fail to meet expectations. There will be additions to the legacy of each administration, as those programs that succeed on the first, second, or nth attempt to deal with a problem are incorporated into the manifold of public policy. From this perspective, the longevity of inherited programs is not evidence that all programs persist but simply that the programs that do persist are the survivors in a trial-and-error process. Insofar as trial and error predominates, then the net growth in the totality of programs will be much less than the total of choices, as policymakers cancel many programs in a search for measures that bring satisfaction.

In the first section of this chapter two contrasting rationales for introducing programs are reviewed. Insofar as the policymaking process involves careful deliberation by politicians and experts, then most new programs should be durable, and inexorable growth result. By contrast, theories based on dissatisfaction as the stimulus to action predict that choices will be adopted in a hurry, when dissatisfaction prompts demands to do something, and any measure, however risky or uncertain, is preferable to inaction. The theories are evaluated by empirical evidence answering two complementary questions. How frequently are new programs chosen? How often are new programs terminated? The second section shows that in postwar Britain the choice of programs does not lead to inexorable growth; it is a trial and error search in which many new programs are stopped as well as started.

Are New Programs Durable or Vulnerable?

The period between the conception of a program and its adoption as a law can be long or short. A lengthy period of incubation provides many opportunities for experts and politicians to consider many alternatives. A technical consensus can emerge about a feasible program, and a political consensus can emerge to support incorporating a measure into the manifold of public policy. Programs that have been through a long process of incubation should persist.

Alternatively, events can create a crisis demand for policymakers to respond immediately. The crisis can result from conditions outside the control of government, for example, an abrupt increase in the price of imported oil, or it can come about because of a sudden change of political mood. When pressures for action are intense, then the technical feasibility of a new program is less important than the political infeasibility of the status quo. Almost any proposal is worth trying, however doubtful its chance of success. In such circumstances policymaking proceeds by trial and error, and many new programs are likely to be found wanting, and terminated.

Incubating Durable Programs

If a program is chosen after a process of deliberation that anticipates and removes faults, this should greatly improve its chances of incorporation in the durable legacy of public policy. Insofar as routine dominates most areas of public policy, there is a lot of time for deliberation. Even though proponents of change argue that too much time is spent in waiting for government to act, time spent in incubating ideas for programs need not be wasted. It makes it more likely that a new program will be effective, because it is based on "much research and reasoned advocacy" (Polsby, 1984: 154).

Time is required to demonstrate the existence of a problem, to canvas ways to resolve it, and to secure a broad base of political support. Polsby (1984: 153ff) describes this as a process of incubation, in which programs are drawn up by "people relatively far in social, temporal and sometimes physical distance from ultimate decisionmakers, such as experts and researchers working in universities or in quasi-academic settings, or technical staff employees of interest groups, government agencies or congressional committees." American politics is full of issue networks in which experts can incubate and transmit information about programs to policymakers. Issue networks are found in Britain, too, clustered around government ministries (cf. Heclo, 1978; Jordan, 1981).

Experts are central in the incubation of new programs, having specialized knowledge of the substantive problems that programs address, and detailed knowledge of what government has been doing and what it can realistically be expected to do. Whereas policymakers making choices come and go from office, expert officials have a permanent commitment to a substantive policy area, are part of a network concerned with issue politics and policy, and some have the entrepreneurial skills needed to market new programs (cf. Doig and Hargrove, 1987).

Technical feasibility is a special concern of experts. Experts do not want to spend years promoting a proposal only to see it fail after enactment. Nor can they maintain credibility as experts if the proposals they advocate appear faulty when subject to hostile scrutiny. Insofar as experts are divided, then the adversary process of political decisionmaking provides opponents and proponents with incentives to test a proposal's feasibility. Kingdon (1984: 139) describes thus the approach of experts to the formulation of new proposals: "The word 'actually' constantly comes into their conversation as they discuss feasibility. 'Will it actually accomplish what we want to accomplish?' 'Can it actually be administered?' "

Incubation can explore the feasibility of a proposal through prospective evaluation, comparing the steps necessary to move from the present to a more satisfactory future state. Prospective evaluation can be purely speculative, mapping the logical requirements to make a program effective. It can be based upon analysis of past trends and present conditions within a given policy area. Prospective evaluation can also draw upon comparisons across space, examining a similar program in effect in another state or nation, in order to draw lessons that will make a proposal more effective (Rose, 1991c).

The formulation of a feasible proposal is not sufficient to secure its endorsement; a second necessary condition is that the topic becomes visible on the agenda of policymakers (Cobb and Elder, 1972; Kingdon, 1984: chapter 8). The circumstances creating a window of opportunity for the adoption of a proposal are often unpredictable and short-lived. Proponents of a technically feasible new idea may have a long wait before it attains a position high on the agenda of policymakers.

Political support is also necessary to secure the adoption of a proposal. In Britain the cabinet minister sponsoring a measure must win the support, or at least neutralize the potential opposition, of other departments and ministers in order to ensure cabinet approval. The Treasury's agreement to fund a measure is also necessary. Once agreement is obtained within the executive, the government of the day can use its disciplined parliamentary majority to defeat amendments that it believes will reduce a bill's effectiveness. It does not have to engage in horse-trading to secure the votes needed for legislative enactment. Thus, acts of Parliament are more likely to be durable than acts of Congress, which are produced by a bargaining process in which the votes of many members of Congress may be contingent upon amendments that reduce a program's effectiveness.

The assumptions of policymaking by incubation are optimistic. Policymakers do not make choices casually; they act only after a lengthy process of deliberation. The programs chosen are doubly desirable, for the time spent in deliberation increases both technical feasibility and political support. Moreover, programs chosen as a result of a lengthy incubation will be durable, thus contributing to the inexorable growth in the legacy of public policy.

Trial-and-Error Responses

A lengthy period of incubation is neither necessary nor sufficient for the adoption of a new program. It is not sufficient because reasoning and research do not of themselves capture the attention of busy policymakers. As long as there is satisfaction within a given area of public policy, there is no need for the government of the day to take any interest in new measures, however carefully they have been incubated. Inherited programs can run by routine.

However, when a gap arises between the performance of established programs and political aspirations, the result is political dissatisfaction. This stimulates policymakers to search for a measure that will put an end to dissatisfaction. Experts who for years have had their views ignored suddenly find themselves sought after, as policymakers are suddenly receptive to listening to expert proposals that they had previously ignored. Policymakers also may also become receptive to harebrained proposals.

When the pressure of political dissatisfaction is strong, there is no time to make a thorough diagnosis of the causes of dissatisfaction. Nor is there time for prolonged consultation with experts about a wide variety of alternatives. As dissatisfaction reaches the acute level, the demand for new measures becomes an imperative; inaction is no longer a politically feasible alternative. The unexpected eruption of a crisis is itself an indication of failure to understand a changing policy environment. Policymakers must satisfice, that is, adopt the first program that meets their minimum needs for action now (Simon, 1979: 503).

The simplest response that policymakers can make is to provide more of the same, that is, increase spending on an inherited program. This is likely to be welcomed by the recipients of the increased benefits, by administrators, and by pressure groups demanding action. It is a low-risk strategy, but it will satisfice only if the policy environment is relatively stable so that an increase in expenditure will produce a proportionately positive effect. If there is a structural change in the policy environment, then a search must commence for a new program.

The existence of a pressing demand does not guarantee the supply of an effective program. A crisis creates opportunities for peddlers of bogus nostrums as well as for carefully incubated expert recommendations. When many proposals compete, contradictory claims create confusion. Kingdon describes the situation as proposals being dropped into a "primeval soup." Cohen, March, and Olsen (1974: 2) speak less appetizingly of the choice facing policymakers as "a garbage can into which various kinds of problems and solutions are dumped by participants as they are generated."

Trial and error is an apt description of searching for a measure that will dispel dissatisfaction. The first priority is not to find the best or the right program (whatever such a term may be thought to mean) but to try *something,* if only to symbolize a willingness to act. The program may even be chosen from the garbage can without any expectation of success. When the political cost of doing nothing is infinite, then choosing a program with an unknown chance of success will be preferable (Rose, 1972).

When the consequences of a choice are indeterminate, policymaking is a learning process in which feedback is critical in deciding whether a newly chosen program should be continued or is a false start and should be terminated (cf. Deutsch, 1963). Difficulties in implementing a new program can give policymakers a better understanding of causes of dissatisfaction. If the new program fails, policymakers can decide to terminate it and choose another. Budget officials will encourage termination and may even make scrapping a program that does not do so a condition of choosing another. In a trial-and-error process, policymakers can continue making choices until satisfaction is achieved.

The trial-and-error hypothesis does not predict that new programs will always fail but that a substantial portion of choices will prove inadequate and soon be terminated. Even if policymakers are good scavengers, refusing to take the first piece of garbage from the can, the likelihood of a new program surviving in the legacy of successive administrations is far less than if programs were chosen after a long period of incubation. However, insofar as choices of policymakers are made with careful deliberation, then inexorable growth will occur.

Lots of Hits and Lots of Errors

Incubation and trial and error can be mutually complementary rather than mutually exclusive. In moments of crisis policymakers may choose a program that has been a long time in incubation, provided there is one at hand. Even if a trial-and-error process is random, some responses to dissatisfaction could succeed first time, and others on a second trial, thus ratcheting up the total number of programs in the legacy of government. A theory of trial and error views the adoption of new programs as a selection process in which policymakers make choices about terminating new programs as well as adding new measures. It also predicts that most programs will not be the object of scrutiny, let alone choice, as long as they routinely produce satisfaction.

Each administration exercises some scope for choice. In the postwar era, 245 new programs have been introduced to the manifold of public policy, an average of 5.6 new programs a year. In a Parliament of four years the government of the day has the opportunity to add almost two dozen programs before it must again face the electorate. If every program that an administration chose was carefully incubated and incorporated into the legacy of successive administrations, then by 1990 the number of programs would be more than treble that at the end of World War II.

In fact, the choices of policymakers are a mixture of hits and errors. Of the 245 new programs that postwar administrations have chosen to introduce, 102, more than two in five, have been terminated. Comparing this 42 percent termination rate with the 17 percent rate for programs adopted before 1945 shows the vulnerability of new choices. As the trial-and-error theory predicts, novelty is a greater cause of failure than obsolescence.

Programs that stop and start are not terminated because of gradual obsolescence; they are short-lived. This indicates that their initial choice was the result of a search under pressure for some means of responding to political dissatisfaction. Of those programs that have started and stopped since 1945, more than half have been terminated

Figure 5.1. Brief existence of start and stop programs

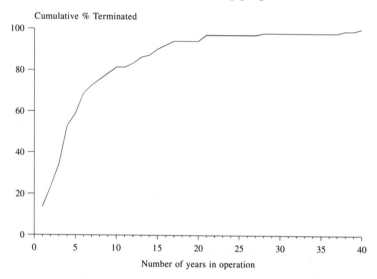

within four years, the normal length of a Parliament. Only 10 percent of new programs that are eventually stopped last as much as 15 years (figure 5.1).

A majority of trial-and-error measures are thus likely to be terminated by the end of the next Parliament—whether or not control of government changes hands. For example, under pressure to deal with the post-1973 energy crisis, the Labour government returned in 1974 started and stopped five programs, and terminated another four inherited from its immediate predecessor. Similarly, the Thatcher administration's response to rising unemployment in the 1980s was to start and stop many measures in a continuing effort to do something in response to the rise in the number of unemployed.

If anything, the foregoing figures underestimate the extent to which new programs both start and stop, for a substantial number of programs introduced in the 1980s will be stopped after the March 1990 cut-off date used in this book. Of the 60 programs adopted since 1983, only eight had been terminated by 1990. The remaining 52 have not yet demonstrated that they will become part of the ongoing legacy of public policy; they are best described as "not having had time to fail." If the failure rate of the postwar era is applied to these programs, then 20 or more are likely to be terminated in the 1990s. If this happens, then more than half of all programs started between 1946 and 1989 may be described as short-term choices not incorporated into the continuing legacy of public policy.

The trial-and-error adoption of programs is a significant factor in containing the cost of policymakers' choices. When initially introduced, the cost of a new program is far less than an established program, for most new programs take several years before they operate at full capacity, and even then a new program tends to cost less than a program that has been expanding coverage and benefits for a generation (OECD, 1985). Costs can also be low in the first few years of a new program because of uncertainties among policymakers about its possible success.

Collectively, programs introduced since 1945 and remaining in the manifold of public policy at the end of 1989 accounted for £37 billion in public expenditure. The average cost of these 143 programs was not large, £260 million, or 0.17 percent of public expenditure. But the average figure is much inflated by the effect of a new housing benefit measure introduced in 1982 and claiming £5.4 billion by 1989. The median, which controls for the effect of a few high-spending measures, was £28 million in 1989, that is, 0.02 percent of public expenditure.

Programs that stop as well as start have a much lower average annual cost than new programs incorporated into the legacy. They have not had decades in which to expand and usually are terminated before becoming fully mature. As failure to achieve success becomes manifest, the program's budget is likely to be cut prior to termination. Average annual expenditure on programs that start and stop was £174 million, a figure substantially inflated by a single, short-term program, the refunds paid for the Selective Employment Tax in the 1960s. The median program that was started and stopped claimed £18 million a year during its relatively short life. In each instance, the cost of stop and start programs is about one-third less than that of new programs that have continued.

Change—and More of the Same

Cumulatively, each administration's choices alter the aggregate legacy of public policy. The longer the span of time, the greater the number of new programs. Yet the termination of programs adopted by a trial-and-error process means that there is nothing inexorable in new programs swamping old. Insofar as inherited programs tend to become more expensive as they become older, then even though the number of new programs grows, more money will be devoted to financing the expansion of old programs.

Choice as Churning

In the short run what matters to politicians is the capacity to make choices during their term of office. Whatever the long-run consequences, the greater the volume of choices, the more "decisive" a politician appears. From this cynical perspective, a program that starts and stops makes policymakers appear twice as active as a program that becomes part of the legacy of public policy, for failure enables one administration to take credit for introducing a program and another to take credit for terminating it! By contrast, a program that has been carefully incubated and remains in place becomes routinized. For example, a minister for social security is not under

Figure 5.2. Churning of program choices, 1946–89

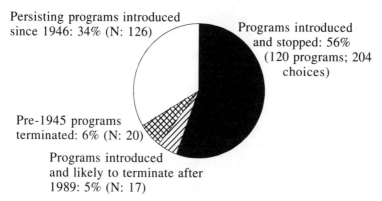

Persisting programs introduced
since 1946: 34% (N: 126)

Programs introduced
and stopped: 56%
(120 programs; 204
choices)

Pre-1945 programs
terminated: 6% (N: 20)

Programs introduced
and likely to terminate after
1989: 5% (N: 17)

pressure to introduce fresh programs. Instead, the minister is under pressure to maintain inherited social security programs.

Churning is an apt term to describe much of the activity of policymakers as they introduce and repeal new programs. Churning involves the intense agitation of everything and everyone caught up in the policymaking process. Instead of standing outside the primeval soup or garbage can, policymakers invest much energy trying to stay afloat within it. Yet the net effect of churning is not to turn public policy by 180 degrees but to come full circle, if new programs have a trial run for several years and are then repealed.

Insofar as we conceive government as making choices, a majority involve churning, undoing programs inherited from predecessors or choosing programs that will subsequently be undone as part of policymaking by trial and error (figure 5.2). Although most programs survive, only one-third of choices involve the adoption of a new program that will survive in the inheritance of successive administrations. Two-thirds of choices taken by postwar British governments are about the introduction of programs that are soon stopped or about stopping programs introduced by previous administrations.

From Annual Choice to Cumulative Change

Because some programs remain in the legacy of public policy after the process of churning is completed, the hypothesis of aggregate equilibrium is therefore rejected. The increase in the aggregate number of programs is achieved in a ratcheting fashion, as the number of programs that survive is greater than the number terminated. When the Labour government entered office after World War II, it inherited 115 programs; it added 25 programs and terminated 8, thus leaving a legacy of 132 programs to its Conservative successor. The Conservative administration that lasted until 1964 terminated six inherited programs, and started and stopped three of the 32 new measures it introduced; it thus left a legacy of 155 programs to its Labour successor. In turn, the 1964–70 Labour government terminated four of the programs it inherited and two of the 33 that it introduced. In consequence, the incoming Heath administration inherited 182 programs. The Heath administration terminated eight programs and added 31; it thus left a legacy of 205 programs to Harold Wilson's 1974 administration. That Labour government terminated 32 programs and added 43, raising to 216 the total number inherited by the Thatcher administration in 1979. In the course of a decade, the Thatcher administration terminated 59 programs and added 81 to the legacy that it left behind, increasing to 238 the total number of programs in effect at the start of the 1990s.

Administrations differ in the number of programs that they subtract and add to their legacy—but to a significant extent that is because they differ in the length of time they remain in office. The Heath administration had only three full parliamentary sessions whereas there were Conservative prime ministers in charge of government for 13 consecutive years from 1951, and the Conservative era launched under Margaret Thatcher in 1979 is even longer. Everything else being equal, the more time an administration is in office, the more impact its choices can have on the legacy that it leaves behind.

Creating an annual index of choice can control for the differential longevity of administrations by calculating the average number of choices made each year as a percentage of the programs that an administration inherits. For example, the Attlee government inherited 115 programs; in six years its choices subtracted eight and added 25 to its legacy. Its 33 choices averaged 5.5 per year, or 4.8 percent of the programs it inherited.

In any one year, choices affect only a few percent of the programs in the manifold of public policy. The 1951–64 Conservative administration made the fewest choices, equivalent to 2.4 percent of its inheritance in a typical year. The 1964–70 Labour government's index rose to 4.0 percent a year. The short-lived Heath administration was most active, but its annual choices were still only 6.9 percent of the inheritance it received in 1970. Since then, the annual rate of choice has remained similar: it was 6.0 percent annually for the 1974–79 Labour government and 6.5 percent for the Thatcher administration.

The cumulative effect of choice upon the legacy of public policy depends upon the *net* increase in programs. As long as the government of the day stops as well as starts programs, it is always less than the total number of choices. A net growth index can be calculated as the percentage of programs annually added (or, if appropriate, subtracted) from the legacy that an administration inherits. For example, the 33 choices of the Attlee administration resulted in a net addition of 17 programs, an average of just under three a year. This produced a net annual addition of 2.5 percent to its original inheritance of 115 programs.

In percentage terms, the rate of growth in programs has tended to decline during the postwar era. It fell to 1.3 percent a year in the 1951–64 Conservative administration, then rose between 1964 and 1974 to 2.8 percent and 4.1 percent under the Heath administration.

However, since 1974 the net annual increase in programs has not exceeded 1 percent a year.

The decline in net growth is due to an increase in churning. Even though the number of choices made has been substantially higher since 1974, the number of terminations has increased greatly too, thus producing less net growth. In the first three decades after World War II, more than half the annual choices were net increases in new programs. But because of churning, since 1974 an administration's gross number of choices has been more than six times its net increase in programs. The frequency of starts as well as stops, and particularly the stopping and starting of recently chosen programs, undermines the rationalistic basis of the hypothesis of inexorable growth and also demonstrates that there are short-term political incentives to terminate many programs. The data support, instead, the trial and error hypothesis.

The Effect of the Present Moving into the Past

While every program was new at some point in time, the programs that constitute an administration's inheritance vary greatly in age; some are less than a decade old, and others more than a half-century old.

The preceding pages have used a single date, 1946, to separate old from new programs. But from the perspective of an administration in the 1990s, programs adopted 15, 25, or 40 years ago are not new; they too are part of the inheritance from the past. It is therefore desirable to distinguish the distant past (that is, the period before 1946) from what is, from the perspective of the 1990s, the postwar past.

Analytically, programs belong to the present as long as they are subject to termination because still on trial; they can be described as incorporated into the continuing legacy of public policy once the probability of termination becomes low. When more than half of trial-

and-error programs are terminated within four years, a program does not need to be half a century old to have a high probability of survival. A program that has already lasted for a decade or two can be expected to remain part of the legacy of public policy into the twenty-first century.

Politics, too, justifies considering many postwar programs as part of the past. Any programs remaining in the manifold of public policy in the 1990s and adopted before the Thatcher administration entered office can be considered secure as part of the legacy of the past, since they have survived an administration pledged to the hostile scrutiny of the whole of its inheritance. Programs adopted between 1946 and 1979 can aptly be described as the postwar inheritance.

When programs are divided into three groups, the inheritance from the distant past, the postwar inheritance, and choices of the present administration, the impact of inheritance is enhanced (figure 5.3). The largest category consists of programs inherited from the distant past, constituting two-fifths of the total. When programs from the postwar inheritance are added, the number of inherited programs rises to 66 percent of the total in effect in 1990. If allowance is made for the fact that some of the Thatcher administration's choices will subsequently be terminated, the significance of the past becomes greater still.

When money is the measure, the impact of inheritance looms larger still. Whereas the majority of programs now in effect were chosen after 1945, 74 percent of public expenditure is allocated to programs in place before the end of World War II. An additional 15 percent is spent on the postwar inheritance of programs. Even though the Thatcher administration viewed public expenditure as central for choice, only 11 percent of the money it spent was allocated to programs that it introduced. Recent programs appear numerous, but in money terms they do not weigh heavily.

To interpret the programs for which the government of the day is

Figure 5.3. Effect of inheritance in 1989

Inherited Programs:

Number

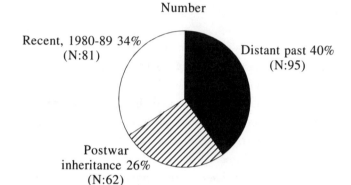

Recent, 1980-89 34%
(N:81)

Distant past 40%
(N:95)

Postwar
inheritance 26%
(N:62)

Public Expenditure

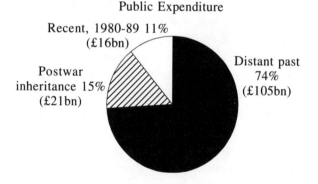

Recent, 1980-89 11%
(£16bn)

Distant past
74%
(£105bn)

Postwar
inheritance 15%
(£21bn)

responsible as the choice of that administration is false to history. At
no point in time did any administration decide how many or what kind
of programs government ought to undertake, or make an ex ante
decision about how much money should be spent, or how it should be
allocated. The record of each successive administration is largely a
record of more of the same; the great bulk of the programs it administers and finances are inherited from the more or less distant past.

Cumulatively, some new programs are added to the manifold of public policy. Because the process is gradual, the causes of choice cannot be found in the record of a single Parliament or a single administration; they must be sought in the whole of the postwar era. The following chapters do just this, testing alternative explanations for the choices registered: parties make a difference, the economic climate matters; and differences in the policy environment of programs accounts for change.

6 Do Parties Make a Difference?

Parties live in a house of power.—Max Weber

Representative government is party government. The choices of voters are not translated directly into public policies; parties aggregate preferences and modify them to reflect their own interests and values. The party winning a general election not only sits in a house of power but also expects to use that power to make choices about public policy. Insofar as parties differ in their political priorities, then the choice of programs should shift when there is a change in the party in power.

The British Constitution gives the governing party great scope for choice. The government of the day can be confident that almost any bill that it chooses to put to Parliament will be approved, for the electoral system manufactures an absolute majority of seats in the House of Commons for the party with a plurality of popular votes. Party discipline ensures that this majority normally endorses the choices of party leaders in government. Whereas an American president can blame a failure to introduce new programs on the refusal of Congress to enact his proposals, in Britain the legislature is no obstacle to party leaders.

Studies of the ideology of political parties imply that the choices made by the government of the day ought to differ because the parties' underlying philosophies differ. The Labour party has been a party of the left, proclaiming a commitment to socialism; the Conservatives are a party of the right, committed to free enterprise or, in a pre-Thatcher era, to an organic Tory view of conserving existing programs rather than enacting new measures. These ideological differences are readily linked to differences between the organized interests of trade unions, an integral part of the Labour party, and business interests allied with the Conservative party (see, e.g., Beer, 1982; Dalton et al., 1984). A left-versus-right theory of party competition implies that both Conservative and Labour parties will be active in promoting programs favoring their respective interests and repealing programs of their adversaries.

The rhetoric of party politics highlights differences in values and goals. In 1945 the Labour party campaigned with a promise to pursue "drastic policies of replanning" to make postwar Britain different from what it was between the wars. In 1951 the Conservatives entered office with a manifesto that called for a "turning point in the fortunes and even the life of Britain." In 1964 Labour won office with a manifesto that called for a "new Britain" achieved through interventionist planning, and in 1970 Edward Heath interpreted the Conservative victory thus: "We were returned to office to change the course and the history of this nation, nothing else." In 1974 the Labour party campaigned with the declared intention of bringing about a fundamental and irreversible shift in the balance of power and wealth (Butler and Kavanagh, 1974: 1, 50; Craig, 1975). The election of Margaret Thatcher as Conservative leader and the swing left of the Labour party after 1979 increased the rhetoric of adversary politics. Shortly before entering office in 1979 Thatcher told an election rally, "I am a conviction politician. The Old Testament prophets did not say: 'Brothers, I want a consensus.' They said: 'This is my faith. This is what I passionately believe.' If you believe it too, then come with me" (qtd. Rose, 1984: 4).

British parties are well organized to prepare programs to convert rhetoric into government choices. In office and opposition, party groups devote a substantial amount of time to developing concrete programs for enactment in government. The opposition party in Parliament is constantly challenged by the government of the day to show why and how it could do better than the current administration. Before each election, party leaders prepare a detailed manifesto that identifies actions to be taken once in office; this manifesto is scrutinized carefully for consistency with the values of the party and for realism, so that it can be defended against hostile criticism from opponents. The body of the manifesto lists specific commitments to action by each government department; rhetoric and slogans are concentrated in the manifesto's introduction (Rose, 1984: chapter 4). Once in office, party leaders constitute the cabinet, and each cabinet minister has a personal career incentive to promote new programs or to repeal inherited programs, for such actions will enhance the minister's political visibility in the party, in Parliament, and with the public (cf. Rose, 1987a).

The programmatic emphasis of British parties contrasts with American campaigners, who promote personal images rather than policies. The approach also differs from the more abstract philosophical tradition of Catholic and socialist parties in Europe, which may enunciate timeless principles but give little weight to specific programs in the haggling that leads to the formation of coalition governments.

Theories of British party competition conventionally postulate that parties are adversaries (Finer, 1975). The Conservative and Labour parties not only contest who should govern but also disagree about how the country should be governed. In the adversary theory, the views of the parties are incompatible; what one does, its adversary will oppose. When control of government changes hands at a general election, the new administration gains the power to repeal programs inherited from its predecessors and to introduce programs that it favors. The starts and stops of programs, in the preceding chapter interpreted as a trial-and-error search, are here viewed as a consequence of adversary politics.

*6.1 (*Adversary politics*). If parties are adversaries, then each administration will repeal many programs inherited from its partisan opponents.

Consensus theories challenge this view of electoral competition, postulating that parties differ very little in the programs that they choose. To win an electoral majority, parties must win votes not only from committed partisans but also from middle-of-the-road voters whose choice is electorally decisive. Since parties seek the support of the same middle-of-the-road electors, programs will tend to converge on the preferences of the median voter (Downs, 1957). In Britain the preferences of the electorate tend to be unimodal, that is, middle-of-the-road voters are the largest group within the electorate. In such circumstances, a party risks electoral defeat if it offers ideologically distinctive programs that are out of sympathy with the electorate (see Rose and McAllister, 1990: chapter 1).

Insofar as competition for votes leads parties to minimize differences, this should produce a consensus in action, even when there is a change in party control of government. Parties can compete on grounds of competence, claiming that their team of ministers is best able to achieve consensual goals (Stokes, 1963). Differences about policy can involve rhetoric and symbols that do not affect what government actually does and, with the help of the media, personalities can be treated as the most important difference between the parties.

Consensus politics is not static politics. In addition to adopting programs that have bipartisan support, each administration is likely to promote some choices to which it gives a high priority but which do not have bipartisan endorsement at the moment of their introduction. The opposition may vote against these programs, but once in office it will accept what it has inherited. Instead of being repealed, new programs will be incorporated into a moving consensus.

*6.2 (*Moving consensus*) If there is a consensus between parties, each administration will accept the great bulk of programs inherited from its partisan opponents.

The termination of programs is consistent with consensus politics, for there can be a consensus that a program once thought worth trying is a mistake or that an old program has become obsolete. From this perspective, the termination of a program is not part of a battle between partisan adversaries; instead, it is part of a continuing search for programs to produce broad satisfaction. Insofar as this is the case, then we would expect that the governing party is as likely to reject programs it has itself chosen as to repeal programs of its opponents.

*6.3 (*Nonpartisan trial and error*). If there is a consensus, the governing party will be as likely to terminate its own programs as programs chosen by its opponents.

Whereas the above hypotheses assume that parties of the left and right are equally active in making choices, a reform model postulates that parties differ in their level of activity. Because a reformist party wants to make changes in society, it will have an election manifesto full of new programs to adopt. New programs can reflect established economic interests or "new" values, such as the environment, gender equality, permissive life-styles, and so forth. The Labour party has long been considered the party of reform in Britain.

Proposals for change can stimulate opponents to defend the status quo on the grounds that it is there. The traditional Conservative party doctrine was to accept programs inherited from its predecessors without promoting further change. In Lord Hugh Cecil's (1912: 243) classic injunction, "Even when I changed, it should be to conserve." Conservative prime ministers such as Winston Churchill, Anthony Eden, and Harold Macmillan did not see the party's role as actively promoting fresh choices. They shared a negative goal: keeping Labour out. The Thatcher administration took a different view. The prime minister explicitly advocated rolling back socialism, that is, introducing new programs to alter the legacy inherited from both Labour and Conservative predecessors.

If a party of change and a status quo party compete for votes, the election outcome can depend upon circumstances. When voters favor new programs, the electoral pendulum will swing to the left, and when consolidation of inherited choices is the majority preference, it will swing in the opposite direction. The performance of parties in office will be very different.

*6.4 (*Reform*). If parties differ in their commitment to change, the party of reform will introduce many more programs than a party of the status quo.

In testing hypotheses, it is important to guard against straw-man theories that parties make absolutely no difference, or that they make all the difference. If it is hypothesized that parties make no difference, then any example of choice, however atypical or marginal, can be interpreted as demonstrating that "parties matter" (cf. Sharpe and Newton, 1984; Castles, 1982). Alternatively, to hypothesize that parties reject all the programs they inherit is to espouse a view of electoral politics as "permanent revolution," a doctrine that can be faulted by a single example of continuity. The first section of this chapter tests the extent to which parties are adversaries or whether programs tend to reflect a consensus. The second section tests the traditional view of the Conservatives as the party of the status quo and Labour as the party of reform.

Adversaries or a Trial and Error Consensus?

Adversary thinking is ingrained in many institutions of British public life. The electorate is asked to choose between the In and the Out party (Schumpeter, 1942; cf. Rose and McAllister, 1992). The first-past-the-post electoral system manufactures an absolute majority of seats in the House of Commons for a party gaining less than half the vote; there is thus no need for the compromise of coalition government. Class theories portray politics as an arena in which classes meet as adversaries. The legal system opposes prosecution and defense in the belief that the truth can be found through an adversary process. The American Constitution, too, institutionalizes adversary politics. Not only do two parties compete at elections, but also the White House and Congress compete, and losers in the electoral process can turn to the courts to try their fortunes there.

Yet consensus is also widespread as a means of reaching decisions. The British cabinet normally takes decisions without a vote; it is up to the prime minister to interpret what Quakers call "the sense of the meeting." A prime minister insensitive to this can lose office through colleagues withdrawing support, as Margaret Thatcher found out in 1990. Political disputes are not meant to be settled in the courts. A consensual method of dealing with difficulties is to appoint a commission to investigate a problem in search of a choice acceptable to both parties. The mistakes of government attract criticism, but when each party has experienced failures in the pursuit of economic growth and full employment, then neither can claim a monopoly of effective programs.

Competing Theories of Conflict and Consensus

The adversary theory of party politics assumes that parties differ not only about the tempo of change but also about the direction. A Conservative government should not just slow the growth of the welfare state but reverse direction, and a Labour government should not just administer a market economy but also promote programs that increase the socialization of resources. Differences not only concern the means of policy (e.g., which program may be a more effective instrument to reduce unemployment) but also the ends (whether a given level of unemployment is acceptable or not). From this it follows that a program endorsed by one party will be opposed by the other. Once in office, the party in power will repeal programs of its predecessors as well as make choices the opposition vigorously contests.

As long as control of government swings back and forth between parties, the legacy that one administration leaves to the next can be subject to subtraction as well as addition. Adversary theory predicts that the cumulative consequence is a continuous reshuffling of programs with the alternation of partisan control of government. S. E. Finer (1975: 16) has described the result as a pattern of "reversals and re-reversals, and in some cases, re-re-reversals of policy."

Adversary politics thus differs from incremental theories, which assume actions of the government of the day will only be changes of degree—for example, affecting spending priorities. The typical incremental policy change is the alteration of public expenditure by a few percentage points at the margin (cf. Braybrooke and Lindblom, 1963; Dempster and Wildavsky, 1979). One party may increase spending on a program by 3 percent annually and another by 6 percent or by 1 percent. In an inflationary era, a small increase in spending in nominal terms can even conceal a cut in real resources—but it leaves inherited programs in effect.

By contrast, consensus theories assume that parties are inclined to agree about programs. Confronted with an unexpected crisis that causes a demand for action, such as the AIDS epidemic, either a Conservative or a Labour government would be expected to act. In such an unprecedented situation, there is no obvious division along left-right lines. Hence, the programs chosen as the result of the combined efforts of experts, civil service advisers, and ministers are expected to be much the same, whatever the party in office. Even if parties do differ, the consensus theory assumes that differences will be matters of degree, not principle, as in differences of degree about priorities for expenditure on different inherited programs.

Differences about political priorities can lead to differences in the programs that each administration introduces while in office. A Conservative government finds it easier to enact laws regulating trade unions, and Labour has a special commitment to devolved institutions for governing Scotland and Wales. These differences reflect distinctive constituencies within each party and can create differences in the choices of different administrations. Even if the opposition party votes against an administration's program when it is introduced in the House of Commons, it does not, however, follow that it would repeal it once it finally regains office. At that stage, an inherited program that was once opposed is no longer a hypothetical proposal; it is a fait accompli.

Consensus theories do not depend upon a coalition government. Insofar as the median voter model of electoral competition is accurate, then any party in office will be centrist. The consensus theory predicts that successive Conservative and Labour administrations will accept the programs that they inherit from their opponents, including those that they voted against when in opposition, and add new programs to the legacy, thus creating a moving rather than a static consensus.

A change of party control of government is more significant than a change of prime ministers by the governing party, or the old administration returning to office in a new Parliament because it has been the election winner. A party winning re-election is likely to accept the commitments it inherits from the previous Parliament, since it has controlled it too.

Government has changed hands between the parties on six occasions since World War II. Labour moved from opposition to office in 1945 and back into opposition in 1951. Three successive election victories under different prime ministers—Churchill, Eden, and Macmillan—gave the Conservatives 13 years in office from 1951 to 1964. Labour returned to office in 1964 under Harold Wilson. It was replaced by a Conservative administration under Edward Heath in 1970. In the crisis election of February 1974, Labour won a plurality of seats and held office until 1979. The Conservatives returned to government in 1979 and have remained in office since. The time span of analysis stops in April 1990, seven months before the end of Margaret Thatcher's 11 years of leadership.

The British pattern is thus very different from a country such as Japan, where one party, the Liberal Democrats, was continuously in office for decades, or Italy, where the Christian Democrats have continuously been the largest party in the governing coalition in the postwar era (Pempel, 1990). It is also very different from the three Benelux countries and Scandinavia, where coalition governments are inevitable or frequent (Bogdanor, 1983). Britain also differs from the United States, where the separate election of the president and Congress frequently divides government between Republicans and Democrats (cf. Thurber, 1991; Cox and Kernell, 1991).

Consensus not Adversary Policymaking

The adversary theory concentrates attention upon the politics of the moment, the confrontation between the government and the opposition parties in the House of Commons. In such circumstances there are immediate incentives for the opposition to criticize anything and everything that the governing party chooses to do, since it is not responsible for government. Rhetorical attacks are part of the perpetual election campaign in which parties engage; as Winston Churchill once declared, "The Opposition's job is to oppose" (cf. Crick, 1970).

From the opposition benches MPs can speak and vote against the government of the day. The Second Reading debate on a pending bill is the best test of the adversary character of the opposition, since at this point the government seeks parliamentary endorsement for the principles of a bill, and government whips expect all its MPs to vote for every government bill. An opposition that considers itself an adversary can make its position clear by voting against government bills at Second Reading. The Opposition's decision about how to vote is the considered decision of the leadership of the opposition party. It is therefore different in kind from opposition that can come from back-bench rebels of the majority or minority parties; such opposition expresses individual opinion rather than collective party judgments.

Notwithstanding the incentives to oppose choices of the government, more than four-fifths of the time the opposition does *not* vote against government bills on Second Reading (figure 6.1). The details of bills are often criticized by MPs of both parties, and critical amendments are often moved. However, the readiness to alter the means by which a program is to be carried out is not opposition in principle. In the postwar era, the Conservatives voted against Labour government proposals only 16 percent of the time, and Labour voted against Conservative proposals only 20 percent of the time. This casts severe doubts upon the adversary hypothesis.

One reason for consensus about public programs is that many measures that the government of the day chooses to introduce are noncontroversial. This is most evident in such matters as emergency measures for flood victims. But an absence of opposition on principle is true in every field of public policy, including health, social security, and employment, where left vs. right differences might be considered especially relevant (cf. Van Mechelen and Rose, 1986: table 5.3).

Many bills are consensual because they are only introduced in the House of Commons after detailed deliberation within Whitehall and with affected pressure groups. An administration does not want to use party discipline to ride roughshod over critics in cabinet or among its own back-bench MPs. It may hesitate to put a measure to a vote until there is a consensus among disparate departments and pressure groups. If a consensus can be developed among major interest groups outside Parliament, the opposition appears a captious minority or risks political isolation if it votes against a popular bill.

The adversary hypothesis should be tested by what a party does in office as well as in opposition. Consensus is carried to the extreme

Figure 6.1. Bipartisan consensus in votes on government bills

Conservative administrations, 1951-83

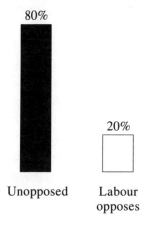

80%

20%

Unopposed   Labour
opposes

Labour administrations, 1945-79

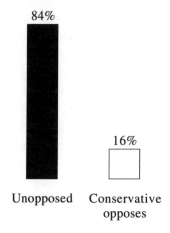

84%

16%

Unopposed   Conservative
opposes

Source: Denis Van Mechelen and Richard Rose, *Patterns of Parliamentary Legislation.*
Aldershot: Gower, 1986, Table 5.2.

when a general election occurs in the middle of a parliamentary session, thus causing all the pending bills of the government of the day to lapse. If it loses the election, the former opposition enters office with the right to introduce a totally different set of choices in the first session of the new Parliament. In fact, there is much continuity. In 1970 a general election caused 23 Labour government bills to lapse without enactment. The Conservatives entered office rhetorically pledged to major changes in public policy. Even though the pending Labour bills were not yet on the statute books, the new Conservative administration reintroduced as its "own" choice 14 bills stranded by the election. After the Conservatives collapsed in midsession in 1974, the Labour administration returned to office with no obligation to introduce the 22 stranded Conservative choices. Yet Labour adopted as its "own" choice 15 programs originally introduced by the Conservatives (Rose, 1984: 88).

Another test of opposition as a matter of principle rather than tactical gesture is whether a new administration repeals programs it has inherited from its opponents. Inherited programs continue to be accepted by each party in power. The limits of adversary government are defined by the 122 programs terminated since 1945, an average of 2.8 programs removed each year. The total of programs stopped includes those adopted before World War II as well as measures adopted during the period of party controversy reviewed here.

The parties terminated programs at about the same rate: an average of 2.8 programs a year when the Conservatives were in office, and 2.7 under Labour. These figures are a very small percentage of the total number of programs inherited by an incoming administration. From 1946 through 1973, about one program a year was stopped. This meant that in a four-year Parliament more than 95 percent of inherited legislation remained as part of the legacy for the next Parliament. Since 1974 the number of programs terminated has increased to more than five each year, but as the total number of inherited programs has increased, the result is that seven-eighths of programs inherited from the previous administration remain in force from one Parliament to the next. The high percentage of programs remaining in place casts further doubts upon the adversary hypothesis.

Terminating One's Own Errors

The repeal of programs supports the adversary hypothesis only if the party in government concentrates upon repealing measures chosen by its opponents. Conservative administrations would only repeal Labour measures, and Labour administrations would only repeal measures introduced during the Conservatives' tenure of office. Undoing the works of Labour would be just as much an expression of Conservative values as the enactment of new programs, and repealing measures inherited from the Conservatives could express Labour values.

The trial-and-error hypothesis predicts a very different pattern of behavior: a Conservative administration would be as likely to terminate measures that it has introduced as to stop those inherited from Labour, and a Labour administration would behave similarly. Just as at one time there can be a consensus in favor of introducing a measure so that there is no opposition in a vote on Second Reading, so the measure's subsequent ineffectiveness can create a cross-party consensus that the measure has failed to work and should be abandoned, regardless of the party initially sponsoring it. No administration wants to defend a measure that causes substantial dissatisfaction, even if it initially chose it.

The evidence supports the trial-and-error hypothesis, for 55 percent of postwar programs repealed are terminated by the party that initially introduced them (table 6.1). The Conservatives have been more active than Labour in terminating programs, but this is not owing to ideological opposition; 57 percent of programs terminated have been introduced by Conservative administrations. Similarly, half the pro-

Table 6.1 Termination of Programs Not Due to Partisanship

| | Termination of programs introduced by: | | | | |
| | Same party | | | Adversary | |
	Own admin.	Earlier admin.	Total (%)	N	Total (%)
Labour govt.					
1946–51	2	n.a.	n.a.	n.a.	n.a.
1965–70	2	1	100	0	0
1974–79	7	5	41	17	59
Total	11	6	50	17	50
Conservative govt.					
1952–64	3	n.a.	60	2	40
1971–73	0	0	0	6	100
1980–89	29	7	63	21	37
Total	32	7	57	29	43
Overall totals	43	13	55	46	45

Note: Excludes 20 inherited programs started before 1946 and terminated afterwards.

grams that Labour has stopped had been initially introduced by Labour. The percentage of "own goals," that is, choices that have had to be stopped, is thus almost the same for both parties.

Contrary to Finer's view that adversary government has been increasing in Britain, an acceleration in the repeal of programs since 1974 has not been due to heightened ideological conflict between parties. Instead, it appears to reflect an increasingly turbulent policy environment, in which trial-and-error searches cause both Conservative and Labour governments to terminate new programs as dissatisfaction continues. This is particularly true of the Conservative administration of Margaret Thatcher, which repealed 29 programs introduced by Conservative governments, eight more than the 21 Labour programs that it repealed. The high proportion of each administration's own goals reflects the fact that policymakers often cannot choose the circumstances in which they act. Political dissatisfaction induced by changes in the policy environment can force them to adopt risky programs that fail to succeed.

Since nine-tenths of inherited programs remain in the legacy that one administration leaves to the next, there is a moving consensus. The realities of office impose many constraints upon the governing party. Inherited programs have supporters who expect them to continue, whatever the election result—and they will make political trouble if a new government threatens to abandon a long-established program. When dissatisfaction produces a demand for new measures, ministers usually turn to expert civil servants for advice; civil servants have a disposition to seek consensus. The state of the economy, reflecting international as well as national conditions, also limits the introduction of new programs. Even though the government of the day has the formal authority to enact many new choices and repeal the works of its partisan opponents, inherited commitments reflect forces that are often stronger than parties (Rose, 1984: chapter 8).

Reform as a March to the Left or Steps Right and Left?

All parties tend to accept their inheritance, but they can differ in their readiness to introduce new programs. Insofar as Labour is the chief party of reform, it would introduce more programs than the Conservatives. Cumulatively, this would create an "unbalanced consensus" as Labour's initiatives would constitute more and more of the inheritance of public policy. The tilt to the left would be greater still if Labour programs also claimed a disproportionate amount of public expenditure. Hypothesis 6.4 predicts that this is the case.

The promotion of reform, in the original sense of making improvements in public policy, need not be viewed as the monopoly of any one party. Conservatives can argue that their priority is to introduce new programs to rectify the shortcomings of Labour administrations. Insofar as this is the case, then Conservative and Labour administrations should add a similar number of durable new programs to a consensus that is moving neither to the right or the left but is balanced, with the two parties contributing equally to the inheritance of public policy.

Claims to the Mantle of Reform

The Labour party has always portrayed itself as seeking to use the powers of government to change British society. In the prewar era it proclaimed socialist goals of redistributing power and wealth. Since World War II Labour has become more a party of amelioration, promoting the improvement of society through government action. The 1945–51 Labour government gave first priority to social welfare measures. Since then, Labour has sought to attract other reform interests, including blacks and feminists.

During the postwar era the Conservative party's position on reform has varied. Conservatives interpreted their election defeat in 1945 as a signal to come to terms with a larger role for government. "Change is our ally" became a party slogan, and party pamphlets trumpeted the programs of earlier generations of Tory reformers. The desire to accommodate change accounts for the 1951–64 Conservative government repealing fewer programs each year than any other postwar government (table 6.1). The priority that its prime ministers, especially Winston Churchill and Anthony Eden, gave to international affairs had the incidental effect of limiting attention to domestic reforms that constitute the stuff of everyday policymaking.

Since 1965, when Edward Heath became party leader, Conservatives have become more activist—although there have been disagreements within the party about the direction of change. Heath's first election manifesto in 1966 was entitled *Action not Words,* implying that a Conservative government would be as committed to change but more effective than the Labour government of Harold Wilson, whose manifesto was equally vague in its title, *Let's Go with Labour.* Under Heath the Conservatives in opposition prepared detailed programs.

Margaret Thatcher's views are paradoxical. Although rhetorically against government interference, she had definite and strong goals for British society, and found much that was wrong in programs inherited from both Labour and Conservative predecessors. The result was a commitment to radical reform, for example the privatization of state-owned industries and new trade-union legislation, measures that Labour regarded as reactionary rather than progressive changes—but government choices nonetheless (cf. Bulpitt, 1986).

Balanced Consensus

Since the Conservative party has been led by activists for more than a quarter century, the postwar portfolio of new programs does in fact show a balanced consensus. Since 1946 Conservative administrations have introduced 144 programs compared to 101 for Labour. The Conservative preeminence remains even after controlling for the fact that Conservative administrations have also repealed more of their own programs. Net of repeals, Conservative administrations have added four new programs for every three new programs that Labour has contributed to the legacy of public policy (table 6.2). The idea that Labour is the party of reform, and that the inertia of public policy lurches to the left, is here rejected.

Table 6.2 Parties Equally Balanced in Introducing New Programs

	New programs			
	Per admin.		Per year	
	Gross	Net	Gross	Net
Labour govt.				
1946–51	25	23	4.2	3.8
1965–70	33	30	5.5	5.0
1974–79	43	31	7.2	5.2
Total	101	84	5.6	4.7
Conservative govt.				
1952–64	32	29	2.5	2.2
1971–73	31	31	10.3	10.3
1980–89	81	46	8.1	4.6
Total	144	106	5.5	4.1

Note: Gross figures refer to new programs introduced by an administration; the net figure subtracts programs that were introduced and repealed by the same party during the same or a subsequent administration.

The Conservative preeminence in introducing new programs is largely due to the longer period of Conservative control of government. When an annual rate for the introduction of new programs is calculated, the figures are virtually the same for both parties, 5.6 programs by Labour and 5.5 by the Conservatives. After controlling for the large number of new programs repealed by the Thatcher administration, both parties average an annual net addition of four to five programs.

Even more strikingly, there appears to be no partisan bias in the subject matter of new programs (cf. Dunsire and Hood, 1989: 55ff). In health, social security, and education, policy areas traditionally associated with the welfare state, Labour has introduced 16 new programs and the Conservatives 17. In economic policy, the Conservatives have introduced 18 new trade and industry programs and Labour 14. The greater number of new Conservative programs in the field of employment, 37 as against 24 under Labour, is not so much a sign of greater Conservative activity as of greater dissatisfaction and pressure to act as unemployment rose to postwar heights during the Thatcher administration.

Money provides a second test of the reform hypothesis. If new Labour programs claimed more public money than programs introduced by the Conservatives, public expenditure would increasingly tilt to the left. This could happen if Labour administrations concentrated upon programs giving benefits to millions of children or pensioners, while Conservative administrations targeted benefits narrowly through means tests or adopted programs that were not costly, such as measures to regulate trade and industry.

When money is the measure, here again the moving consensus is balanced. In the postwar era the initial cost of new programs introduced by Conservative administrations totalled £22.7 billion in constant pounds, double the £11.1 billion initial cost of new programs introduced by Labour administrations. Even after allowance is made for the fact that the Conservatives introduced more new programs, the average cost of a single new program is much higher for Conservative administrations. Even after controlling for the effects of inflation, each Conservative administration has spent more on new programs than its immediate Labour predecessor. The Thatcher administration too has surpassed its Labour predecessor in the money annually committed to new programs.

The initial cost of new programs is not the best indicator of their impact on the public purse, for the amount spent on a program in time

Figure 6.2. Aggregate costs of programs by party

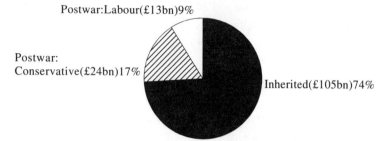

Postwar:Labour(£13bn)9%

Postwar:
Conservative(£24bn)17%

Inherited(£105bn)74%

can balloon out of all proportion to initial expenditure. Proponents of major spending measures may even adopt the "camel's nose" approach, intentionally introducing programs with a low level of expenditure but designed to increase in cost as demand for the program grows. It could be argued that Labour would do this knowingly, because of the belief that a long-term increase in public spending on social and economic programs is desirable, whereas Conservative administrations would "front-end load" new programs, claiming credit for measures where spending is initially high and then quickly recedes.

In fact, the cumulative increase in the cost of programs is not affected by party: Labour is no more likely than Conservatives to introduce programs that become increasingly costly. The programs initiated by the Attlee government after the war have more than doubled in cost, but this is an exception to the overall pattern. The total cost today of programs introduced by the two subsequent Labour governments is actually less than their initial cost. Similarly, the current cost of programs introduced by two of the three Conservative administrations is less than their initial cost. The total spent on new programs does not balloon up, because the increase in some programs tends to be offset by the termination of errors.

Expenditure on the manifold of public policy today shows political inertia claims far more money than partisan will. Programs inherited from the distant past predominate; programs in place before the end of World War II today account for almost three-quarters of public expenditure (figure 6.2). Collectively, new Conservative programs account for almost twice as much money as new Labour programs. Instead of expenditure on new programs causing a progressive move to the left, it has increased the weight of Conservative measures in public policy.

The introduction of new programs shows greater differences between administrations of the same party than between the parties. The Attlee administration was much less likely than the 1974 Labour government to introduce new programs, to commit large sums of money to new programs, or to introduce programs that were terminated because of failure. The same is true of the difference between the 1951–64 Conservative administration and the much more active, bigger-spending and more-often-in-error Heath and Thatcher administrations. The Thatcher administration has been much readier to spend money initiating new programs (£12.2 billion) than previous Conservative and Labour administrations. This indicates a secular shift in the postwar era in the frequency of introducing and repealing programs, a change more likely to be accounted for by alterations in the economic climate or the policy environment of specific programs than by the rhetoric of parties.

7 Economic Constraints on the Scope for Choice

There is no such thing as a free lunch—An adage of economists

Politics is meant to be a happy art. Politicians want to be identified with what is popular, and spending money on the "good" goods and services that government provides, such as education, health care, and social security benefits. This is much more popular than refusing demands for new and popular programs. If politicians had their choice, the economy would always be booming, for economic growth makes it possible to enjoy "policy without pain" (Heclo, 1981: 397).

Economics is often known as the dismal science, because no program is free of costs; these costs must be met by taxation, borrowing, an inflationary expansion of the money supply, or a combination of all three. The state of the economy is thus a constraint upon the choices of policymakers. When the economy is in recession, tax revenue declines and expenditure and deficits rise, putting pressure on inherited programs and leaving little fiscal scope for new choices.

Yet in good times the economy can produce treble affluence. An economic boom raises tax revenue without any increase in tax rates. If national income rises by £10 billion, then applying fixed tax rates to this increase will yield about £4 billion in additional revenue from income and value-added taxes, social security contributions, and other taxes. The extra revenue can be used to expand inherited programs or fund new choices, and the fiscal dividend of economic growth can finance an increase in take-home pay too.

In the short term, economic growth is measured in a few percentage points. Two percent annual growth in the economy may not sound like much, but in Britain it amounts to more than £10 billion in a single year, and in the United States to more than $100 billion. In four years in office, the compounding of a two percent annual rate of growth increases the national product by more than £50 billion in real terms. Compounding a 2 percent annual growth rate for a decade would generate a real increase of £110 billion in the national product. Like spending programs, tax laws are sustained by political inertia; as a result, every decade adds tens of billions to public revenue (cf. Rose and Karran, 1987). In 1946 total tax revenue in current money terms was £4.1 billion; in 1989 it was £198 billion. Inflation eroded some but not all of the purchasing power of this almost 50-fold increase.

Whatever the amount of additional tax revenue generated by the economy, inherited spending commitments have the first claim. The more programs a new administration inherits, the more its tax revenues are committed in advance. Moreover, the commitments are dynamic, not static. Programs can increase through routines sustained by laws and political inertia: indexation of pensions, an increase in the number of people entitled to claim health care or unemployment benefits, wage increases of public employees, and so forth. An increase in the claims of inherited programs can preempt the fiscal dividend of growth. When recession causes a shortfall in tax revenue, increased expenditure on inherited programs can exceed any increase in tax revenue, thus boosting the public deficit.

If spending on inherited programs increases as fast or faster than the growth of public revenue, this can lead to a crowding out of new programs, for everything else being equal, the greater the total increase in the claims of inherited programs, the less money is available for the government of the day to spend on new programs of its own choice. Even though public expenditure grows in aggregate, there is no revenue free to finance new programs, because the whole of the year's increase in taxation is already committed to inherited programs.

*7.1 *(Crowding out)*. As claims of inherited programs increase, the scope for new programs decreases.

This hypothesis implies that the lower the growth rate, the greater the extent of crowding out.

The fiscal dividend of a high rate of economic growth tends to offset the effects of crowding out.

*7.2 (*Growth finances more growth*). As the gross national product increases, new programs increase.

Many politicians regard it as self-evident that the growth in public policy is desirable. Public choice theorists often assume that politicians want to buy reelection by introducing more and bigger programs. Advocates of a constitutional limit upon public expenditure believe that if spending is not thus constrained, the cumulative effects of the choices of hyperactive politicians cannot be sustained economically. In Britain the ceiling imposed by economic growth is lower than in the average advanced industrial nation, because growth in the British economy has been below the international average.

The sequencing of events loosens economic constraints, for the amount of revenue obtained by government in a given year from economic growth is only known after the fact, whereas the choices that politicians make about the year's spending commitments are based upon ex ante expectations of economic growth. There are always a multiplicity of forecasts of the state of the economy in the months ahead, each based upon varying theoretical and empirical assumptions and producing significantly different results. Differences in forecasts thus give politicians some discretion in choosing the revenue estimate to be taken as the constraint upon choice. A rosy scenario allows much more scope for choice than a dire forecast.

Projecting past trends into the future is the simplest way to form expectations of public revenue. However, this is risky because of the short-term ups and downs of the economic cycle, and over the years there are structural changes in the rate of economic growth. Statistical models of the future path of the economy can take into account the ups and downs of economic cycles, but anticipating shocks from abroad is much more difficult, and such shocks are important as an open economy is increasingly subject to international influences.

Our expectations fluctuate too. In Victorian times there was a consensus that favored strict limitations upon activities of government. When the government claimed only a few percent of the national product, this was sometimes considered "too much." In 1931, at the height of the world depression, the Labour government of Ramsay MacDonald cut spending in the belief that it had no choice but to balance the budget. After World War II the Keynesian paradigm recommending an active role for public policy in promoting economic growth gained sway. But this paradigm was undermined in the 1970s by stagflation, the coincidence of rising unemployment, inflation, and low rates of economic growth. Today, a variety of Keynesian and monetarist paradigms compete in claims to predict how the economic system works. Confronted with conflicts between economists, politicians are forced (or free) to choose which set of expectations to adopt (Hall, 1989; Rose, 1989b).

Subjective political factors are important in shaping the economic expectations of policymakers. Because expectations concern the future, it is impossible to demonstrate that they are wrong until after the event. Faced with political difficulties, policymakers are apt to choose expectations that are most congenial for their political circumstances, even if they rest on dubious assumptions, evidence, and reasoning. Whatever the source, expectations influence politicians' perceptions of the scope for choice.

*7.3. (*Expectations*). As expectations of economic growth rise and fall, the scope for new programs rises and falls.

Given that economic constraints are material and not just imagined, the first section of this chapter tests the extent to which inherited programs crowd out the choice of new programs. Since the crowding-out hypothesis is not supported, the second section tests the extent to which the expectations of policymakers loosen or tighten constraints upon choice.

Crowding Out Choice?

Political choice is contingent upon resources. Whereas in third-world countries an absolute lack of money is often the problem, in advanced industrial nations the risk is more likely to be the preemption of revenue by inherited programs. In 1906 the reformist Liberal administration had great scope for choice because public expenditure claimed about one-tenth of the national product. The 1945 Labour government inherited many more program commitments, but it also inherited the greatly enhanced revenue-raising powers of wartime government. By the 1970s, the inheritance had continued to grow, but there was no readily available resource for expanding revenue.

The scope for choice depends upon the number and cost of inherited programs. As the legacy of public programs expands from one administration to another, each new administration inherits a larger number of prior commitments from its predecessors. Insofar as inertia forces also push up the cost of inherited programs, then there is an increasing "front-end load" upon public revenue. When government must raise more and more revenue to finance the programs it inherits, this can crowd out new choices.

Inertia Growth of Inherited Programs

The cost of inherited programs is not a constant; it tends to increase each year (see OECD, 1985: chapter 2). In an era in which it is normal for government to run an annual deficit, each year's deficit is added to next year's total debt, increasing the total amount of interest that must be paid. If interest rates rise, this increases even more the cost of financing inherited debts. Interest on debts inherited from previous administrations is a primary charge upon public revenue. The payment of interest on the national debt inherited from previous administrations today is the biggest line in the budget, and is bigger than the amount that most departments have to spend in total on 20 or more programs.

Many of the most expensive programs, such as pensions and education, confer entitlements to benefits upon all who meet stated criteria. An increase in the number of older people entering retirement pushes up the cost of social security. If individuals tend to live longer in retirement, this further increases the costs of social security and of health care. Growth in the number of young people entering university inexorably forces up expenditure on higher education.

Indexing cash benefits against inflation pushes up the cost of inherited programs. In response to inflation, legislation has incorporated provisions to increase the value of benefits more or less automatically in line with a rise in the cost of living, economic growth, or changes in both (Weaver, 1988). Since inherited social security measures are the largest set of programs in the budget, indexing exerts a strong annual upward pressure on public spending.

When program outputs are the services of public employees, as is the case of health care and defense, public sector wages can rise faster than productivity grows in the service sector, thus raising prices relative to growth in the economy overall (see Baumol, 1967; Heller, 1981). Public employees constitute more than a quarter of the British labor force and, in an era of economic growth, it was assumed that public sector wages would be inflation-proofed and grow with the economy. Since productivity in the capital-intensive private sector tends to rise faster than productivity in the labour-intensive public sector, the cost of producing public services increases relative to manufactured goods. In a period of fiscal stress, administrations have sometimes increased public sector wages less than the rate of inflation and economic growth. Such a practice is part of a strategy of containing costs that also implies a crowding out of new programs.

The bulk of spending on inherited programs is often described as uncontrollable, because the government of the day has no choice but to carry out statutory commitments inherited from its predecessors. Politically, the line of least resistance is to accept increased expenditure on inherited programs. Beneficiaries of established programs constitute a formidable lobby, and a government can allocate money to inherited programs with confidence in how the money will be spent. By contrast, doubts can be voiced about whether a new program can be successfully implemented or whether it will be effective, because it is not a known quantity (cf. Pressman and Wildavsky, 1973; Bowen, 1982). By definition, a new program has been unable to institutionalize support from producers and recipients of its benefits, and it is harder to mobilize support for potential benefits than to defend established benefits.

Since financing new programs from the fiscal dividend of existing taxes is politically much more appealing than raising new taxes to finance new programs, the cumulative growth of spending on inherited programs threatens to crowd out new programs.

Crowding Expenditure but Not Number of New Programs

The inheritance from the distant past has definitely not crowded out the introduction of new programs. The 1945 Labour administration commenced peacetime policymaking with 115 programs inherited from the past. Since 1945 a total of 245 new programs have been adopted, and 143 were still in effect in 1990. Since the majority of programs in effect today are postwar programs, the legacy of the distant past has not prevented fresh choices (figure 7.1).

Stronger evidence against the crowding-out hypothesis is that the number of new programs chosen annually has tended to increase

Figure 7.1. Growth in inherited and new programs compared, 1946–89

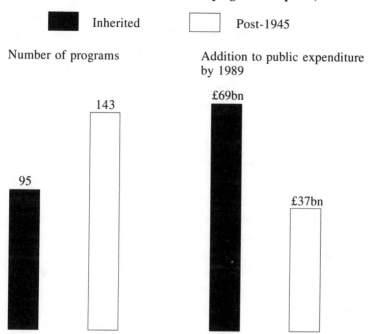

rather than decrease with the passage of time. At the start of the postwar period a new administration could be expected to introduce three or four programs a year; since 1970 the rate of introducing new programs has averaged more than eight new measures each year. Even though many choices have subsequently been abandoned in a trial-and-error process, the critical point here is that the increase in the number of inherited programs has not prevented successive administrations from adding more choices to the total (cf. table 6.2).

Inherited programs can crowd out expenditure if they claim the bulk of additional tax revenue. Crowding out hypothesizes that there will be an inverse correlation between the amount of additional money spent on each year's inherited programs as against new programs. However, this is not the case. On an *annual* basis, decisions about spending on new programs appear to be independent of increased spending on inherited programs. There is only a weak statistical correlation between the two ($r = .07$), and the positive association implies that both types of program go up or down together. The annual increase in spending on new and inherited programs is also independent of the rate of economic growth, which explains less than 1 percent of the variance in the annual increase in spending on inherited programs and on new programs.

Cumulatively, the picture is different. Between 1946 and the end of the 1989 fiscal year, public expenditure quadrupled, increasing in real terms by £106 billion. If that increase had been divided in proportion to the number of programs inherited from the distant past and programs introduced in the postwar era, then new programs would have claimed 61 percent of additional postwar expenditure.

Spending on new programs has been squeezed, but not crowded out, by programs inherited from the distant past. Programs inherited from the distant past have accounted for almost twice as much additional expenditure as their numbers would appear to justify. New programs have claimed 35 percent of additional expenditure in the postwar era, much less than their proportion of total programs. The average inherited program in 1989 cost £1.1 billion; less than one-quarter this amount, £257 million, was spent on the average new program.

The disparity between the increased number of new programs and increased expenditure on such programs reflects trial-and-error choices. New programs are adopted when pressures to act increase—and these pressures have been great in recent decades. The sums spent are smaller, because programs adopted under conditions of uncertainty are likely to be less generously funded, and new programs cannot enjoy the bulk of the fiscal dividend of economic growth, for that is already committed to finance programs inherited from the distant past.

Expected Growth Influences Program Growth

If policymakers did not expect the economy to grow, then the inheritance of public policy would be an extremely tight constraint upon choosing new programs, for new programs could only be financed by raising taxes or terminating inherited programs. But the more policymakers expect economic growth, the easier it is to choose new programs without facing hard choices about how they are to be paid for.

Economic trends tend to be cyclical; sometimes the rate of growth is high or rising, and sometimes it is decreasing or even negative. It is unusual for an economy to follow a steady path throughout a Parliament. The postwar British economy has been especially subject to stop-go cycles of expansion and low growth or contraction. During a recession a spending-oriented politician can argue that the cycle is about to reverse and there will be more scope for choice by the time new programs come into effect. A politician opposed to the growth of government can argue that the recession will continue, or a boom will not last if government increases its expenditure.

The climate of economic expectations is constructed, not given (cf. MacKuen et al., 1992). Policymakers can form their expectations retrospectively, as a response to what has been happening in the economy. If the economy has been growing, further growth can be projected, and this will encourage the choice of more new programs. If the economy is contracting, the projection of recession discourages the choice of new programs or can put the brakes on expenditure for inherited programs. Alternatively, policymakers can form their expectations prospectively, placing more weight upon the future than the immediate past. Because accurate data about the state of the economy only arrives after the fact, disputes about the state of the economy in the year of concern to policymakers can only be resolved empirically when it is too late to affect current choices.

Decisions about how much tax revenue is available to finance new choices must be made in advance of the fact (cf. Mosley, 1984: chapter 3). In the year in which policymakers are asked to decide about choices to be put into effect in the following year, the only hard numbers available are about the past. Forecasts about the state of the economy next year and the tax revenue can only be estimates, and all estimates are subject to a margin of error. Different economic assumptions can cause forecasts of revenue to differ marginally. A 1 percent difference in forecasts may not sound large, but represents at least £2 billion in Britain and $12 billion in Washington. Figures of this magnitude are great enough to pay for six or eight new programs in a year.

By definition, expectations cannot be disproved by empirical evidence, for the future is not yet here. Policymakers can "shape" the future, that is, make a subjective judgment about the economic climate for the next few years. In the words of a Washington analyst, "Revenue estimating has *become* policy" (quoted in Crenshaw, 1993: 22). The increased use of empirically based economic models to forecast the future places limits on the credibility of alternative scenarios. Policymakers do not propose that the economy double in wealth in five years, but differences in econometric forecasting methods allow policymakers a choice of more or less politically congenial forecasts. For example, during the growth mania of the 1960s, both Conservative and Labour administrations announced public expenditure decisions based on economic expectations without any historical precedent. In the 1980s both the Thatcher administration and the Reagan administration showed the capacity to make forecasts based on pure theory, such as monetarism and supply-side economics.

Expectations in the Budget Process

At the start of the budget process expectations about the economy are critical in determining the scope for choice. From a macroeconomic perspective, whether or not new programs are introduced is less significant than the net impact of all changes in programs, whether inherited or new. A year before a budget is due to go into effect, public officials forecast what the state of the economy is expected to be in the following year, what revenue the government can expect to collect, and the cost of inherited programs.

The budget forecast also includes, however, an estimate of the expected increase in the cost of inherited programs. If cost increases are above average, say, because of a large wage award to public employees or a big increase in interest rates, and if revenue is not increasing as expected because of a recession, then the forecast produces a very tight constraint upon the choice of new programs.

Expectations about public expenditure are evaluated by the Treasury within an overall macroeconomic policy framework. In the mixed economy of Britain, the Treasury's first priority is to maintain an uneasy balance between growth, inflation, the foreign-exchange value of the pound, and unemployment. Public expenditure is regarded as a means of attaining these macroeconomic goals. If there is a desire to stimulate economic demand, then greater increases in public expenditure and deficits may be tolerated; if inflation is the primary worry, then there is less scope for choice of new programs that increase public expenditure.

The total sum allowed for increased expenditure on inherited and new claims on the fisc is set at the beginning of the budget cycle. The public expenditure division of the Treasury, headed by a cabinet minister, then engages in political bargaining with the heads of spending departments in an effort to keep the total increase of spending within the agreed macroeconomic limit. Outcomes are determined by political bargaining; the extent to which the Treasury must concede funds for new programs depends upon the political climate (e.g., the approach of a general election) as well as upon the economic climate. It also depends upon the pressures to raise or to cut taxes (cf. Rose and Karran, 1987: chapter 7; Heclo and Wildavsky, 1981).

Because economic forecasts are statements about the future, the figures involved are not a hard constraint, like a run on the pound in the foreign exchange markets. During the months in which the budget is in preparation, forecasts are modified to take into account observed changes in the national and international economy and their anticipated consequences for the following year's budget. These changes increase or decrease the potential scope for choice. Revision of official expectations is an ongoing process. It continues even after the budget has come into effect. Over a period of years, the average error in the Treasury forecast of economic growth has been about 1 percent, a sum equivalent to more than £2 billion in revenue (Britton, 1991: 204; Treasury and Civil Service Committee, 1991).

The decisions made about each year's budget are ultimately political decisions. Insofar as there is a gap between what is desired and what is expected, the gap can be closed by sacrificing political choices, or by altering economic expectations, or adjusting both. Cabinet ministers see little point in risking a split in the party for the sake of half a billion pounds, when such a sum is well within the normal margin of forecasting error and adjusting forecasts can "create" the money needed to bridge divisions within the cabinet.

Expectations as a Function of the Retrospective Record

A simple materialist approach is to assume that the economic expectations that policymakers have are retrospective, an extrapolation of what has been happening in the immediate past. The invocation of experience always has force in politics, and this is true whether projections from the recent past show a booming economy, with much scope for choice, or tight constraints. Grounding expectations in recent events greatly reduces malleability. Whereas the future is protean, the past is a given.

The expectations hypothesis predicts that if the economy has been growing, then more new programs will be enacted and more spent on inherited programs, and if it has been contracting, the opposite will occur. These general propositions may be tested three ways.

First, if the actual growth rate of the economy determined the number of new programs adopted, there should be a good fit between the growth rate in one year and the number of programs adopted in the following year. In fact, there is not; the pattern is completely random (r^2: .00). Since there was a major increase in the number of programs adopted annually after 1964, the test was also rerun for two periods. From 1946 until 1964 there was a limited correlation between annual economic growth in one year and the number of new programs adopted in the following year (r^2: .24). However, since 1965, when policymakers became more active in adopting new programs but less effective in promoting economic growth, the relationship has been very weak (r^2: .04).

Secondly, the state of the economy could influence *spending* on new programs; the higher the rate of growth, the more likely the government of the day would be to introduce expensive new programs; the lower the growth rate, the more likely it would be to approve choices costing very little money. This hypothesis too must be rejected, for the relationship between the economic growth rate in a given year and program expenditure two years hence (a period allowing time to adopt a new program and its spending pattern to be established) is completely random (r^2: .00).

Squeezing inherited programs achieves real cash savings, whereas the rejection of new proposals only constrains the rate of expansion.

Thus, a third hypothesis is that the material state of the economy could influence inherited programs, with spending rising substantially with an increase in growth, but much less in recession. In fact, there is virtually no association between spending on inherited programs and the state of the economy the year before (r^2: .01).

On all three counts, increases in expenditure and in the number of programs are not a retrospective reflection of recent economic growth. The influences that make the economy grow faster or slower, such as alterations in the international economy, or macroeconomic conditions, hardly influence individual programs. The pressures that push up expenditure on inherited programs are specific to their structure; for example, the effects of demographic changes on health services or education. New programs reflect political priorities or responses to dissatisfaction forcing trial-and-error measures.

The failure to find a fit between new programs and economic growth is not proof of the unimportance of the economy for the choices of policymakers. It may simply indicate that a retrospective measure of the state of the economy is unimportant as an influence on policymakers compared to future expectations.

Political Climate Shapes Economic Expectations and Program Choices

The climate of economic expectations reflects political judgments as well as economic data. There is considerable fashion in political judgments, including judgments about the economy, and disagreement among economists (Ricketts and Shoesmith, 1990). While growth, inflation, and unemployment rates are persisting features of every economy, the attention given to each fluctuates with the political climate.

The optimism or pessimism with which the future is viewed is subject to fashion at both the mass and elite level. Since 1960 the

Gallup Poll has annually asked Britons about their economic expectations for the year ahead. Pessimists consistently outnumber optimists,
but the percentage of pessimists varies from a low of 20 percent at the
beginning of 1964 to 85 percent pessimistic at the beginning of 1975.
Given the consistency in pessimism, it is not surprising that mass
expectations do not correlate with changes in the choice of programs.
When the percentage of persons with optimistic expectations for the
year ahead is used as the independent variable, the r^2 value for the
number of new programs introduced in the year ahead is .00; for
spending on new programs in the year ahead, .01; and change in
spending on inherited programs, .04.

The expectations of policymakers ought to be much more important than mass expectations, since the formulation of economic forecasts is in the hands of a political and technocratic elite. In the postwar
era British policymakers have veered between assumptions of economic stability, relatively optimistic beliefs in growth, and pessimistic expectations of decline. The ideas dominant among policymakers
have greater duration than a single business cycle, and are also independent of short-term reactions of public opinion. We can identify
five different periods of contrasting elite economic expectations (for
details, see citations in the bibliography of Britton, 1991: 337–59):

1. *Austerity: 1946–51* (annual growth in gross domestic product [GDP]: 0.5 percent). After the end of World War II, the
Labour government saw major economic difficulties in convert-
ing a wartime economy to peacetime; the gross domestic product
fell substantially in real terms as a consequence of reconversion
from war. Instead of expecting growth, the Attlee government
cautiously sought to avoid recession by stabilizing the economy
and maintaining full employment. Symbolic of the austerity
approach was the government's reliance upon rationing to re-
strain demand at a time of scarcity. This climate should be a

constraint upon the creation of new programs, and spending on inherited and new programs.

2. *Stability: 1952–64* (annual growth in GDP: 3.7 percent). The Conservative government returned in 1951 sought to make a bonfire of austerity's controls and rationing, but shared Labour's goal of an inflation-free economy with full employment. Depression, not rapid growth, was viewed as the alternative to stability. When a leading Labour economist and adviser to Hugh Gaitskell, Anthony Crosland (1956), published a political manifesto anticipating an expansion of public policy financed by an ever-expanding national income, his calculations were widely distrusted by Labour colleagues as well as by Conservatives (cf. Butler and Rose, 1960). In fact, the national product grew at the relatively high rate of 3.7 percent annually. However, in a climate of political expectations anticipating little growth, one would not expect big increases in public programs and expenditure.

3. *Expected boom: 1964–73* (annual growth in GDP: 3.2 percent). In the 1960s both the Conservative administration of Harold Macmillan and Labour administrations became converted to a faith in continuous and high economic growth. Both parties assumed that government actions could and should promote growth, and their expenditure calculations anticipated a fiscal dividend. Whereas in the 1959 election Hugh Gaitskell had been scorned for proposing to finance increased pensions from economic growth, by 1964 the Conservative government campaigned with a Treasury document promising to finance an annual increase in public expenditure of 4 percent annually from the fiscal dividend of economic growth. Both the Wilson and Heath administrations expected to achieve an historically unprecedented growth rate and planned public expenditure in ex-

pectation of a boom. We would thus expect a high rate of growth in programs and public expenditure, even though the actual annual growth rate was less than in the period of expected stability.

4. *Fiscal stress: 1974–82* (annual growth in GDP: 0.7 percent). The British economy was already in difficulty when the 1973 OPEC oil crisis and the subsequent world recession hit. The average annual growth rate was very low, and in four years the economy actually contracted. The 1974 Labour administration initially sought to spend its way out of recession, but this policy failed. In 1976 an IMF loan was sought to stabilize the economy, and cash limits on public expenditure were set at levels lower than the rate of inflation. The return of a Conservative government under Margaret Thatcher in 1979 intensified the pressure to deal with the fiscal effects of recession. Hence, both public expenditure and the number of new programs would be expected to grow slowly in a period that could aptly be described as the Healey-Thatcher years, because it started under a Labour chancellor, Denis Healey, and was continued in the Thatcher administration.

5. *Political stress, 1983–89* (annual growth in GDP: 3.8 percent). Margaret Thatcher entered office when economic forces had placed tight constraints upon expanding public policy. Hence, the anti-spending pressures of her first term of office cannot be ascribed simply to political principles; they were also a continuation of measures inherited from her Labour predecessor. The real test of Thatcherite convictions came when the economy again began to boom. The Thatcher administration, uniquely among postwar British governments, gave first priority to spending the fiscal divided of growth on tax cuts. The result can aptly be described as "political stress," a conflict between proponents

of the Thatcher view and proponents of expanding popular programs. In seven years from 1983, the economy grew at a rate of 3.8 percent, higher than at any previous postwar period, and higher than the overall growth rate for the Thatcher administration. Political stress implies that notwithstanding economic growth, the threat of a prime ministerial veto prevented the big expansion of public programs.

Because economic expectations are often the opposite of economic outcomes, they constitute a valid independent influence upon the choice of programs. In the 1950s era of stability, the economy was not expected to grow a great deal—but in fact it did. The growth rate of 3.7 percent was very high by comparison with the postwar average. When the economy was expected to boom in the late 1960s, the rate of growth was well below the average. Political stress was not generated by low growth but by Margaret Thatcher's unwillingness to conform to the expectation that all politicians, including Conservative leaders, should allocate most of the fiscal dividend of economic growth to expanding public policy.

Insofar as expectations are important and variable, the readiness of administrations to start new programs should vary with changes in political climate. This is the case (table 7.1). For two decades after World War II there was no expectation of economic growth. When policymakers believe that no growth in the economy is likely, they adopt few new programs, and those adopted cost little money. Fewer new programs were initiated annually from 1952 to 1964 than in any other economic climate, and their total cost in real terms was the lowest in the postwar era. Consistent with stability, the administration also terminated the fewest number of programs. The austerity of the Attlee administration was similar, for new programs claimed little money. However, more programs were started and terminated each year in the adjustment from war to peace, and because the Attlee

Table 7.1 Effect of Economic Climate on New Programs

	New Programs (per annum)			Total Spending on New Programs* (£mn per annum)
	Started	Terminated	Net	
Austerity	4.2	1.3	2.9	584
Stability	2.5	0.7	1.8	480
Expected boom	7.1	1.6	5.5	2,148
Fiscal stress	7.1	4.9	2.2	1,449
Political stress	8.6	6.7	1.9	1,306

*In third year of program in effect to allow time for full cost to build up. If a program is terminated after two years, the average expenditure for both is used.

government wanted to introduce social programs that Labour had been promoting for decades.

When policymakers expect the economy to boom, they are most ready to spend money on expensive new programs, and this is true of both Conservative and Labour administrations. From 1964 through 1973 an average of seven programs a year was launched at a total annual cost of more than £2 billion. The ten-year period thus saw a very large number of programs added to the manifold of public policy and few subtracted, and there was the biggest boom of the postwar era in spending on new programs too.

The fiscal stress that followed in 1974 reduced the net number of programs added to the manifold of public policy to a level similar to the era of austerity. It also reduced the additional cost of new programs by one-third from the preceding decade. However, this was not due to inactivity but because of a frantic trial-and-error search for measures that would reduce dissatisfaction. The number of new programs introduced each year remained at a high level; fiscal stress showed its biggest impact in the increase in the number of programs terminated.

The Thatcher administration was definitely *not* conservative with a small *c*; it rejected the laissez-faire approach of its 1951–64 Conservative predecessor. It was radical in inclinations and prepared to face up to the stress of refusing to expand public programs. Notwithstanding the extra money generated by the boom of the mid-1980s, the Thatcher administration reduced the net number of new programs added to a level almost as low as in the 1950s. However, it could do this only through a trial-and-error process of abandoning as well as launching programs. The level of expenditure on new programs dropped in total and even more on a per program basis.

Inherited programs are also subject to expectations in the economic climate, since programs inherited by the government of the day constitute the bulk of its responsibilities. Even though marginal changes in inherited measures do not change the manifold of public policy, collectively they are much costlier in money terms.

Expectations and economic resources are in equilibrium when growth in spending on inherited programs is in accord with the expansion of the economy. This can occur at high levels of expansion or by constraining expenditure during a recession. Equilibrium was maintained during the era of austerity, for the low rate of growth of the economy was matched by little growth in spending on inherited programs; the difference between the two rates was only 0.3 percent (table 7.2). Equilibrium was also maintained at a high level of economic growth in an era in which stability was the norm. From 1952 to 1964 spending on inherited programs grew by about 4 percent, and the same was true of the economy.

Disequilibrium has persisted since 1964. In anticipation of economic growth, public spending on inherited programs grew by 6.5 percent from 1964 through 1973, the highest rate in the postwar era. However, the economy grew at less than half that rate and had to finance a much-expanded set of new programs as well as inherited programs. Hence, a relatively high rate of economic growth of 3.2

Table 7.2 Effect of Economic Climate on Inherited Programs

	Public expenditure (1)	GDP (2)	Difference (2-1)
	(% growth per annum)		
Austerity	0.2	0.5	0.3
Stability	4.4	3.7	−0.7
Expected boom	6.5	3.2	−3.3
Fiscal stress	3.0	0.7	−2.3
Political stress	0.6	3.8	3.3

percent was insufficient to meet commitments undertaken in expectation of a level of economic growth that did not materialize (table 7.2). The disequilibrium created fiscal stress.

The 1974 Labour government inherited overextended commitments from both Conservative and Labour predecessors. It succeeded in putting the brakes on the growth of spending on inherited programs; the 3.0 percent per annum average increase was less than in the previous two decades. But because the economy grew at less than 1 percent a year, the gap between economic growth and public expenditure was the second largest in the postwar era.

The political will of the Thatcher administration reversed the long-term increase in public expenditure on inherited programs, with the result that it grew much less than the economy as a whole. Even though the economy was booming in the mid-1980s, public expenditure on inherited programs scarcely increased in real terms. The result was a new type of disequilibrium: public expenditure grew far less than the economy as a whole. This created political stress due to conflict between government and opposition about priorities for private as against public expenditure.

Political Climates Stronger than Partisanship

In two major postwar periods—that of expected boom and fiscal stress—there was a bipartisan economic climate. The big boost in programs and expenditure from 1964 through 1973 occurred under both Labour and Conservative administrations. In a complementary manner, after the 1974 Labour government had slammed the brakes on public expenditure, the successor Conservative administration of 1979 kept its foot hard on the brake.

Even though austerity occurred only under the Attlee government, there was a high degree of bipartisanship in the House of Commons. The Conservative opposition did not criticize the Attlee government for doing too little but too much, and the Labour government spent its final year in office, 1951, promoting a budget that put the brakes on the national health service. The period of political stress is exclusive to the Thatcher administration, but part of Margaret Thatcher's time in office involved fiscal stress inherited from her Labour predecessor.

Major differences between administrations of the same party identified in chapter 6 can be explained by changes in the economic climate. The three postwar Labour administrations differed from each other because they held office in different climates of opinion—the Attlee administration in a climate of austerity, the first Wilson government in expectations of a big boom that never came, and the second Wilson government inherited fiscal stress. Conservative administrations too held office in different climates. The Conservatives entered office in 1951 when stability was expected. The Heath administration expected economic growth, but it did not come. The Thatcher administration inherited fiscal stress from the failure of the expected boom of the Wilson-Heath years to materialize. Unusually among administrations of both parties, its head imposed distinctive values upon the political climate.

Differences in economic climate also account for administrations of the same party differing in their propensity to introduce programs. In times of austerity and stability, both Conservative and Labour administrations were less inclined to start or stop programs. In times of expected boom, both parties were ready to start but not stop programs. Since 1974 administrations of each party have been active in stopping and starting programs. Variations in economic climate can explain the overall pattern of starts and stops, but to understand which particular types of programs stop and start, we must look more deeply into the attributes of programs.

8 Program Goals and Policy Environment

In the past ten years both the Keynesian and the monetarist explanations have been found to be inadequate. I think all economists are to some extent at sea in describing how the economy works.
—Sir Douglas Wass, former head of the British Treasury

Programs matter because two-fifths of the gross national product is collectively spent on hundreds of measures intended to benefit individuals, groups, and society collectively. Ordinary people expect public policy to provide education for their children, health care when sick, and a secure income in old age or unemployment. Employers and workers want government to provide conditions in which the economy can flourish. Everyone looks to government to maintain law and order at home and security in a troubled world.

Insofar as a democratic government is meant to provide people with what they want, then programs should be consistently popular, and there would be no need to terminate any measure. However, there are evidently big differences in the capacity of programs to provide satisfaction, since more than one hundred programs have been terminated since 1945. Why do some programs persist and others not?

Studies of public policy tend to concentrate upon the processes leading up to the adoption of programs: the problems they are meant to address, the interests involved, the personalities of participants, and the politics of adoption. Some studies go further, examining implementation too. But it is unusual for attention to be given to a program's "afterlife," that is, what happens after it is routinized, and subsequently persists or is terminated. Case studies usually end with a program appearing as an addition to the inheritance of public policy.

Whatever the problem at hand, the policy process is assumed to work much the same. The system of Whitehall decisionmaking is characterized by what is common to all measures: the need for parliamentary approval, Treasury endorsement of finance, and administration according to standard civil service procedures. Studies of Washington likewise concentrate upon similarities in the process of policymaking.

Models that assume policymaking is much the same whatever the subject matter cannot answer the question: Why are some programs more likely to persist in the inheritance of public policy and others to be terminated? Theories of party government certainly do not offer an explanation, and the economic climate has only a marginal affect on this legacy. Durability of purpose is one reason for the continuation of programs. Some programs address continuing concerns of every administration, such routine matters as fire protection or primary education. But other programs have short-term ad hoc purposes, such as an emergency flood program, and can stop soon after they start. Even programs that address durable concerns may be stopped if they are ineffective in reducing dissatisfaction; this can be the fate of programs intended to promote employment when unemployment continues to rise.

Differences in policy environment are a second reason for programs to differ in their capacity to persist. A program that operates in a predictable environment can continue undisturbed by routine. By contrast, a turbulent environment can destabilize a program, as measures that once operated routinely no longer produce satisfaction, forcing a search for new measures to remove dissatisfaction. The second section of this chapter differentiates between the turbulence and unpredictability of the market and the much more predictable environment of social and defining programs. Differentiating programs by purposes and policy environment produces a fourfold classification. The concluding section of this chapter shows that the distribution of programs is strongly skewed: the bulk have persisting purposes and a relatively predictable policy environment. Chapter 9 then identifies the systematic differences that can account for the differential durability of programs.

Persisting and Finite Goals

Models of policymaking as purposeful action usually focus on decisionmakers. A simple description is given of why programs start and stop; they are the choices of the government of the day. If one knows the preferences of policymakers, one can then predict what choices will be made. But this statement is not really an explanation, for it does not say why an administration should want to start some programs and terminate others, or start and then stop a program.

An alternative is to examine what is chosen rather than the choosers: some programs may have finite goals while others have open-ended persisting goals. Business management theories often conceive goals as terminal objectives. From this perspective, programs are a means to achieving finite objectives, such as a corporate takeover or the development of a new product. Once a finite goal is achieved, there is no further need for a measure. However, functionalist theories of government emphasize persisting goals, such as national defense. Programs concerned with persisting goals have a promise of longevity—as long as they produce satisfaction.

Goals as Finite Objectives

A finite goal not only justifies the adoption of a program but also its termination once the objective is achieved, for example a program to host the Olympics in the year 2000. Because programs with finite goals are designed to achieve a terminal objective, their stoppage is not an indication of failure, as in a trial-and-error search, but of achievement.

From a political perspective, programs with goals that can be achieved in a fixed period of time are particularly attractive, for the administration can claim credit for their immediate success rather than waiting for promised benefits to be produced after its term of office has expired. The privatization programs of the Thatcher administration are good examples of finite choices. The goal of each program was clear: to end government ownership of a specific nationalized industry. A series of programs was required, not only for legal reasons but also because industries differed in their structure and in the means chosen for their sale. Acts of Parliament authorized the means by which each state-owned industry was to be privatized. Once the sale of a particular industry was accomplished, the program terminated.

Ad hoc events can unexpectedly challenge policymakers to adopt programs to deal with immediate difficulties. For example, a dramatic natural disaster can stimulate an hoc program to provide relief for its victims. This differs from a program to establish a public emergency relief program to deal with floods, gales, and other natural disasters whenever they recur.

Programs designed to achieve a transition from one policy to another are also likely to be finite. For example, the grant of independence to Burma, India, and Pakistan, previously ruled from Westminster, required a special program for the transition from colonial status to independence in 1948. The reorganization of the national health service in the early 1970s was carried out by a three-year program. Subsidies paid by the 1974 Labour government for rail freight and lending by building societies were meant to tide these sectors of the economy over the difficulties arising from a turbulent recession and an energy price shock.

Goals as Persisting Concerns

Persisting programs address perennial political, social, or economic concerns of society, many of which predate the contemporary welfare state, for example, health and security in old age. Until the twentieth century, these were household concerns but they were not commitments of public policy. When policymakers adopted programs addressing these concerns, they did not assume that health, social security, and education were finite objectives that could be achieved on a once-for-all basis, like winning a war or granting independence to a colony. These are continuing needs. Health care must always be at hand for that percentage of the population suffering from illnesses, social security is needed for that percentage of the population in old age or without an income from employment, and each cohort of children must be educated in reading, writing, and arithmetic.

When a concern is persisting, the instrumental goal of policymakers is to maintain programs that can produce persisting satisfaction. Instead of thinking how quickly a program can achieve a finite goal, policymakers must think in terms of stamina: How long can a program last? A program concerned with elementary education has a time horizon of decades, for the first group of children will not leave primary school until more than a decade after a decision is taken to introduce a new measure. A program to modify university education, if it depends upon changes in youths' previous schooling, takes even longer to implement. Universities require massive commitments in buildings and tenured faculty; they cannot be started and stopped like a flood relief program or a plan to build a supersonic plane.

The choice of a program addressing a persisting concern of society is an open-ended commitment, for there is nothing inherent in its purpose to cause it to be stopped. Whereas capital investment programs such as the construction of a highway system can be accomplished, a program to combat crime addresses a continuing concern of society. In a given year's budget, persisting programs are classified as current expenditure, but they are better conceived as recurrent, since they remain part of the legacy of each successive administration.

The concept of persisting concerns can link programs inherited in

1946 and still persisting, and "new" (that is, post-1945) programs still in effect today. For the purposes of exposition, the distinction was necessary since as of today one cannot show empirically that a program adopted in 1950 has a minimum duration of 50 years. However, whenever adopted, it is possible to describe programs as addressing persisting concerns of society. For example, health programs adopted in 1948 address perennial rather than finite and terminable goals. Since it is simply a matter of time before such programs become half a century old, they can be classified as having persisting goals, however many years they have been in effect.

Persistence can be identified prospectively, since it is usually the result of a durable purpose. A program less than a decade old can be considered persisting if its object is long-lasting. For example, a program for AIDS victims initiated in 1989 concerns a problem that is literally in the bloodstream of society. Policymakers cannot contemplate the termination of AIDS programs until methods are found to eradicate the disease from the inheritance of society.

The logic of continuing concerns is that they sustain long-term additions to the legacy of public policy. But some programs are terminated that address persisting concerns. Why should an administration want to or be forced to do this?

Predictable and Turbulent Policy Environments

The persistence of a program depends not only upon choices of policymakers but also upon what happens in a policy environment that government can influence but not control. If the policy environment alters, then without any change in the intrinsic characteristics of the program, this will alter the impact of a program.

In principle, every public program is to some extent vulnerable to changes outside the control of policymakers. For example, the birth rate has a significant impact upon many areas of public policy from primary school enrollment through the cost of pensions. But British government has eschewed having a population policy. As a Cabinet minister told the House of Commons, this would mean "a policeman in every bedroom" (qtd. Wood, 1971). Even measures that incidentally affect birth rates are usually not undertaken as part of an explicit population policy.

Predictability or turbulence of the policy environment differs greatly from one area to another of society. A policy environment is predictable insofar as changes tend to be foreseeable and gradual. A policy environment is turbulent insofar as changes are unexpected, of large magnitude, and frequent. Unpredictable changes in the environment may fortuitously increase the satisfaction that a program brings, but they are more likely to create dissatisfaction with measures previously deemed satisfactory.

Predictability Is Contingent

Everyday phenomena vary greatly in predictability, from the regularity of sunrise and sunset through probabilistic forecasts of population trends to the unexpectedness of natural disasters. This is also true of the policy environments of public policy.

Established programs are predictable in the sense that those administering the program operate by routine. When a program is concerned with the organization or procedures of government itself, in the first instance the enactment of a law will produce a predictable effect, for example, the abolition of old local government boundaries and their replacement by new boundaries. The certain establishment of new local government institutions does not, however, guarantee the predictability of subsequent second-order consequences.

Programs producing goods by established engineering technologies have a high degree of predictability, for example, building new public highways, dams, and transport. Military procurement is about the supply of weapons, aircraft, or other materials produced to very carefully specified standards. Even when there is political controversy about the cost of arms or of a new motorway, there is little doubt that government can achieve what it proposes.

Major social programs operate according to well-established social technologies. Health programs have expanded in cost and variety, with advances in medical knowledge making treatment predictable to a high degree. Many education programs have predictable social technologies for training teachers. New primary and secondary schools are built to serve new suburbs on the assumption that new schools can produce the same effects as existing schools. Social security programs are even more predictable, for bureaucratic procedures routinely record births, payments of social security contributions, and, when an individual attains pensionable age, computers are programmed to print out social security checks.

An unprecedented problem is difficult to deal with predictably, and some policy areas are unpredictable. For example, even though most social programs are predictable, measures directed at groups in poverty often fail to produce satisfaction, because the causes of poverty and the means by which government can reduce poverty are only very imperfectly understood.

Even when technologies are predictable, political satisfaction is not always certain, for conflicts can arise about whether programs are to be assessed by engineering, economic, or other criteria. For example, the building of highways, hydroelectric dams, and other large projects is no longer evaluated solely on grounds of engineering feasibility and economic costs. Increasingly, there are demands to evaluate such programs in terms of their impact upon the natural environment and upon established communities.

The interaction of policy environment and programs requires policymakers to monitor the effects of programs by routinely obtaining feedback. If the policy environment is steady, then the feedback to policymakers will reinforce routine operations. Changes in the policy environment can produce negative feedback, forcing inherited programs to be replaced if a persisting goal is to be attained.

Social security for the elderly is an example of a program in a policy environment that changes slowly and predictably. Individuals now in retirement were born more than 60 years ago; in order to qualify for a pension, they have paid social security contributions for up to 40 years. The median contributor to social security today is unlikely to be drawing a pension before the year 2015. Policymakers can use actuarial criteria to forecast the number of persons of retirement age for decades or even half a century ahead. A "crisis" in social security is not a problem that arises overnight but advance warning of an imbalance between social security income and benefits at some point 20 to 30 years in the future.

Predictability is a matter of degree. The number of older people drawing a pension depends not only upon past birth rates but also upon mortality rates. If the next generation lives longer than the present one, more money will have to be paid out. The income from social security contributions depends upon the number of people currently in work. If the work force in the year 2020 is larger or smaller than expected, this will affect the amount of money available for pay-as-you-go financing of pensions. In the United States, the size and volatility of immigration, which is disproportionately youthful, also affects estimates of the future ratio between persons of working and retirement ages.

Predictability does not preclude choice; it informs choice. Policymakers are better able to produce a program that will bring continuing satisfaction if they can reasonably foresee the circumstances in which it will be in effect a decade or more ahead. Given some foresight, it is possible to make a prospective evaluation of the impact of a projected program, so that a new program, when tried, is more likely to be a success than an error (cf. Rose, 1991c).

The Turbulence of the Unexpected

In a given policy environment, changes can occur independently of or in spite of actions by government. For example, the nation's economy is subject to the impact of activities in other countries and fluctuations in the international economy. A program's impact can also destabilize a policy environment in predictable ways; for example, a new urban highway may generate so much additional traffic that it creates more traffic bottlenecks than it resolves.

A turbulent policy environment disrupts routine behavior and expectations. Instead of predictable satisfaction, policymakers receive shocks. The two OPEC oil shocks of the 1970s were disturbing not only because of the magnitude of the price increase but also because each was unexpected. Policymakers could not incubate energy conservation measures over a long period of time, as would have happened if the increase had been due to a gradually increasing shortage of oil. Instead, they had to respond with emergency energy programs.

The magnitude of change is also important, even if unexpected small-scale changes in the policy environment do not normally cause large amounts of dissatisfaction. However, continuous compounding over many years can result in what was initially dismissed as a small change, because calculated on an annual basis, turning into a big change. For example, an annual inflation rate of 5 percent becomes, by a process of compounding, a 28 percent increase in prices in five years. Even a 1 or 2 percent change in a program can have a large impact if it is an increase in interest rates; such an increase can add as much as 25 percent to the monthly cost of a mortgage or loan.

In a turbulent policy environment, shocks succeed each other sooner rather than later. Instead of events following a familiar cyclical pattern, they can generate an uncharted course for structural change. The market is the paradigm example of a turbulent policy environment, for flux rather than continuity is its primary characteristic. Whereas the number of elderly in the population changes very slowly, the number of people unemployed, stock market prices, and foreign currency rates fluctuate daily. Well-publicized monthly reports of unemployment show whether the change is a cause for satisfaction (low or falling) or dissatisfaction (a rising or high level of unemployment). Monthly reports of inflation are similarly watched as an indication of the direction in which the economic winds are now blowing. A generation ago policymakers often believed that mathematical models could forecast trends and help them control the national economy. Events since have undermined such faith.

When changes are frequent, large in scale, and occur unexpectedly, turbulence can create such shocks that inherited programs must be terminated because they are no longer satisfactory. *Turbulence in the policy environment thus constitutes a force equal to or greater than the force of political inertia.*

Effects of Turbulence on the Government of the Day

At a maximum, policymakers can hope to make choices that achieve their intended purpose, and become a continuing part of the legacy of public policy. At worst, they may be forced to make choices in a turbulent environment in which errors are likely and fledgling programs fail. Differences in policy environments influence the capacity of policymakers to achieve the maximum or avoid the worst.

Turbulence gives policymakers the opportunity to make fresh choices—but not necessarily in circumstances that they want. Turbulence produces unpredictable changes in programs that had previously produced satisfaction. In a turbulent environment, policymakers are not so much free to choose but forced to choose. Because causes of unpredictable problems are often not understood, it is difficult to estimate the consequences of whatever choice they make. A high degree of uncertainty reduces the likelihood that choices will become part of the continuing legacy of public policy. A forced trial-and-error search is not the ideal situation for choice.

Predictability in the policy environment makes it easier for policy-makers to act with confidence in the consequences of choice. The greater the number of predictable programs that an administration inherits, the easier it is to achieve the minimalist ambition of avoiding frequent failures. But predictability also reduces the opportunity to make fresh choices. There is no need for choice if goals are persisting and programs run by routine. In such circumstances policy-makers must be content with taking credit for programs inherited from others or create dissatisfaction in order to justify the choice of new programs.

Insofar as programs address a persisting goal, every administration will be committed to maintain some measures addressing it. Programs can be classified as having a persisting goal if they have been in effect continuously since 1945 (e.g., civil service pensions). Programs can also be classified as having a persisting goal if they address open-ended concerns, whether through a single program (for example, the dental program of the National Health Service) or through several programs seeking a common end, such as youth unemployment.

By contrast, programs with finite goals have an attainable objective and can be terminated once they have achieved (or failed to achieve) their goal. Finite goals differ in the extent to which their environment is predictable. Payments to prisoners of war after 1945 occurred in a relatively predictable policy environment, whereas many wartime programs seek to attain specific goals in a turbulent environment.

Combining distinctions about program goals and policy environment identifies four conditions influencing whether programs remain

Figure 8.1. Impact of difference in goals and policy environment

		Goals	
		Persisting	Finite goals
	Predictable	CONTINUING INHERITANCE	PLANNED ACHIEVEMENT
Policy Environment			
	Turbulent	TRIAL-AND-ERROR ADAPTATION	AD HOC

in the legacy of public policy (figure 8.1). An administration's scope for choice depends upon how the 360 programs in effect at some time since 1945 distribute among these four categories.

1. *Continuing inheritance*. If a program addresses a persisting concern of society and operates in a relatively predictable environment, it is part of the continuing inheritance of public policy. Durability of purpose is independent of the age of a program. Some programs adopted in the 1980s address persisting concerns of society, for example, road safety or the administration of estates of individuals who die intestate.

An absolute majority of programs, 55 percent of the total, are part of the continuing inheritance of the government of the day (figure 8.2). This group is divided almost equally between programs inherited from the distant past and those adopted since 1945. Programs that are part of the continuing inheritance of government cover a wide range of concerns, such as policing, water supply, and hospitals. In money terms, programs in the continuing inheritance of the government of the day are even more dominant, accounting for 87 percent of calculated public expenditure (figure 8.3).

The importance of the continuing inheritance of public policy implies that public officials ought to devote considerable attention to program management. Just because there is no need for new social

Figure 8.2. Continuing inheritance accounts for most programs

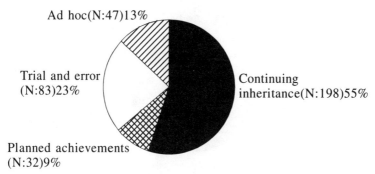

Ad hoc(N:47)13%

Trial and error
(N:83)23%

Continuing
inheritance(N:198)55%

Planned achievements
(N:32)9%

security legislation it does not follow that administering programs spending tens of billions occurs automatically or easily. When programs are costly, even small gains in efficiency can save significant sums of money, and when programs affect millions of people, fine-tuning amendments to inherited measures can improve conditions for tens or hundreds of thousands. In addition, predictable changes in the policy environment can be met by preparing plans for future developments after a given Cabinet minister has left office. However, managing an inheritance from previous administrations is politically less attractive than making choices about new programs.

2. *Planned achievement.* If a program addresses a clear, finite goal and operates in a predictable policy environment, then the prospects of a choice being successful are high. Policymakers can adopt such programs with confidence that their efforts will not be blown off course, and the results of their choice will be visible. Moreover, they are not just administering programs inherited from predecessors.

In government, programs that are 'doable' according to plan are very much the exception. In the postwar era, only 9 percent have been planned achievements. These include politically controversial measures such as the privatization of Britoil, British Airways, and the

Figure 8.3. Continuing inheritance makes biggest claim for money

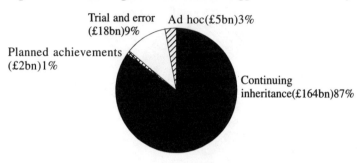

Trial and error
(£18bn)9%   Ad hoc(£5bn)3%

Planned achievements
(£2bn)1%

Continuing
inheritance(£164bn)87%

electricity industry, each achieved by an administration making a choice and enacting and implementing an act of Parliament within a limited period of time. However, most planned achievements are relatively small in scale, for example, a reduction of personnel at the Royal Ordnance Factories, a measure that was within the power of government to accomplish in a limited amount of time. The establishment of a royal commission or a committee of inquiry are other examples of goals that are finite and achievable. The sums of money involved are usually small, in total affecting 1 percent of calculated public expenditure.

3. *Trial-and-error adaptation.* When the purpose of a program is persisting, then the government of the day inherits a commitment to act and programs embodying this commitment. But in a turbulent environment, sooner or later dissatisfaction is likely to force policymakers to begin a search for a new program that might bring satisfaction. In such circumstances, policymakers are not making a voluntary choice between carefully considered and incubated alternatives but responding as politicians to pressures to act.

Actions taken on a trial-and-error basis may succeed in the first attempt and become part of the continuing inheritance of public policy. But if this does not happen, then the government of the day must terminate the program and try again. A second attempt has the advantage of building on the knowledge gained from an earlier failure, but it occurs in turbulent circumstances that make repeated failure possible. Yet even if failures are recurrent, the government of the day cannot stop trying to address a persisting concern.

Programs are trial-and-error measures if, even though addressing a persisting concern, they do not persist themselves, being adopted and then abandoned without producing satisfaction. Programs also come under this heading if they have recently been introduced to deal with a persisting problem that has been the subject of chronic dissatisfaction. In fields such as unemployment in the late 1980s, it is more accurate to describe a program in effect for two years as not yet having had time to fail rather than call it part of the continuing inheritance. Altogether, 23 percent of programs are trial-and-error measures that have been rejected or are vulnerable to termination because they are part of a turbulent policy environment. Their cost is substantial, 9 percent of calculated public expenditure.

4. *Ad hoc programs.* Turbulence in the policy environment can sometimes reflect transitory disturbances. A foreign policy crisis, such as the Iraqi invasion of Kuwait, is an example of turbulent events forcing a government to act—but not requiring a persisting program. A measure to give emergency aid to the National Coal Board in the early 1970s, when the Heath adminstration had problems with both miners' pay and energy prices, is an example of an ad hoc domestic program without a persisting commitment. An ad hoc response does not commit a successor administration to act, because the goal is finite. There is no long-term cost, for an unsatisfactory response is not the occasion for another try. Equally, there is no long-term success, for the impact of ad hoc measures is not lasting. Ad hoc measures are relatively infrequent. In the postwar era only 13 percent of programs can be classified as ad hoc, claiming 3 percent of calculated expenditure.

Changes in the policy environment put pressure on the government of the day. But the opportunities for choice are not on terms that policymakers welcome when the stimulus to act reflects dissatisfaction with inherited commitments. Choices that result in satisfaction, whether on the first attempt or after several tries and errors, become part of the continuing inheritance that constitutes a constraint upon the choice of the government of the day. Ironically, the most satisfactory choices of government, planned achievements in a predictable environment, are short-lived, infrequent, and do not involve substantial sums of money. Every administration makes all four types of choice, but it does not make them in equal numbers and, as the next chapter shows, the chance of having a long-term impact by contributing programs to the continuing inheritance of government varies greatly from one field of public policy to another.

9 Why Programs Matter

Programs differ in their purposes; some face backwards in time and others are directed at current dissatisfactions or the future. The inheritance of each new administration contains many programs that will remain in the legacy that it leaves to its successors, and some that will soon be terminated. What accounts for the difference between these two types of programs?

Since inheritance emphasizes the importance of the past, a systematic analysis of the evolution of the program concerns of modern states since the mid-nineteenth century offers an appropriate basis for differentiating programs (Rose, 1976). By the end of World War II, all states had programs addressing three major purposes. First in point of time were the defining *sine qua non* policies of the state, without which it could not exist: defense against external attack, maintaining public order and collecting taxes to finance its activities. Second came the mobilization of economic resources, starting with transportation by canals, railways, roads and the postal service and extending to the promotion of trade, industry, and employment. In the twentieth century a third persisting set of purposes developed: promoting the welfare of individuals through education, social security, and health care.

Although purposes can be persisting, particular programs can be terminated if they do not succeed in achieving these goals. Success is problematic. It requires established means-ends technologies, so that programs are not based upon trial-and-error searching. It also requires a stable policy environment, so that policymakers can adapt measures to changes in the world about them. Three hypotheses can be offered about the likelihood of a program persisting in the inheritance of public policy.

Social policies promoting individual welfare through education, health, and security of income are relevant throughout an individual's lifetime. Programs in such fields cannot be terminated on the grounds that they have accomplished a specific mission, since the needs are continuing if society is to reproduce itself. To start and stop such programs with each fluctuation in the electoral cycle would interrupt important phases in the life cycle of tens of millions of citizens. The means of delivering health care, education, and income maintenance are well understood social technologies; hence, there is limited trial and error. The importance of demography in determining demand makes changes in the environment of social programs especially predictable.

*9.1 *(Welfare)*. If programs are about lifelong welfare concerns of individuals, they are likely to remain in the continuing inheritance of each administration.

The goals of defining programs are persisting by definition. In national security, programs are not about responses to particular crises, for example, what message the Foreign Office should issue during a Middle East crisis or what troop movements should be made. Policymakers respond to crises by using resources of established programs, such as diplomatic representation and the army, navy, and air force. In the administration of justice, precedent, and thus persisting, is important; people must know what acts are and are not legal in order to organize their affairs in a law-abiding way. In fiscal programs, routinization of taxation is necessary to finance contemporary commitments of big government. It is far easier to alter tax rates at the margin than to introduce major new taxes in place of old, for the former provides a predictable source of new income but the latter does not (cf. Rose and Karran, 1987).

*9.2 *(Defining concerns)*. If programs are about the defining concerns of government, they are likely to remain in the continuing inheritance of each administration.

Economic programs depend for success upon conditions in the market, and the market is a turbulent environment for public policy. Whereas each generation of children looks to British government to provide education, each generation of consumers does not necessarily look to British manufacturers for automobiles or consumer durables. Even though many economic concerns are persisting, such as the promotion of trade and employment, changes in the policy environment threaten programs with termination. Because cyclical and structural changes in the market occur in a matter of months or a few years, pressures to act can be unpredictable and force trial-and-error responses.

*9.3 (*Market*). If programs are about problems of the market, they are likely to be trial-and-error or ad hoc responses.

Lifelong Commitments to Individual Welfare

The purpose of social programs is to advance the welfare of individuals—but this purpose is confused by terminology. Services that people regard as essential in everyday life—education, health care, and social security in old age—are undoubtedly public policies, paid for by public finance, administered by public employees, and subject to public laws. In economics, however, the outputs of these public programs are described as *private* goods, that is, goods and services that benefit identifiable individuals, families, or other users. From a political economy perspective, characteristic programs of the welfare state such as primary schooling or social security meet *private* needs.

Ordinary people do not think of having their welfare depend upon the outcome of an election, nor do people expect politics to enter into a trip to the doctor, the education of children, or the enjoyment of old age. Nor is an election outcome expected to alter principles of medical care or the teaching of arithmetic. The welfare hypothesis predicts that once chosen, programs concerned with the lifelong needs of individuals are likely to persist as part of the legacy of each administration.

Individual Needs Persist

From the perspective of an individual, health care, education, and a secure income are not political demands; they are essential needs for life in a modern society. People cannot imagine growing up as illiterates. Nor do people accept that they should do without health care because they cannot afford to pay a doctor or hospital charges. The idea of elderly people being forced to work because of penury is an anachronism too.

The growth of government has intertwined the lives of tens of millions of people with the spending of tens of billions of public money. Although the state is not the sole source of welfare, 90 percent of British families receive at least one major welfare service from government each year, and the average family receives more than two benefits (Rose, 1989a: 22ff). Social security programs provide an income for elderly persons. Medical and hospital care is available as required. Education programs meet needs of children and their parents. The poor and handicapped benefit from a host of specialized social safety net programs. At a given point in time, it is the exceptional family that is not receiving a benefit, and usually it is because they are between those stages in the life cycle where social welfare programs are important.

Family budgets rely on benefits from social welfare programs. The value to the average British family of cash transfer payments and health, education, and housing is equivalent to 44 percent of its gross income (Central Statistical Office, 1988: table 5.15). If the state did not finance these measures, then a family would have to pay the full cost of educating its children, face a big monthly bill for health insurance, and saving for old age would be a major anxiety. In addition, public programs also deliver services to neighborhoods and communities, such as sewage and water, refuse collection, and measures that protect and conserve the household's immediate environment.

Even though politicians may not be very interested in the unglamorous task of administering inherited commitments, public opinion surveys demonstrate that welfare programs benefiting the great majority of citizens (as distinct from programs stigmatized as "welfare" because they benefit only a small number of poor people) have a very broad base of popular support. There is also widespread public acceptance of the requirement to pay taxes to finance these programs (see, e.g., Rose, 1989a: 24f; Hadenius, 1985).

Even administrations headed by persons ideologically against welfare programs, such as Margaret Thatcher and Ronald Reagan, have not sought to repeal measures popular with the electorate. It is politically easier to take credit for benefits, as if the government of the day had actually chosen what it inherited. For example, the 1987 Conservative election manifesto boasted: "Expenditure on pensions and other benefits has risen by £13 billion on top of inflation since we came into office. Most of that has gone to provide better standards of help and support to more elderly people, families with children, disabled people and those suffering long-term illnesses." Of the four programs cited, two were inherited from the very distant past and two from the Heath administration scorned by Thatcherites.

An incoming administration inherits contractual commitments between government and millions of ordinary citizens. Retirement pensions are funded by national insurance contributions committing government to pay pensions to millions of people when they reach retirement age in up to half a century. Younger members of society pay contributions for pensions that they expect to be receiving in the year 2050—and beyond. As Sir Patrick Nairne, a former civil service head of the program, has emphasized, "The character of social se-

curity derived from legislation and the payment of contributory benefits leaves policymakers very little room for maneuver" (qtd. Pollitt,
1984: 71).

Borrowing money for the construction of housing by local councils
has created long-term contractual obligations to repay loans. Housing
expenditure is capital expenditure, and the cost is amortized over a
period of up to 60 years. Thus, a commitment to finance a council
house can be five times longer than a program commitment to educate
an individual. Payment of interest and repayment of capital on borrowing to finance houses built in the years immediately after World
War II will persist into the next century. Borrowing to finance new
council housing creates obligations due for repayment in the second
half of the next century.

The commitment to inherited programs can also be demonstrated by
considering what would be necessary to repeal social security, health,
and education programs. In theory, this could produce tax cuts that
would enable families to finance such benefits through means of their
own choice. But there would be very large "transition" problems,
arising from the fact that many families would not be able to buy
welfare services. For example, unemployed people cannot buy unemployment insurance in the private market, people in hospital cannot
buy health insurance because they have a bad medical history, and
older people cannot begin saving for old age if they are already retired.

Because welfare programs provide long-term services, any decision to terminate such programs would take many decades to implement. For example, to abolish social security pensions in old age
could not be done by the state returning pension contributions already
paid with accumulated interest, for it would be beyond the capacity of
government to raise such large capital sums in a short period. An
alternative would be to allow younger people to stop paying social
security benefits if under the age of 40 and to refuse those under the
age of 25 the right to pay contributions for a social security pension.

Such a technically feasible solution would hardly be considered politically feasible, for it would force policymakers to defend giving half the citizenry social security while denying it to the other half. If such a policy were nonetheless chosen, inherited commitments would require the provision of benefits for upwards of 15 Parliaments.

When people think about welfare, they do not think of the government's electoral cycle but of their own and their family's life cycle. Whereas a government's budget covers one year and the maximum life of a Parliament is five years, the life expectancy of an individual is 70 years, a span equal to 18 average Parliaments. Throughout the life span, public programs are significant. The health service provides everything from ante-natal care for the mother to geriatric treatment in extreme old age. Adults have received a dozen years education and are likely to want more for their children. Throughout a working lifetime people want protection against the loss of income through unemployment, ill health, or disablement, and the assurance of an income for a decade or more of life in retirement.

The family's life cycle can be extended indefinitely, because of the ties that bind together generations. Older people are not only concerned about their own pension but also about the education of their grandchildren, and middle-aged parents worry about the health and economic well-being of grandparents and the future of their children, as well as about their age-specific problems.

Predictable Needs

Because social security, health care, and education programs are concerned with important stages in the life cycle, there is very little turbulence since entitlements to these benefits are demographically driven. Education is compulsory between the ages of 5 and 16; pensions are payable as of right from the age of retirement until death; and health care is disproportionately concentrated upon the elderly and the very young. Actuarial forecasts of population trends can thus give policymakers forewarning of changes in demand decades ahead. Although the demographic composition of the population is not constant, it is very slow to change.

When policymakers have a long lead time to prepare for changes in demand, there is time to respond in ways that can maintain satisfaction, albeit often at a much higher level of expenditure. An increase in the number of children requires building new schools, an increase in the number of retired people requires paying more pensions, and an increase in the number of very elderly requires building more centers for geriatric care. Predictability does not mean stagnation; it means gradual but steady change.

Policy networks in education, health care, and social security are continuously discussing possible changes in welfare programs. The discussions reflect technical concerns as well as partisan goals. Since any new program is likely to be expensive and difficult to terminate once introduced, the incubation process is lengthy, which also makes changes more likely to be durable.

Predictability leads to routinization, and the lack of scope for choice limits the attraction of social welfare programs to politicians. Even though the programs are usually the biggest spending commitments of government, the ministers in charge have a low standing in Cabinet. At times in the postwar era, ministers responsible for social programs affecting the lives of tens of millions of people have not even been included in Cabinet. In Washington health, human services, and education are regarded as "Outer Cabinet" posts of no interest to the White House (cf. Rose, 1987a; Cronin, 1980: 274ff).

Persisting and Predictable Needs Sustain a Continuing Inheritance

Because the life of an individual is far longer than the life of the government of the day, the welfare hypothesis states that these programs should continue in the legacy of successive administrations, and this is the case. Of nearly one hundred education, health, social security, housing, and environmental services programs in effect since 1945, 86 percent are part of the continuing inheritance of public policy (figure 9.1).

Programs directed at needs of individuals through the life cycle are not started casually or abandoned easily. The few that start or stop are scattered almost equally between planned achievements, such as the reorganization of the national health service in the 1970s, ad hoc responses to help people in need during the economic crisis of 1974, and a few trial-and-error measures, such as inner-city programs. The exceptions do not detract from the predominance of inheritance in social programs.

When money is the measure, the dominance of inherited programs becomes greater still; 97 percent of expenditure on programs promoting individual welfare is claimed by measures inherited from earlier administrations. Moreover, the total sum claimed by inherited programs is vast, £94 billion in 1989. Virtually no money is spent on programs that are at risk from trial and error; for example, student loans, an experimental program of the Department of Education and Science, claims only 0.04 percent of the department's calculated expenditure. In social security, trial-and-error programs claim 0.4 percent of calculated expenditure, and in housing and environment 0.5 percent. The only expensive noncontinuing program was the £2.2 billion advanced on an ad hoc basis to building societies during the 1973–74 economic crisis.

Examining the continuing inheritance at the departmental level shows the variety of ways in which inherited programs meet current needs and future expectations of tens of millions of families. The 1945 Labour government inherited five health programs that covered part but not the whole of the population. By the time it left office it had added seven health programs to its legacy, the measures that made the

Figure 9.1. Welfare programs: goals and policy environment

Number of programs

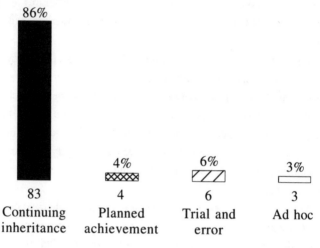

Expenditure

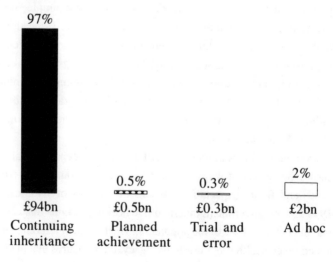

health service national (that is, comprehensive). Five more programs have been added in the four decades since, such as a program for the disabled. The two programs that started and stopped concerned planned reorganization of services. The postwar addition of 12 programs to the legacy of health policy reflects cumulative choice, but it also means that in the course of four decades each successive administration has received a larger legacy of programs.

A youth is in school for more than a decade, and a family uses the education services for upwards of two decades. There are changing fashions in educational practice that affect classroom activities of teachers. Education ministers like to announce "new" priorities for education. But ministerial speeches are far distant from the classroom, and the application of education theories usually occurs through established programs. The postwar structure of primary and secondary education was established in the 1944 Education Act, and many commitments, for example, to teacher training and pensions for teachers, long antedate World War II. A new measure for funding universities and polytechnics, introduced in 1989, is not a crisis measure but the response to a predictable expansion of the number of places in higher education. All but one of the 19 education programs are part of the continuing inheritance of public policy.

Social security programs are commitments to individuals extending beyond the time that any MP serves in Parliament. The 1945 Labour government inherited seven social security programs, the oldest based on claimant contributions made prior to World War I. It amended but did not terminate this inheritance, adding four new programs. An additional 13 programs were adopted in the 1970s and 1980s. The biggest in money terms is housing benefit, introduced in 1982 in order to shift public subsidy from building houses to low-income tenants. A grudging tribute to the strength of inherited commitments was given by the Thatcher administration. It set up a major review of social security under Secretary of State Norman Fowler, but the review found very little scope to alter inherited commitments (Cmnd. 9691, 1985). Altogether, 18 of the 22 postwar social security programs are a continuing part of the inheritance of public policy; two others have been trial-and-error measures; and two ad hoc responses.

In housing and environmental services public policy has shown the addition of a large number of inexpensive programs to a small core of expensive persisting programs concerned with refuse collection, housing subsidies, and housing repair, increasing the six programs in the field in 1945 to 32 as of 1990. Of these additions, five-sixths address persisting concerns and have been incorporated into the legacy of each new administration. Because the physical environment changes slowly, few programs are trial and error or ad hoc; the biggest short-term program, a Department of Environment measure about the finance of building societies, was stimulated by problems in the market.

Great Growth with Little Choice

Growth has been a major feature of social policy since World War II. At the start of the period, British government had 32 programs in this field. The 1945–51 Labour government added 12 programs to the continuing inheritance of postwar administrations, and its Conservative successors added another nine. Since 1964, 33 more programs have been added to the inheritance. By 1989, the total number of welfare programs had increased more than two and one-half times.

But cumulative growth does not give much scope for choice by a particular administration, for the total increase has occurred by adding an average of about one program a year for half a century. In a Parliament lasting four years, the government of the day may expect to add a program or two for health and social security, and two or three programs for housing and environment. Since nearly all the choices made are additions to the continuing inheritance of public policy, the legacy of each new administration becomes larger, and its impact relatively smaller at the margin. The predictability of the policy environment leaves little scope for choice through trial and error.

The first concern of a social welfare minister is the cost of inherited programs. Because welfare programs provide private benefits to individuals and families, costs tend to be proportionate to the number receiving benefits. Even though a £5-a-week increase in pension payments may not sound big, when the extra £260 per year per person is multiplied by 10 million pensioners, the additional cost to the fisc is £2.2 billion.

Policymakers do not choose to become big spenders on social programs; they inherit large and growing spending commitments. Expenditure on inherited programs increases due to demographic changes increasing the number entitled, the indexation of cash benefits, the relative price effect, and increased utilization of established services. Marginal changes in entitlement qualifications or in the value of benefits represent the most—and the least—that the government of the day alters. While heralded by the minister making them, such choices are strictly marginal by comparison to the expansion of expenditure on inherited programs.

Total spending on welfare programs has increased almost ten times in the postwar era, principally due to the ripening of inherited obligations. In real terms expenditure on welfare rose from £9.5 billion in 1946 to £94 billion in 1989. Of this, £60 billion was allocated to programs that had already been in effect at the end of World War II and an additional £7 billion to programs adopted by the 1945–51 Labour government. Thus, three-quarters of increased expenditure on social programs has been claimed by programs inherited from the distant past, and 97 percent of welfare expenditure is claimed by programs that are a continuing part of the inheritance of public policy (see figure 9.1).

Defining Programs: A Continuing Inheritance

Defining concerns of the state require collective action; they cannot be looked after by individuals. A central decision must be taken about diplomatic relations and treaties between states, about military alliances and declarations of war. Taxes must be stipulated by legislation and paid into a collective fund. Courts and the police enforce law and order on behalf of society as a whole. If individuals had the choice of opting out of war, not recognizing the courts, or not paying taxes, then a modern state would not exist.

The essential concerns of the modern state, what it must do by definition if it is to survive, are givens in the inheritance of each new administration. At a minimum, a modern state must defend its territorial integrity by diplomacy or armed force, maintain internal order, and mobilize the finances necessary for these purposes. If a state does not have programs that achieve goals central to its existence, then it will collapse because of external invasion, internal disruption, or both. Because the defining concerns of government are few, a minimum of programs are required (Rose, 1976: 250ff).

Fixed Goals with Some Flexible Means

Each new administration takes an oath of office to maintain the state; this purpose is fixed, and so are many programs intended to achieve this purpose. An incoming administration inherits programs that maintain a defense establishment. Inherited diplomatic commitments cannot be ignored because of an election result. Inherited programs for police, prisons and a fire service continue whatever the government of the day. Decisions of the courts are based upon precedents inherited from past generations or centuries. Inherited taxes finance the cost of inherited spending programs.

The simplest way of responding to changes in the policy environment is to alter funding. A more threatening international climate can justify increased expenditure on defense forces, and a less bellicose policy environment can justify spending less money, but not the abandonment of an army, navy and air force. An increase in crime can be met by an increase in the number of police or pay of police. Such changes in expenditure do not make programs more or less essential; they simply reflect shifts in an administration's views about what it costs to maintain effectiveness.

Insofar as the policy environment is stable, there is no pressure to introduce programs on an ad hoc or trial-and-error basis. Predictability must be high in taxation in order to meet the high claims of public expenditure. The government of the day may change the rate at which a tax is levied, but rate changes have only a marginal effect on revenues collected. They leave in place the basic structure of taxes on income, customs, and excise that have endured for generations or even centuries. Although levels of crime fluctuate, the basic programs of police, prison, and courts remain in place. The international security environment can change abruptly, but defense programs are designed to maintain forces that can react to unexpected events. The Gulf War, for example, did not require the enactment of new programs but the use of forces at the ready under existing programs. In the Foreign Office, change is most often signified by modifying verbal statements of intent.

Policymakers sometimes add new programs in response to changes in the policy environment, for example, immigration in the 1960s. Policymakers can occasionally introduce new programs to achieve persisting goals, for example, legal aid reducing financial barriers to individual access to the courts. Unexpected changes in the policy environment can stimulate ad hoc responses, such as an emergency program to deal with foreign exchange.

The logic of defining programs creates a high probability that any program dealing with defining goals will remain a part of the continuing inheritance of each new administration. A regime should not meet defining concerns on a trial-and-error basis, for failure could risk its very existence.

Inheritance Dominates

The Whitehall departments responsible for defining programs are the oldest departments of British government, some tracing their origins back to medieval times: the chancellor of the exchequer in charge of the Treasury and answerable for tax collection agencies; the Lord Chancellor's Office and the Home Office, responsible for courts and maintaining internal law and order; and the Foreign & Commonwealth Office and the Ministry of Defense, each in their own way concerned with national security. To create a modern government, it was necessary for these departments to develop a minimum of effective means of maintaining security at home and abroad and financing its minimal programs. This was achieved by the first half of the nineteenth century (cf. Rose, 1965; Chester, 1981).

Altogether, departments concerned with defining purposes of government have been responsible for 71 different programs since the end of World War II. The largest number, 31, have been in the field of defense; the fewest, five, have been the concern of the Lord Chancellor's Office. Consistent with expectations, more than four-fifths of all defining programs have been a continuing part of the inheritance of public policy (figure 9.2). Of these, more than half have been in effect since before the end of World War II, and programs concerned with such aims as the pay of the army and the collection of customs and excise taxes date back centuries.

The nine programs that have started and/or stopped in the postwar era have usually been ad hoc responses to unexpected events, such as Treasury measures concerning exchange control or the purchase and sale of silver or defense measures consequent to the ending of World

Figure 9.2. Defining programs: goals and policy environment

Number of programs

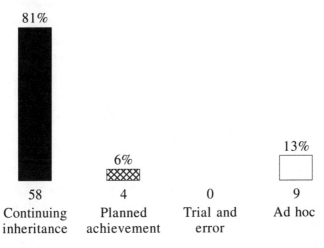

81%	6%		13%
58	4	0	9
Continuing inheritance	Planned achievement	Trial and error	Ad hoc

Expenditure

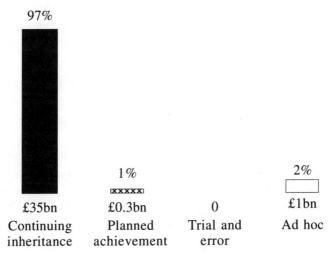

97%	1%		2%
£35bn	£0.3bn	0	£1bn
Continuing inheritance	Planned achievement	Trial and error	Ad hoc

War II, or else planned achievements, such as the reorganization of military reserve forces.

When money is the measure, the dominance of inheritance is greater still. Inherited measures account for 97 percent of total public expenditure on defining programs. Ad hoc programs are almost invariably inexpensive, for the cost of meeting an emergency that comes and goes quickly is much less than that of an inherited program that has had years to expand to its full cost. Planned changes usually involve small costs too, for example, reductions in force in the royal ordnance factories.

Defense programs are the most numerous of defining policies and account for three-fifths of money spent. Whatever the international situation, it is necessary to recruit and pay soldiers, sailors, and air force persons, and civilian staff too. Equipment, fuel, buildings, research and development, retirement pay, and other mundane activities are needed to maintain armed services at the ready for whatever eventuality occurs, whether near at hand, such as Northern Ireland (itself an inheritance from centuries past) or the Falkland Islands (which became a British Crown Colony in 1832). Although purposes are continuing, the policy environment can change, requiring short-term responses to ad hoc problems, such as payments to Polish troops that were a British responsibility after World War II. Changes in the international policy environment also create pressures to adapt programs; major British defense reviews in the 1960s scaled down Britain's forces in the light of America's assumption of the role of global superpower.

The goals of the Foreign and Commonwealth Office are persisting; whatever the state of the world, diplomats must represent Her Majesty's Government to other countries. The policy environment changes slowly, though sometimes to major effect. The postwar era has seen the winding down of colonial administration, and the Heath administration made Britain a member of the European Community. Subsequent administrations have not chosen membership but inherited it, being bound not only by an Act of Parliament but also by a predecessor's signature of the Treaty of Rome.

The maintenance of law and order through the police and courts is another persisting concern; programs are relatively expensive, claiming almost £8 billion. Of the 19 programs of the Home Office and the Lord Chancellor, 18 are part of the continuing inheritance of government, usually from the distant past. Programs introduced in the postwar era, such as criminal injuries compensation, can be expected to remain in the inheritance of each administration, because they address persisting concerns of society. Even a program that has been stopped, such as the state management of public houses in the Carlisle area, was introduced as a local anti-drink measure in World War I and inherited by successive administrations for more than half a century until terminated in 1973.

A majority of the Treasury's programs, accounting for 95 percent of its audited expenditure, are part of the continuing legacy of government. These programs deal with such classic financial responsibilities as customs and excise, the inland revenue, and the national debt. The remainder reflect a response to ad hoc but finite problems, such as the advance of money to allies after World War II or responsibility for a single contribution to the Kennedy Memorial Fund in 1965. The uncertainties of the market do not affect these programs as they do the measures for which Employment and Trade & Industry are responsible.

A Ceiling on Choice

Defining goals establish a floor or minimum for what government must do. Implicit in this idea too is the prospect of a ceiling on the number of defining measures that a government need undertake. A government needs so much and no more of diplomats, soldiers, courts, police, and tax collectors. Once its defining programs are in place and effective, there is no need for making further choices in this field.

A ceiling does exist, for the number of defining programs has changed very little in the past half century. At the end of World War II, there were 38 programs in place; four and one-half decades later there were 53. Ad hoc stimuli and changes in the policy environment gave occasion to start, stop, or start and stop some programs involving small sums of money. On average, the government of the day can reckon on making one choice a year that adds to or reduces the number of defining programs. A foreign secretary or a chancellor of the exchequer is constrained in what he or she can do by what predecessors have done. Policymakers in this field are not so much concerned with launching new programs as they are trying to manage the legacy of choices left by their predecessors.

Because defining programs are collective goods, their cost is not proportional to the number of people benefiting. Because they are political goods, increased expenditure is not necessarily a sign of success. Spending more money on defense indicates an increased military threat; it is not a sign of peace. Similarly, spending more money on police and prisons is an indication of increased crime.

In the postwar period, spending on defining programs has almost doubled in real terms from £18.7 billion to £34.5 billion, an increase of 85 percent. Yet defense, which claims the most money, has had its total expenditure reduced in real terms by almost £2 billion. This is due to a high level of expenditure on defense at the end of World War II and the fact that as long as its purpose can be achieved, there is no need to spend more. The increase of more than ten times in spending on Home Office programs has not produced more law and order but reflects a strategy of responding to a rising crime rate by spending more on established programs.

Forced to Choose: Trial and Error in the Market Place

Policymakers concerned with economic programs, like directors of large business firms, are vulnerable to what happens in the market place. Each wants their particular choices to succeed yet recognizes that the overall state of the economy has a significant impact upon outcomes. A stable environment cannot be assumed for economic programs, for market conditions fluctuate much more than does the demographic structure of the population. Because Britain is part of an international economic system, changes in the international environment frequently produce unpredictable and unwanted shocks.

In the abstract, policymakers might welcome continuous economic flux because it widens the scope for choice. But when programs must be changed in turbulent circumstances, policymakers are driven to a trial-and-error search for new measures. Whereas a business firm risks going bankrupt if its measures are consistently unsuccessful, policymakers whose programs fail to produce satisfaction must try and try again.

The Turbulent Environment of Economic Programs

The economic goals of government—growth, full employment, stable prices, and a balance-of-payments surplus—are constants. Every postwar British government has asserted the desirability of all four of these objectives. Policy debates are about the priority to be given each goal, since advancing toward one may cause difficulties in pursuit of another. Each objective requires a distinctive set of programs.

Economists offer conflicting advice about the programs best suited to pursue these persisting goals (cf. Ricketts and Shoesmith, 1990). They disagree in their basic assumptions about how the economy works. Disagreements also reflect differences in interpretations of empirical evidence. Even if there is a consensus among economic advisers about the program best suited to achieve a given goal, advice is usually proffered *ceteris paribus*—all other conditions remaining equal. However, in the market place all other conditions usually do *not* remain equal, making the outcome of economic programs problematic. Even if a target goal is achieved, a program may produce side effects that cause such dissatisfaction that the program itself becomes discredited; for example, anti-inflation measures can also produce recession, just as anti-unemployment measures can also produce inflation.

The market is a continuing arena of choice in which consumers signal demands and producers determine supply. Hundreds of millions of choices are made each day as people go about their everyday routines. International money markets are capable of moving hundreds of billions of currency each day, far more than the Bank of England can command in efforts to stop speculation against the pound. Large enterprises monitor their cash flow on a daily or weekly basis. The stock market assesses the value of companies on the basis of their quarterly, semi-annual, or annual reports.

Changes outside the control of British government can so alter market conditions that a program that once produced satisfaction becomes unsatisfactory. Throughout the postwar era, world economic conditions that influence the price of such imported necessities as food, and the demand for exports needed to maintain the country's standard of living, have been major determinants of the state of the British economy. No British government has been able to base policy solely upon the choices of British producers and consumers. During the postwar period, a variety of factors—global economic growth, Britain's entry into the European Community in 1973, and the rise of Japan and revival of Germany—have reduced Britain's influence upon the world economy and increased the impact upon Britain of fluctuations in the international economy.

The turbulence of the British economy in the postwar era is illustrated graphically in figure 9.3, which traces the annual ups and

Figure 9.3. Ups and downs in the British economy since 1946

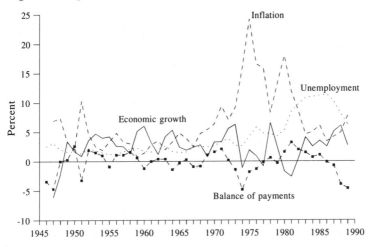

Sources: Growth in GDP, *Economic Trends.* Unemployment, *British Labour Statistics: Historical Abstract 1886–1968* and *Annual Abstract of Statistics.* Inflation, *Internal Purchasing Power of the Pound.* Balance of Payments as % of GNP, *Annual Abstract of Statistics.* All publications, HMSO, London.

downs of economic growth, unemployment, inflation, and the balance of payments since the end of World War II. The extent of turbulence can be expressed arithmetically by frequent reversals in direction in all four of these economic targets and statistically as the coefficient of variation, that is, the standard deviation in each year's change divided by the mean.

Economic growth is a necessary condition for funding significant increases in spending on inherited programs and financing new programs. For most of the postwar era, British policymakers have regarded the growth rate as too low. Increasing the rate above the mean of 2.4 percent has been a perennial goal of economic policy, but success has been intermittent. Although policymakers may claim credit for a rise in the growth rate, none will choose to make it fall.

High rates of growth have not been sustainable. From year to year the growth rate has reversed, either down or up, in 24 of the 43 years under review here. A given year's rate of growth is often substantially higher or lower than the mean, producing a standard deviation of 2.6 percent and a high coefficient of variation, 1.08.

The rate of unemployment has been less turbulent in the short run, but only because a long period of very low unemployment immediately after the war was followed by a long period of high structural unemployment since. Until 1964 the mean annual rate of unemployment was 1.9 percent, with little fluctuation around that figure. Since 1965 the mean annual rate has been 5.7 percent, with a tendency for unemployment to be higher still in the 1980s. Given an overall mean of 4.0 percent unemployment and a standard deviation of 3.1, the coefficient of variation is high too, 0.78. In one year in three the rate of unemployment has reversed, but this lower level of turbulence is bad news for policymakers: it reflects a relatively steady rise in unemployment for more than two decades.

Inflation rates are higher and fluctuate more widely than unemployment or growth; the mean rate of inflation since 1946 is 6.6 percent. The annual inflation rate has ranged from 24.0 percent in 1975 to 0.8 percent in 1959. Here too there is a sharp upward step. Until 1964 the annual rate of inflation averaged 3.5 percent; since then it has averaged 8.9 percent. Because high rates of inflation are regarded as undesirable by policymakers, a great deal of political effort is devoted to reducing the rate of inflation. Even though the path of inflation is upward, it is not steady. In 19 of 43 years the rate of increase in prices has reversed direction from the year before. Ironically, intermittent success in lowering inflation can also cause turbulence, for a drop of 8 percent between 1975 and 1976 can be just as much a shock as an increase of 8 percent between 1974 and 1975. With the inflation rate having a standard deviation of 5.1 percent, the coefficient of variation is high, 0.77.

The balance of payments is not a figure that consumers think about, but it is a statistic that policymakers monitor because it summarizes Britain's international trade. The goal is to have a positive balance of payments, with exports exceeding imports. During the postwar era the balance of payments has on average been negative, -0.2 percent of the gross national product. This low mean and a standard deviation of 1.9 percent produce a very high coefficient of variation, 9.5. Equally relevant as an indicator of turbulence is the reversal of the annual balance of payments in 19 years since the end of World War II.

The difference between the economic cycle and the life cycle is aptly illustrated by government statistics. *Social Trends* reports data about individual behavior on an annual basis, and census trends are based on data collected once every ten years. By contrast, *Economic Trends* reports employment and inflation statistics on a monthly basis; interest rates are reported in the press on a daily basis; and the foreign exchange markets value and revalue the pound on a minute by minute basis during a trading day that extends from morning in Frankfurt to nightfall in Tokyo and Hong Kong. Economic programs must operate in an environment in which trends are reported thousands of times as fast as social trends.

Turbulence in economic conditions, especially in conjunction with upward trends in inflation and unemployment, generates political dissatisfaction. It puts pressure on policymakers to do something about economic difficulties. Even if ministers would like to dismiss economic problems as not really their fault, they cannot ignore them as long as they are considered an important determinant of the government's electoral success. The coincidental reporting of economic statistics and public opinion polls encourages the belief that fluctuations in the former cause fluctuations in the latter (but see Hibbs, 1987; Rose and McAllister, 1990: chapter 7).

When turbulence in the economy generates political dissatisfaction, then notwithstanding the many uncertainties involved, policymakers must make choices, adopting programs through a trial-and-error search in which many new measures are introduced, some becoming incorporated in the continuing legacy of government, but others failing. Whatever the amount of expenditure, errors are accepted as politically less costly than doing nothing. When structural change occurs more or less predictably, such as the decline in British manufacturing, policymakers can plan a transition program, such as running down a cotton industry based on nineteenth-century markets. But when structural difficulties do not have predictable solutions, policymakers must make ad hoc or trial-and-error responses in search of satisfaction.

A Fitful Record of Starts and Stops

When turbulence forces policymakers to act, they will review available knowledge about a program, insofar as the constraints of time and political ideology allow. But whether or not the program chosen will reduce dissatisfaction only becomes evident after a choice is made. Success is not the avoidance of error. It is being right more often than wrong, or at least, getting the program right on the second or third try, if not the first.

Responsibility for economic programs is spread widely in Whitehall. Department of Employment programs deal with a labor market in which tens of thousands of people change jobs every day, and billions of pounds are spent to promote employment and assist the unemployed. Department of Trade & Industry programs deal with industries and trade flows in which billions of pounds change hands each day. The programs of the Energy Department are affected as much or more by world markets as by acts of Parliament. Transport is a daily necessity of the economy; the condition of roads, rail, air and shipping depend upon investment decisions so long-term that the consequences of choice are realized by distant inheritors. Agriculture programs are oriented toward the market, albeit in a perverse way, seeking to protect farmers from fluctuations in prices and international competition.

More than half the programs in effect since World War II deal with the market. But because of its turbulence, seven-eighths have either started, stopped, or started and stopped in the postwar period. Only 25 programs concerned with the market have been part of the inheritance of public policy since 1946. Economic policymakers concerned have thus had lots of opportunities for short-term choices but few to add programs to the continuing inheritance of public policy.

Hypothesis 9.3 is confirmed. The largest group of economic programs, 40 percent, has been part of a trial-and-error process, having started and stopped, or is likely to terminate in response to changes in the market place (figure 9.4). In addition, one-sixth of economic programs are ad hoc, adopted in response to unexpected developments in the market. This is most evident in energy, where two unexpected oil price shocks have prompted more than a dozen different ad hoc measures. Trade and industry have ad hoc problems arising from specific problems of major companies or industries threatening to collapse. Altogether, 56 percent of programs with market goals operate in conditions of *unwanted* choice, a policy environment so unpredictable that policymakers must proceed uncertainly on a trial-and-error or ad hoc basis.

Only three in ten economic programs can be described as part of the continuing inheritance of public policy. Most are routinized measures addressing persisting goals, for example, testing motor vehicles or inspecting health and safety. At least in the short term, policymakers can develop programs to achieve a finite objective. Privatization measures are examples of such programs and have been prominent in energy and industry. Even though its goals are persisting, employment has a turbulent policy environment. In labor markets there is no such thing as a once-for-all solution.

Figure 9.4. Market programs: goals and policy environment

Number of programs

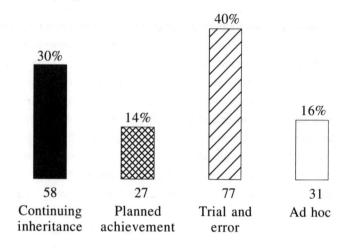

Expenditure

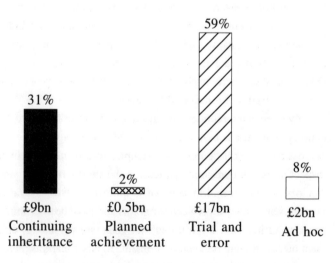

When money is the measure, the effects of market turbulence are even more clearcut. Trial-and-error programs account for almost three-fifths of total expenditure on economic programs, and ad hoc measures for an additional 8 percent. Thus, economic programs with a high risk of failure claim more than two-thirds of money spent on market measures (figure 9.4). Programs that are part of the continuing inheritance of government account for less than a third of total expenditure. The discrepancy in costs remains even when one controls for the greater number of trial-and-error programs. The mean expenditure on these risky programs is almost half again that on economic programs forming part of the persisting inheritance. Many persisting in this field involve very small sums and are insulated from the turbulence of the market, for example, a £6 million annual subscription to the International Labour Organization.

Trial-and-error economic programs tend to cost more because they often address big problems, e.g., rising unemployment or industrial restructuring, and sometimes just because they are unsustainable. When unemployment causes great dissatisfaction, expensive new programs can be launched since, if they are successful, they become self-liquidating as unemployment falls. If the program fails to stop dissatisfaction, it can be terminated and the money saved through cancellation used to finance another measure in its place. Alternatively, an expensive unsuccessful program, for example, to subsidize shipbuilding, can be terminated when it becomes evident that the money spent is not an investment but an economic waste.

The foregoing figures understate the extent of turbulence in the market, because agriculture programs are included among the market programs. In practice they are not responsive to the market but designed to insulate agriculture from the market. Of 16 postwar agricultural programs, 14 are part of the persisting inheritance of public policy. Before and after World War II, protection from the market was justified on national security as well as interest group grounds. Britain's entry to the European Community in 1973 compelled it to accept the legacy of the Community's agriculture subsidy programs. Subsidy programs that draw the ire of economists on the grounds of inefficiency are not without a justification: the insulation of agriculture from the market produces political satisfaction among farmers. If agricultural programs are reclassified as social measures to preserve rural families and communities or national security measures defending an island nation's capacity to feed itself, then the turbulence of market programs appears greater still.

Employment, which accounts for the largest number of programs with market goals, is today the paradigm example of making policy in a turbulent environment. When the 1945 Labour government entered office it inherited nine programs. For nearly two decades afterwards there was widespread satisfaction at an unemployment rate averaging less than 2 percent. To promote economic growth, the 1964–70 Labour government introduced seven new programs concerned with prices and incomes, industrial relations, and productivity; it did not terminate any inherited programs. The Heath administration sought to prevent inflationary boosts in wages and prices and create a corporatist system for administering employment programs; it therefore introduced new programs and phased out some inherited programs, thinking it would thereby be adding a large number of carefully incubated measures to the continuing inheritance of public policy. Events soon showed this assumption was a mistake.

Since 1973 employment programs have had to respond to a turbulent policy environment. Unemployment passed one million in 1975, then two million and finally the three million mark, 10 to 15 percent of the labor force, depending upon which set of statistics were used. Trials and errors have characterized the 45 employment programs started since 1975, and 29 had been stopped as of the end of 1989. Most programs stopped were measures introduced and abandoned a few years later as failures (for details, see Rose and Page,

1990). Because so many employment programs have been abandoned, the annual budget of the Department of Employment is far lower than would be assumed by summing average annual expenditure on each of its programs. Trial-and-error programs account for 89 percent of calculated expenditure in the turbulent environment of employment.

Trial-and-error search is equally evident in energy. In 1946 there were two energy programs in place, and in the quarter century subsequently 12 more were adopted and none was terminated, for the policy environment was then predictable. The 1973 oil price shock led to the creation of the Department of Energy, a classic administrative attempt to "control" policy inputs, as if that were the same as controlling the policy environment. Turbulence in international markets is not subject to administrative control from Whitehall. The Energy Department has since chosen two dozen programs, but the great majority have been trial-and-error measures stopped soon after starting, such as subsidies to users or producers of energy. The Thatcher administration managed to achieve planned objectives, but only by making the privatization of energy resources a major policy goal.

Although the Department of Trade and Industry traces its administrative origins back three centuries, its programs are subject to frequent starts and stops in response to turbulence in international markets since the conversion of the British economy from a wartime to a peacetime footing. The result is that of 45 trade and industry programs, only 12 are part of the persisting inheritance of government, and a majority are trial-and-error or ad hoc attempts to cope with continuing goals, such as increased investment, or ad hoc problems of industrial reorganization. Ironically, the most predictable way in which the Department of Trade & Industry can achieve success is by withdrawal, privatizing state-owned enterprises.

Transport, too, is an environment where changes occur through market pressures, for example, the growth of road as against rail traffic, and technological change, such as the development of jet airplanes. Whereas only five transport programs were in effect at the end of the war, 20 operated in 1989. Three-fifths of transport programs are part of the continuing inheritance of government, such as capital investment and road maintenance, or planned achievements, such as the privatization of British Airways. Ten are trial-and-error measures. Inherited transport programs tend to concern capital investment, whereas those that are trial and error address such persisting problems as the economics of London transport.

Increasing Turbulence Increases Tries and Errors

For the first two decades after World War II, the British economy was relatively predictable and policymakers expected it to remain so. Up to 1964 only 22 new economic programs were introduced and 11 terminated, a rate of less than two a year. Since many of the programs terminated were temporary postwar measures, these figures actually understate the predictability of the market environment at that time.

The 1964 Labour government opened a period of elite-led initiatives to stimulate the British economy. It assumed that the market was relatively predictable, so that the plans of a Labour government could be achieved by introducing new programs intended to sustain long-term growth. It quadrupled the annual rate of choice of market programs and only terminated three. At this high point of confidence in economic planning, there was no thought of trial and error.

Since the beginning of the 1970s the initiative for starting and stopping programs has come from turbulence in the market. The Heath administration was much more active, starting an average of six programs a year. However, economic turbulence led to a big increase in the number of programs stopped, almost four a year. Since 1974 the rate of adopting and stopping new economic programs has accelerated. In a trial-and-error search for means to dispel dissatisfaction about the failure to advance toward perennial goals of economic policy, the 1974 Labour government started 34 programs and stopped 30, an average of more than 10 changes a year. The Thatcher administration started 57 programs with market goals and terminated 37, and left more than a dozen trial-and-error measures vulnerable to termination in the 1990s.

The aggregate effect of stopping as well as starting so many measures is that spending on market programs has not grown greatly and today does not claim a large share of total public expenditure. At the beginning of the postwar era, these programs accounted for £3.1 billion; in 1989 they accounted for £13.8 billion. If every economic program operating at some point in the postwar era had persisted at its average level of annual expenditure until 1989, then total spending on market programs would have been nearly £28 billion, more than double its current level. Frequent failure makes it easy to finance frequent fresh trials.

The Alternatives: Durable Success or Forced Choice

If a policymaker's only goal were to maximize opportunities for choice, then devising economic programs would be desirable, for this is a field in which there are lots of choices to be made. In a turbulent economy the distant past is of little significance compared to the current demand to "do something" to remove current dissatisfaction. Whereas defining policies are the object of about four choices in an average Parliament and social welfare about six, in the past two decades policymakers have been able to make several dozen choices during an average Parliament. In the postwar era overall, British government has had 183 economic programs as against 96 programs with social welfare goals and 71 with defining concerns.

But the stimulus to act in economic policy also threatens failure, for the pressures to act are due to the fact that the majority of measures introduced by successive Conservative and Labour administrations to deal with economic problems fail to bring satisfaction. Failure on this scale cannot be blamed on individuals or collective institutions such as a party or even civil servants, particularly when many measures have initially been welcomed in the belief that they would improve conditions. The underlying explanation is that four-fifths of economic choices must be made in unstable market conditions in which it is uncertain whether a program will be effective, and programs are terminated because they fail to produce satisfaction. Instead of describing economic policymakers as free to choose, they can be said to be *forced* to choose.

If the object of policymaking is to achieve durable success, welfare and defining concerns offer the best opportunities. Because their policy environments are usually predictable, it is very likely that a program, once chosen, will become part of the persisting inheritance of public policy. Whereas less than half of economic programs concern predictable policy environments, 87 percent of defining programs and 90 percent of welfare programs are introduced in predictable environments (figure 9.5).

When expenditure is the measure, the gulf is wider still between different types of programs. Programs that are part of the predictable policy environment account for 98 percent of expenditure on welfare and the same percentage on defining programs. By contrast, they account for only 33 percent of expenditure on economic programs. Two-thirds of the money invested in market programs finances high-risk programs that often fail.

There is an inverse relationship between the cost of programs and the scope for choice by the government of the day. The biggest claims on expenditure in the legacy of each administration are programs to promote welfare. The programs are expensive because they provide

Figure 9.5. Predictability by types of program

Share of programs predictable

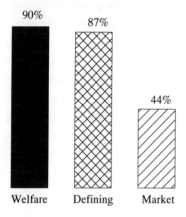

Share of expenditure on predictable programs

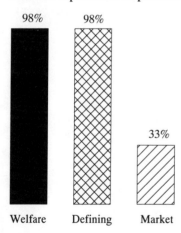

benefits through their lifetime for almost every British family. Thus, they remain part of the persisting legacy of public policy. When policymakers are choosing new programs, they are likely to be facing a turbulent market environment and have limited sums to spend and a much higher chance of failure. Thus, a policymaker who sees himself or herself as a decisionmaker is likely to be kept busy in a trial-and-error pursuit of policies that succeed briefly, at best, and are likely to be undone soon after. A policymaker who wants to make a durable impact on public policy must be patient, for opportunities to do so are few. In fields where government spends most money, the main task of policymakers is to administer what they have inherited.

10 Change without Choice

The expense is not noticed because it does not come all at once, for the mind is led astray by the repeated small outlays, just like the sophistic puzzle. "If each is little, then all are little." This is true in one way, but in another it is not, for the whole total is not little, but made up of little parts—Aristotle

President Clinton will submit his own budget—totally rewriting the one President George Bush comes up with this week
—Associated Press news story, 6 January 1993

The short-term effects of the inheritance of public policy are stabilizing, but the cumulative effect is destabilizing. More than two millennia ago Aristotle described the flaw in the politician's sophistical claim that short-term choices had no long-term consequences: in the fullness of time seemingly small annual changes add up to big changes. This is true in Britain—in almost half a century since the end of World War II the total number of programs has more than doubled, and program expenditure has more than quadrupled—and throughout the OECD world.

The pervasive public policy issue of the 1990s—the deficit—is a direct consequence of the unnoticed inheritance of change without choice. In an era of slow economic growth and continuous pressures to increase public expenditure without proportionate increases in taxation, each incoming administration, whatever its partisan color, is likely to run a deficit. The deficit is primarily due to commitments inherited from predecessors. In the annual budget process, there is thus a gap of a few percent between revenue from inherited taxes and expenditure committed to inherited programs.

The annual deficit is small relative to the total budget. In public finance, £6 billion is equal to 2.5 percent of total public expenditure and 1 percent of the national product. Moreover, the cost of financing the deficit (that is, the interest on borrowing £6 billion), is much less still, about 0.2 percent of current public expenditure or 0.08 percent of the national product. Such sums are within the range of measurement error of macroeconomic forecasts. Few politicians will want to risk the political unity of the government of the day for the sake of a few tenths of one percentage point in the budget. The easy way out of disputes about the budget is to add just "a little" to the deficit. Within the framework of a 12-month budget cycle, the reasoning is understandable. Moreover, the fact that previous administrations ran deficits legitimates doing so too.

In the annual budget cycle, last year's deficit is forgotten—but it does not disappear. Instead, it is incorporated in the public debt, a figure that represents the sum of deficits inherited from the distant and not-so-distant past. Moreover, the £6 billion added to the public debt increases the interest that must be paid in the current year's budget by £400 million to £500 million. In the course of a four-year term of office, the total debt thereby increases by £24 billion, and annual interest on the debt by up to £2 billion. An increase of £24 billion is not a small sum; it is equivalent to 4 percent of the total national product. Moreover, any marginal increase in debt is added to the public debt inherited from previous administrations. The consequence, in Aristotle's terms, is that even though each year's deficit may appear just a little bit, "the total is not little."

The puzzle of public policy is how so much change—and so much *unwanted* change—can occur with so little choice. Confronted with the prospect of responsibility for choices in the budget, Richard Darman, head of President Bush's Office of Management and Budget, spoke of being overwhelmed by the budget as "the *Ultimate Cookie Monster.* . . . Its motivation is clearly not malevolent. What harm it may cause is largely unintended." It restricts the White House scope for choice because the monster "cannot quite control the way in which he behaves." (Office of Management and Budget, 1990: 7; italics in original). Joseph White and Aaron Wildavsky (1989: xix) conclude, "Deficits persist because all choices are bad." Although this is accurate as description, it is does not explain how policymakers have landed in a situation that is not of their choice.

The theory of inheritance before choice explains how change without choice has come about. To understand change in public programs, we must think first about the impersonal force of political inertia. It maintains the great bulk of public programs from the less or more distant past and imposes spending increases through statutes authorizing entitlements and the indexation of benefits. The first section of this chapter summarizes the cumulative changes wrought by this inheritance in postwar Britain.

But is it reasonable to expect programs in other countries to be as rooted in the past as in Britain? To test this, the second section examines the United States, a nation with much less stable and centralized institutions of government. Notwithstanding this, policymakers in Washington are as much in thrall to inheritance as is Whitehall. Washington's current problems of budgeting are a legacy of choices by previous administrations. Social security expenditure is based upon legislation initially introduced in President Roosevelt's New Deal. Defense expenditure reflects President Truman's commitment in the 1940s to provide American forces as a global shield for allies. Medicare and Medicaid were enacted at the beginning of the Johnson administration. Debt interest is a perennial line in the budget; its present height owes much to the Reagan administration. As Steven Mufson wrote in the *Washington Post* (1992), "For the first time this century, the federal government is spending more on the interest on past debts than on investment." No one, certainly not Bill Clinton, chose the budget commitments that he inherited. The second section asks: How large a proportion of the president's total budget is a statement of the president's choices? Whereas statements about the scope for choice emanating from the president-elect are an expression of faith untempered by experience, the answer given here is based on what actually was done.

From a normative perspective, the critical political question is whether freedom of choice or the constraints of inheritance make for better public policy. Freedom of choice is considered desirable for individuals as voters and as consumers, yet individuals act within a society in which many benefits of public policy are assumed to continue. The conclusion argues that there are good reasons to prefer the continuity of inherited public policy to disruption of individual welfare through frequent choice.

The Accumulated Inheritance

By comparison with most advanced industrial nations, the British crown is a very old state with an uninterrupted lineage from medieval times. However, antiquity is not the cause of inheritance. The programs reviewed here are quintessential modern programs addressing the problems of industrial and postindustrial societies.

Inertia Leads to Unintended Growth

The bequest that each administration leaves to its successor is larger than the legacy it inherited, for each administration introduces more new programs than it terminates, and these are retained by the moving consensus of successive Conservative and Labour administrations. In the course of almost half a century the total number of programs has more than doubled, rising from 115 to 238. However, this change occurred very gradually; it was not the choice of any one administration. The net increase of 123 programs is at the rate of a dozen programs in a typical four-year Parliament. The adoption of new programs has been greater since 1964 and even more since 1974, but because many involved the trial-and-error starting and stopping of programs, they have not greatly accelerated the increase in the legacy. The bias toward growth is steady but not inevitable. In eight years the total number of programs actually contracted, and in four it remained the same. The manifold of programs thus expands in about three years in four. This is enough to create substantial long-term expansion, although far less than would be the case if all 360 programs operating at some point in the postwar era had remained in effect.

The tipping point—that is, the year in which new programs outnumbered old programs—was 1973, more than a quarter century after the end of World War II. As of that year just under half of all programs in effect were inherited from before World War II; a quarter dated from prior to 1964 and a quarter from the enthusiasms of the Wilson-Heath years. As previous chapters have documented, many of these new programs turned out to be errors and were soon terminated. By the beginning of the 1990s the proportion of pre-1945 programs in the manifold of public policy had hardly declined further. The big change occurred in the definition of newer programs; only one in five programs is less than 20 years old.

The impact of inheritance upon expenditure is even greater, for the total cost of programs has quadrupled. Programs inherited at the end of World War II claimed the equivalent of £36 billion in constant pounds. Following postwar demobilization, in 1947 inherited programs claimed £29 billion and then began a slow but cumulatively great rise. On entering office, each administration finds that it is committed to spend a larger sum than its predecessors. In some instances, such as the 1951–64 Conservative administration, increased expenditure was financed by the fiscal dividend of economic growth. At the other extreme, an administration may find that spending on inherited commitments rises almost twice as fast as the economy grows, causing the deficit to escalate further.

Figure 10.1. Gradual change in the legacy of program expenditure

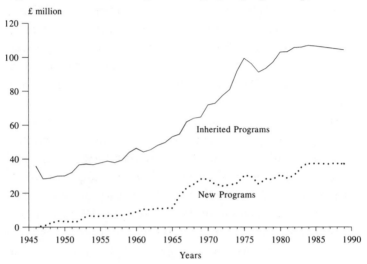

Expenditure growth is a recurring tendency but not an iron law; in 13 of the 43 years reviewed here, total expenditure actually contracted in real terms. In times of crisis, the contraction can be substantial. For example, in 1977 the Labour government made a cut of 7.5 percent in real expenditure in keeping with conditions of an International Monetary Fund loan financing recovery from an earlier acceleration of spending. Most reductions are small, often less than 1 percent of the total; thus, they do not reverse the long-term bias toward growth in the cost as well as the number of public programs. *In public expenditure, the force of inertia is so great that the center of gravity has not yet tipped into the postwar era.*

At the beginning of the 1990s, 74 percent of expenditure was devoted to programs that had been inherited from a half century ago or longer (figure 10.1). Even though the number of programs in effect from the distant past cannot increase, the amount of money spent on these programs can and does increase. Because the rate of spending on inherited programs has been greater than that on new programs, inherited programs will cost more than post-1945 choices well into the twenty-first century. Even if total expenditure on inherited programs did not increase from its 1989 level of £104 billion, at the current trend rate of increase, total spending on new programs would not be as much as the inheritance from the distant past until after the year 2060!

Changes in the Composition of the Manifold

While the bias toward growth has affected all types of programs, it has not affected them equally; there has thus been a cumulative shift in the *composition* of public policy, altering the share of the budget claimed by different types of programs (figure 10.2). Immediately after the end of World War II, defining programs were the most numerous, accounting for 39 percent of programs in effect. In expenditure terms, too, defining programs were also most important, claiming 66 percent of total expenditure. Since then, the number of defining programs has only increased by seven, in keeping with the logic of a ceiling as well as a floor. Defining programs have claimed a limited amount of additional money; spending has gone up £11 billion in real terms, and defense has even had its total expenditure contract in real terms. Within the category of defining programs, there has been a shift from programs concerned with international security to measures addressing law and order at home.

Programs concerning the market have almost trebled in number to 100, but spending has only increased by £11 billion, because so many starts have been trial-and-error measures that have subsequently been terminated. The increase in market programs has been greatest in employment; there were three programs in 1946 and 32 in 1989. Many market programs in effect in 1989 are likely to be terminated

Figure 10.2. Changing composition of public policy

A) Number of Programs by Type

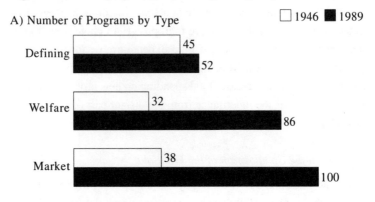

B) Expenditure on Programs

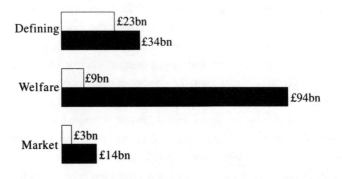

because they do not produce satisfaction. Yet since promoting the economy is a continuing purpose of government, the total stock is likely to remain very large as new measures are substituted for abandoned ones.

Welfare programs have more than doubled in the postwar era, too. In number, the biggest increase has been in local government and environmental services, which has added 26 programs. But in terms of money, the biggest increase has been in social security, where continuing programs have claimed an extra £41 billion, and health, which has had expenditure rise by more than £23 billion.

The manifold of public policy is today very different than at the beginning of the postwar era. Today, programs for individual welfare constitute two-fifths instead of one-quarter of the total, and in cash terms welfare programs now account for 66 percent of public spending, more than double their share of a much smaller budget in 1946. Market programs have grown greatly in number and increased in expenditure, but not so much in relative terms. Defining programs have contracted in relative importance.

Differences in growth rates of contrasting types of programs do not reflect conscious policy choices. Each field of public policy has its own distinctive purposes and policy environment. Cumulatively, differences between programs in the legacy that each administration leaves to its successor compound to produce a major structural shift in the composition of public policy. The shift is not the choice of a particular administration; it is due to what is inherent in programs and changes in policy environments.

Change is inevitable, but many changes are a by-product of choice rather than the conscious purpose of the government of the day. When old means to old ends claim tens of billions of additional expenditure for social security, health, education, and defense, there is limited money to finance the choice of new programs. Opportunities for choice tend to arise in unwanted circumstances, when the failure of market programs to produce satisfaction leads to a trial-and-error search.

In the 1990s the first claim on the government of the day is the inheritance of the past. This is reflected in the cost of financing past deficits and the current cost of past commitments. In the 1993 financial year the cost of interest payments on past borrowings is almost £20 billion, more than 3 percent of the gross national product and nearly 7 percent of total public expenditure. The payment of debt interest is thus one of the biggest spending programs of British government and is an inescapable legacy of the past. Moreover, an annual deficit of up to £50 billion adds approximately £3.5 billion to the debt interest that must be paid in the following year (Treasury, 1993: 8). Interest on the inherited deficit is now growing faster than expenditure on the legacy of social welfare programs, adding more to the cost of each year's public expenditure than the few choices that the government of the day can afford to make.

Different Histories but the Same Constraints

Testing general ideas against the experience of a single country makes it possible to examine in detail the program lines in the budget over many years. But are findings from British experience applicable elsewhere?

Comparing Washington with Westminster is a robust test of the model of inheritance, for American politics focuses upon the present and how today's choices affect tomorrow. The annual budget battle is a free-for-all. What goes in and what goes out of the budget is not subject to centralized control by the executive office of the president, as the British budget is centrally controlled by the Treasury (cf. Heclo and Wildavsky, 1974; Wildavsky, 1988). The same is true of legislation. The president's State of the Union message is the start, not the end, of the choices inscribed as law at the conclusion of each session of Congress. In such an open, unstable system we would expect far more scope for choice and much less persistence of inherited commitments.

The Reagan Years: A Legacy of Debt

When Ronald Reagan entered the White House, his rhetorical goal was to cut the size of government. He inherited from President Carter a set of programs that were costing $678 billion a year. The great bulk was financed by taxes. The deficit was only 11 percent of total federal expenditure. To reduce the size of government Reagan had three choices: to cut spending, cut taxes, or do both.

Tax cuts were the prime successes of the Reagan campaign against big government. The 1981 Tax Act was a typical "Christmas tree" measure, containing gifts for many groups represented in the White House and Congress. The tax cuts were justified by supply-side economics, which claimed the measures would stimulate economic growth, thus generating sufficient revenue to finance inherited federal programs, and new measures for defense expenditure too. Although the economics was dubious, the political attractions of tax cuts were irresistible. Moreover, many Reaganites believed that even if revenue did not increase, the resulting deficits would constitute a major pressure preventing the adoption of new programs and forcing cuts in established programs (cf. Stockman, 1986).

The 1986 Tax Act was a very different but equally significant victory for Reagan. It was revenue-neutral, that is, it did not reduce the amount of money that the federal government collected in taxes. What it did was to cut the rate at which income tax and other taxes were levied and broaden the base of taxable income by repealing many loopholes. The repeal of loopholes was deemed an important step in making the system fairer and economically more efficient. An incidental consequence was that it left no "soft" targets for repeal by a future president intent on finding new sources of revenue.

However, instead of cutting federal expenditure, the Reagan administration watched it balloon. By the time Ronald Reagan left the White House in 1989, federal expenditure had risen to $1.144 trillion, an increase of more than two-thirds in current dollars and of a quarter in constant terms. Since tax revenues had not risen in proportion, the federal deficit doubled to $155 billion and was higher still in 1984, an election year, when more than a quarter of federal spending was financed by borrowing rather than taxation.

The fate of the Gramm-Rudman-Hollings Act of 1985 illustrates the great difficulties that Washington faces in trying to make choices about taxes and spending. The act sought to place a strict ceiling on the federal deficit by introducing "automatic" cuts in spending if Congress and the White House could not agree to keep the deficit within specified limits. However, the act explicitly exempted from such cuts inherited programs accounting for 66 percent of the federal budget, such as social security and benefits for low-income households, debt interest payments, federal retirement benefits, the postal service, unemployment compensation programs, veterans compensation, and $109 billion of defense expenditure (Office of Management and Budget, 1990: A-34ff). In short, a third of the budget was expected to bear the whole cost of budget cuts of up to $100 billion or more. Rather than see this happen, Congress and the White House first sought to "stretch" the ceiling on the deficit through optimistic forecasts of tax revenue assumptions and then abandoned the Gramm-Rudman ceiling.

The Reagan legacy shared one feature with its inheritance: federal spending was higher in 1989 than it was under the previous administration. But it also had three novel features. First, the federal deficit was higher than ever before. Secondly, the next president's scope for choice on spending programs was greatly reduced because some success in squeezing discretionary expenditure resulted in 91 percent of total federal expenditure being immediately uncontrollable. Thirdly, the next president's scope for choice was very slight because a big deficit required increasing amounts of revenue simply to meet debt interest payments, and there were virtually no significant tax loopholes that could be repealed.

Choice Between Horns of a Dilemma:
The Inheritance of George Bush and Bill Clinton

Proponents of politics as public choice normally write as if the freedom to choose was a welcome freedom. Policymakers are portrayed as choosing between competing goods, or between programs favoring supporters rather than opponents. Yet policymakers also have a choice when they face a dilemma, and each alternative has unacceptable consequences.

George Bush faced a dilemma when he ran for the Presidency in 1988. As the author of the phrase "voodoo economics" and vice president under Ronald Reagan, he was aware of the problems in President Reagan's legacy. But as a candidate facing a tough election fight, he needed an issue that could benefit him. Taxation was the issue that he chose. In his acceptance speech to the Republican convention, Bush declared: "I'm the one who will not raise taxes. My opponent now says, my opponent now says he'll raise them as a last resort, or a third resort. Well, when a politician talks like that, you know that's one resort he'll be checking into. And my opponent won't rule out raising taxes. But I will. And the Congress will push me to raise taxes, and I'll say no, and they'll push, and I'll say no, and they'll push again. And I'll say to them: Read my lips. No new taxes" (*Congressional Quarterly,* 1989: 23). The good news for Candidate Bush was that he won the election; the bad news was that he inherited the Reagan budget deficit—and President Bush's campaign pledge landed him "in deep voodoo" (Rowen, 1990).

The extent to which a President is a prisoner of inheritance can be illustrated by examining the problem confronting President Bush in 1990. In the words of his budget director, Richard Darman, this was the year when "*there is an obligation to be serious*" (Office of Management and Budget, 1990: 20; italics in the original). The president's inheritance is summed up in the current services budget, an estimate of what it would cost to fund inherited programs "if programs and activities were carried on at the same level as the current year without a change in policy" (qtd. Muris, 1989: 6). The current services budget not only recognizes that inherited programs must be maintained but also that the cost of inherited programs can increase. A similar calculation can be made for tax revenue. The estimates of expenditure on inherited programs and revenue from inherited taxes produce an initial calculation of the likely size of the inherited deficit (e.g., Kamlet and Mowery, 1986; Kamlet et al., 1988).

President Bush delivered as "his" 1991 budget programs costing a total of $1.339 trillion; nearly all of this total was allocated to programs that he had not chosen (figure 10.3). Of this total, 42 percent was claimed by mandatory entitlements to programs promoting individual welfare throughout the life cycle, such as social security, Medicare, and Medicaid. The budget statement explicitly recognized that the president has no choice about these programs; he had inherited "a moral obligation to the people who are counting on them for future support" (Office of Management and Budget, 1990: 215). The Bush administration also had no choice but to pay interest on the inherited federal debt, a sum estimated at $176 billion, or 13 percent of total expenditure. Its own laws bind the federal government to make payments on loans it guarantees and to meet the cost of compliance with its own regulations. The Bush administration inherited credit and insurance guarantees to banks, insurance companies, home loans, and government-sponsored enterprises of more than $5.8 trillion—and an $82 billion savings and loan bail out inherited from past guarantees. Defense and international commitments are uncontrollable in the short term, for not only is national security a defining purpose of government but also defense programs involve very long-term commitments to career military personnel, and procurement and

Figure 10.3. Inherited federal programs—discretionary and non-discretionary

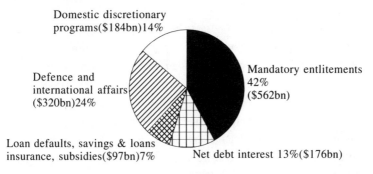

Domestic discretionary
programs($184bn)14%

Defence and
international affairs
($320bn)24%

Mandatory entlitements
42%
($562bn)

Loan defaults, savings & loans
insurance, subsidies($97bn)7%   Net debt interest 13%($176bn)

Source: OMB (1990) 157, 163, 208, 215, 229, 245f, 258, 271.

maintenance of military equipment. Altogether, 86 percent of the president's budget, accounting for well over a trillion dollars, was immediately uncontrollable.

Programs are described as discretionary if they can be altered without amending the legislation authorizing them or repudiating contractual obligations. Measures classified under this heading are not luxuries; they cover such activities as mass transit, sewage treatment plant construction, postal rates for government mail, fossil energy research, and grants to libraries (see Office of Management and Budget, 1990: 271ff; Office of Management and Budget, 1992: I-376ff). Within the field of domestic discretionary programs, the president can choose to recommend new programs or to alter or terminate inherited programs. His proposals for extra expenditure were few and inexpensive, such as altering expenditure by a few million dollars (e.g., the National Endowment for the Arts); tens of millions of dollars (e.g., expanding the FBI's anti-drug activities); hundreds of millions of dollars (e.g., federal funding of programs for the disadvantaged in elementary and secondary school); and very occasionally, adding billions of dollars (e.g., the Strategic Defense Initiative). Inexpensive choices make little difference to the budget in aggregate.

President Bush did propose to reduce spending on 51 different domestic programs, including 10 recommended for termination, such as measures dealing with disaster loan funds and construction grants. The estimated saving from the president's proposed cuts in discretionary programs totaled $15 billion. Almost one-third was calculated as saved from four programs described as "one-time events," where the program was a planned achievement not suited for continuous funding, for example, prison construction or a decennial census (Office of Management and Budget, 1990: 277). Three food assistance laws due to expire under sunset legislation were calculated as yielding additional savings of almost $15 billion. However, sunset legislation does not guarantee termination; a program can be renewed. The chief program scheduled for expiration, the 1977 Food Stamp Act, was in fact continued, though its temporary expiration was counted as a "saving" in the president's budget.

Because discretionary expenditure is a small portion of a large total, any cut is relatively small compared to the manifold of public policy. The savings from discretionary cuts proposed in Bush's 1991 budget amounted to only 1 percent of the budget, and savings from the presumed expiration of sunsetted laws to another 1 percent. In consequence, nearly all the spending commitments that George Bush inherited were left behind for his successor. The Bush White House was aware of this: "Because future mandatory spending is usually automatic, these programs tend to lock future voters and their representatives into spending priorities established in the past" and do "not leave much room in the budget for priority initiatives" (Office of Management and Budget, 1990: 183f).

President Clinton won office by successfully navigating between pressures to cut the deficit from supporters of third-party candidate

Ross Perot and pressures to increase public spending from liberals in the Democratic party. From the Reagan administration he inherited a tax system that offered very few politically palatable choices for raising more revenue. From President Bush he inherited a federal debt that had ballooned from less than $1 trillion in 1981 to more than $4 trillion—and was threatening to grow at a rate of more than $300 billion a year.

The first Clinton budget was introduced with the title *A Vision of Change for America*. But the contents reflected the dead weight of the past. Insofar as President Clinton wished to take credit for increasing federal expenditure, this was easy to do for the current services budget projected an increase in federal spending of $286 billion in his term of office. However, it also forecast a deficit of $340 billion in the first full year of office and the addition of more than $1.4 trillion to the federal debt—without the president making any choices whatsoever (Office of Management and Budget, 1993: 141).

The inheritance from the past has left President Clinton with limited scope for choice. The current services budget projected a four-year $116 billion increase in spending on entitlements for Medicare and Medicaid; a $62 billion increase on social security; and a $73 billion increase in interest on the federal debt. Of the total anticipated increase in expenditure, 91 percent was claimed by mandatory programs (Office of Management and Budget, 1993: 141).

In Washington as in Westminster, the compounding of seemingly small annual changes gradually leads to big changes in the priorities of public expenditure. Inherited programs have become increasingly important, and domestic discretionary programs have declined to relative insignificance (for background, see Ippolito, 1990). The growing federal deficit in the United States is not the choice of the White House or of Congress; it is an unintended consequence of an accumulation of changes without choice. While commentators credited President Clinton's first budget with recognizing the seriousness of

the deficit, understanding the depth of the dilemmas further constrained choice: "The crucial point is that the Clinton Plan was never a
sharp break from the past" (Prowse, 1993).

The Same Elsewhere Too

The reasons for each new administration accepting inherited program
commitments are common to governments on every continent. There
is not time enough to review every program that a new administration
inherits. Complaints about "too much" spending or "too big" a
deficit are vague; they do not identify the programs that should be
abolished or subject to big cuts in order to achieve savings on expenditure. As long as programs produce satisfaction, they are likely to
continue. A decision to abolish a program usually stirs up more political controversy than a decision to carry on with inherited measures.
Social welfare programs persist because they are commitments to the
life cycle of individuals. Expenditure on welfare programs has almost
doubled its share of the gross domestic product in the average OECD
nation in the past quarter century (cf. OECD, 1985). In 1960 social
expenditure claimed 13 percent of the gross national product, more
than half of total public expenditure; by 1986 the total had increased
to more than 25 percent of gross domestic product. The increase is
bigger still if the end of World War II is taken as the starting point.

Given the force of inertia, the biggest choice facing policymakers is
about how to live within the constraints of their inheritance. Experts
in budgeting are increasingly conscious of how little scope there is for
choice, whether the annual review is conducted under circumstances
of centralized control, as in Britain, or in the free-for-all arena of
Washington. A host of different practices are recommended for keeping spending commitments within limits. But skeptics can note that
such proposals have yet to mobilize the political support necessary to
stop the inertia of inherited commitments.

What Do We Want: Continuity or Discontinuity?

The limitations that inherited programs place on the scope for choice of a popularly elected government raise fundamental questions about the nature of democracy. If democracy is about giving people what they want, should not a popularly elected government be free to choose what the people want? If representative government is about the governing party answering to the electorate for what happens during its time in office, should it not be able to make choices about actions for which it is held responsible?

Continuity is also highly valued in everyday life. The contrast between choice and persistence is paralleled by differences in outlook between economists and sociologists. As Mancur Olson (1968: 117) perceptively noted in an essay on "Economics, Sociology, and the Best of All Possible Worlds":

> In an economist's ideal society, things would constantly be in flux, because of the need to re-allocate resources to achieve optimal conditions in regard to ever-fluctuating popular demands. In a sociologist's ideal society, by contrast, alienation can be minimized and a sense of community achieved only by minimizing social change. The economist's ideal of constant flux is a nightmare to the sociologist; the sociologist's vision of a stable community implies the negation of economic change. Between these two extreme theoretical ideals, the real world reflects an equilibrium, balancing continuing change and the maintenance of social solidarity.

A desirable equilibrium point cannot be determined scientifically; it is a choice that *"must be made by the political system"* (Olson, 1968: 117, italics in the original). Olson is correct in regarding a preference for choice or continuity as a normative, not a technical, matter. But he is mistaken in implying that government has great scope for choice or that a complex collective entity such as government can make choices as an individual might. Government is not so much a mechanism for choice as it is a complex of institutions producing outcomes as a by-product of inherited choices.

Representative government is a social institution, and a society cannot be rolled over like a portfolio of stocks or currencies. Government is different from business, for it is about maintaining society rather than about making profit through the continuous transformation of resources. The everyday "business" of government is the delivery of programs to individuals, families, organizations, and communities. The most costly program of government, social security, is the program that places the greatest premium on continuity and affords the least scope for choice, for it is a commitment to pay individuals benefits into the second half of the twenty-first century.

Even the disruption of a regime by war or revolution is insufficient to repudiate programs inherited from previous regimes. Changing the constitution does not alter the need of children for education, of older people for social security, or of people of all ages for health care. Therefore, welfare programs of an earlier regime are likely to be part of the legacy of administrations ruling under different constitutions. The importance of defining programs for defense, diplomacy, law and order, and taxation may even be increased by a dramatic change of political regime. "Assumption" is the principle controlling public programs in a time of transition from one regime to another. A new regime is expected to assume commitments inherited from the old regime, unless there is an explicit reason not to do so.

The 1958 transition from the Fourth to the Fifth Republic in France was based on the assumption that all the laws of the Fourth Republic (and of previous Republics too) remained in place unless there were explicit decisions to the contrary. Even in Germany, a paradigm example of regime change, many programs in the contemporary legacy are inherited from earlier regimes. Since 1870 Germany has had the Wilhelmine Reich under a kaiser, the Weimar Republic, the Third Reich of Hitler, and the Federal Republic of Germany, established in 1949 and enlarged in 1990. Yet studies of the rise of the welfare state since the time of Bismarck usually stress continuity (see, e.g., Flora and Heidenheimer, 1981: 18; Alber, 1982).

"Repudiation by exception," like management by exception, is a consequence of the shortage of time to review all the programs that the government of the day inherits. The changes that a new regime wants to introduce usually concentrate on a small number of defining programs that have caused the old regime to become discredited and collapse. For example, a new regime may introduce civilian control of the military, or place responsibility for public order in the hands of officials committed to respect civil rights. The upheavals of twentieth-century Europe have *not* been about programs for education, health care, and social security; these have continued under democratic and authoritarian regimes alike.

Public Continuity and Private Choice

In matters affecting everyday life, ordinary people are likely to prefer continuity to discontinuity. When issues of education, health, and security in old age arise, people are inclined to be risk averse. Parents do not want their children to keep changing schools in search of something better; they want a satisfactory school. People do not want to spend all their time with a doctor or in a hospital; they want to know that medical services will be available as and when needed. People do not want their security in old age, whether in a year, a decade, or a quarter-century hence, to be at the mercy of frequent political choice.

Recurring changes in programs involved in the market show that continuity is preferable only as long as programs produce satisfaction. Because the market is turbulent and conditions can change quickly, an elected government is often forced to choose new economic programs. However, this is not choice for its own sake, but choice with the purpose of adapting the means of public policy to make the nation's economy work better.

Representative government maintains a framework of order, rules, and benefits within which individuals can make their own choices. The object of education is not to teach people what to think but to teach people how to do things for themselves. A national health service does not prescribe what people must do to maintain their health; it offers preventive medicine and recuperative treatment. Older people are not compelled to enter publicly run retirement homes in order to qualify for social security; they receive pensions to spend as they choose.

From the perspective of ordinary people, government coexists with institutions of civil society that offer individuals opportunities to satisfy themselves independent of the state. This point may seem obvious to people raised in a liberal society, but it is a right that could not be taken for granted by people who lived under totalitarianism (cf. Shlapentokh, 1989). In a free society government does not supplant the choices of the market, the choice of friends, or the affection of family. Individuals do not want to turn to the statute book, to bureaucrats, or to elected politicians to be told what to do. The purpose of government is to increase the capacity of individuals to make their own choices.

Just as elected governments depend upon voters, so people in their roles as students, sick and infirm, unemployed or retired persons depend upon public programs. The interdependence of public policy and private welfare is a major characteristic of the contemporary mixed society (Rose, 1989a). The inherited commitments that reduce the choice of policymakers increase the capacity for choice of ordinary people.

References

Alber, Jens. 1982. *Vom Armenhaus zum Wohlfahrtsstaat*. Frankfurt: Campus Verlag.

Allison, Graham T. 1971. *The Essence of Decision: Explaining the Cuban Missile Crisis*. Boston: Little, Brown.

Almond, Gabriel A. 1960. Introduction to Gabriel A. Almond and J. S. Coleman, eds., *The Politics of the Developing Areas*. Princeton: Princeton University Press, 3–64.

Arthur, W. B. 1988. "Self-Reinforcing Mechanisms in Economics." In P. W. Anderson, K. J. Arrow, and D. Pines, eds., *The Economy as an Evolving Complex System*. Santa Fe, N.M.: Santa Fe Institute Studies in the Sciences of Complexity/Addison-Wesley, 5: 9–32.

———. 1989. "Competing Technologies, Increasing Returns and Lock-in by Historical Events." *Economic Journal* 99, no. 1: 116–31.

Bachrach, Peter, and Morton Baratz. 1962. "The Two Faces of Power." *American Political Science Review* 56, no. 4: 947–52.

Baldwin, David. 1990. *The Politics of Social Solidarity:* Class Bases of the European Welfare State 1875–1975. New York: Cambridge University Press.

Barnett, Joel. 1982. *Inside the Treasury*. London: Deutsch.

Baumol, W. J. 1967. "Macro-Economics of Unbalanced Growth: The Anatomy of Urban Crisis." *American Economic Review* 57: 415–26.

Becker, Gary. 1976. *The Economic Approach to Human Behavior*. Chicago: University of Chicago Press.

Beer, Samuel H. 1982. *Modern British Politics*. 2d ed. London: Faber and Faber.

Bendor, Jonathan, and Thomas H. Hammond. 1992. "Rethinking Allison's Models." *American Political Science Review* 86, no. 2: 301–23.

Blais, Andre, and Stephane Dion, eds. 1991. *The Budget-Maximizing Bureaucrat: Appraisals and Evidence*. Pittsburgh: University of Pittsburgh Press.

Bogdanor, Vernon, ed. 1983. *Coalition Government in Western Europe*. London: Heinemann.

Bowen, Elinor R. 1982. "The Pressman-Wildavsky Paradox." *Journal of Public Policy* 2, no. 2: 1–22.

Braybrooke, David, and C. E. Lindblom. 1963. *A Strategy of Decision*. New York: Free Press.

Britton, A. J. C. 1991. *Macroeconomic Policy in Britain. 1974–1987*. Cambridge: Cambridge University Press.

Bulpitt, J. G. 1986. "The Discipline of the New Democracy: Mrs. Thatcher's Statecraft." *Political Studies* 34, no. 1: 19–39.

Butler, D. E., and Dennis Kavanagh. 1974. *The British General Election of February 1974*. London: Macmillan.

Butler, D. E., and Richard Rose. 1960. *The British General Election of 1959*. London: Macmillan.

Castles, F. G., ed. 1982. *The Impact of Parties*. Beverly Hills, Calif.: Sage Publications.

Cecil, Lord Hugh. 1912. *Conservatism*. London: Williams and Norgate.

Central Statistical Office. 1988. *Social Trends*. Vol. 18. London: HMSO.

Chester, Sir Norman. 1981. *The English Administrative System, 1780–1870*. Oxford: Clarendon Press.

Clarke, Harold D., Marianne Stewart, and Gary Zuk, eds. 1989. *Economic Decline and Political Change*. Pittsburgh: University of Pittsburgh Press.

Cm. 540. 1988. *Employment for the 1990s*. London: HMSO.

Cmnd. 9691. 1985. *Reform of Social Security: Programme for Action*. London: HMSO.

Cobb, Roger W., and Charles D. Elder. 1972. *Participation in American Politics: The Dynamics of Agenda-Building*. Boston: Allyn and Bacon.

Cohen, Michael D., James G. March, and Johan P. Olsen. 1972. "A Garbage Can Model of Organizational Choice." *Administrative Science Quarterly* 17, no. 1: 1–25.

Congressional Quarterly. 1989. *President Bush: The Challenge Ahead*. Washington, D.C.: CQ Press.

Cox, Gary W., and Samuel Kernell, ed. 1991. *The Politics of Divided Government*. Boulder, Colo.: Westview Press.

Craig, F. W. S. 1975. *British General Election Manifestos, 1900–1974*. London: Macmillan.

Crenshaw, Albert B. 1993. "It's Just a Guess, But It Better Be on the Nose." *Washington Post National Weekly Edition*, 31 May.

Crick, Bernard. 1970. *The Reform of Parliament*. 2d, rev. ed. London: Weidenfeld and Nicolson.

Cronin, Thomas E. 1980. *The State of the Presidency*. 2d ed. Boston: Little Brown.

Crosland, C. A. R. 1956. *The Future of Socialism*. London: Jonathan Cape.

Currie, Martin, and Ian Steedman, Ian. 1990. *Wrestling with Time: Problems in Economic Theory*. Manchester: Manchester University Press.

Dahl, Robert A. 1957. The Concept of Power. *Behavioral Science* 2, 201–15.

———. 1961. *Who Governs? Democracy and Power in an American City*. New Haven: Yale University Press.

Dalton, Russell J., Scott J. Flanagan, and Paul Allen Beck. 1984. "Electoral Change in Advanced Industrial Societies." Princeton: Princeton University Press.

David, Paul A. 1985. "Clio and the Economics of QWERTY." *American Economic Review* 75, no. 2: 332–37.

Davies, Phillip L. 1989. *Continuity in Programme Expenditure: British Data since 1946*. Glasgow: University of Strathclyde Studies in Public Policy, no. 179.

Davies, Phillip L., and Richard Rose. 1988. "Are Programme Resources Related to Organizational Change?" *European Journal of Political Research* 16, no. 1: 73–98.

Dempster, M. A. H., and Aaron Wildavsky. 1979. "On Change, or There Is No Magic Size for an Increment." *Political Studies* 27, no. 4: 371–89.

Deutsch, K. W. 1963. *The Nerves of Government*. New York: Free Press.

Doig, Jameson W., and Erwin Hargrove, eds. 1987. *Leadership and Innovation: A Biographical Perspective on Entrepreneurs in Government*. Baltimore: Johns Hopkins University Press.

Dowell, S. 1884. *A History of Taxation and Taxes in England*. London: Longman.

Downs, Anthony. 1957. *An Economic Theory of Democracy*. New York: Harper.

Dunsire, Andrew, and Christopher Hood. 1989. *Cutback Management in Public Bureaucracies*. Cambridge: Cambridge University Press.

Durr, Robert H. 1993. "What Moves Policy Sentiment?" *American Political Science Review* 87, no. 1: 158–70.

Dyson, Kenneth. 1980. *The State Tradition in Western Europe*. Oxford: Martin Robertson.

Easton, David. 1965a. *A Framework for Political Analysis*. Englewood Cliffs, N.J.: Prentice-Hall.

———. 1965b. *A Systems Analysis of Political Life*. New York: John Wiley.

Eckstein, Harry. 1960. *Pressure-Group Politics*. London: Allen and Unwin.

Edelman, Murray. 1964. *The Symbolic Uses of Politics*. Urbana: University of Illinois Press.

Ehrmann, Henry W. 1976. *Comparative Legal Cultures*. Englewood Cliffs, N.J.: Prentice-Hall.

Etzioni, Amitai. 1988. *The Moral Dimension: Toward a New Economics*. New York: Free Press.

Finer, S. E., ed. 1975. *Adversary Politics and Electoral Reform*. London: Anthony Wigram.

Flora, Peter. 1983. *State, Economy and Society in Western Europe 1815– 1975: A Data Handbook*. Vol. 1. Frankfurt: Campus.

Flora, Peter, and Arnold Heidenheimer, eds. 1981. *The Development of Welfare States in Europe and America*. Brunswick, N.J.: Transaction.

Gandhi, V. P. 1971. "Wagner's Law of Public Expenditure: Do Recent Cross-Section Studies Confirm It?" *Public Finance* 26, no. 1: 44–56.

Hadenius, Axel. 1985. Citizens Strike a Balance: Discontent with Taxes, Content with Spending. *Journal of Public Policy* 5, no. 3: 349–64.

Hall, Peter A., ed. 1989. *The Political Power of Economic Ideas*. Princeton: Princeton University Press.

Headey, Bruce. 1974. *British Cabinet Ministers: The Roles of Politicians in Executive Office*. London: Allen and Unwin.

Heald, David. 1991. The Political Implications of Redefining Public Expenditure in the United Kingdom. *Political Studies* 39, no. 1: 75–99.

Heap, Shaun Hargreaves, Martin Hollis, Bruce Lyons, Robert Sugden, and Albert Weale. 1992. *The Theory of Choice: A Critical Guide*. Oxford: Blackwell.

Heclo, Hugh. 1974. *Modern Social Politics in Britain and Sweden: From Relief to Income Maintenance*. Yale Studies in Political Science, 25. New Haven: Yale University Press.

———. 1978. "Issue Networks and the Executive Establishment." In A. S. King, ed., *The New American Political System*. Washington, D.C.: American Enterprise Institute, 87–124.

———. 1981. "Toward a New Welfare State." In Flora and Heidenheimer, 1981 (q.v.), 383–406.

Heclo, Hugh, and Aaron Wildavsky. 1981. *The Public Government of Private Money*. 2d ed. London: Macmillan.

Heidenheimer, A. J. 1985. "Comparative Public Policy at the Crossroads." *Journal of Public Policy* 5, no. 4: 441–66.

Heller, Peter S. 1981. "Diverging Trends in the Shares of Nominal and Real Government Expenditure in GDP." *National Tax Journal* 34, no. 1: 61–74.

Hennessy, Peter. 1992. *Never Again: Britain, 1945–51*. London: Jonathan Cape.

Hewart, Lord. 1929. *The New Despotism*. London: Ernest Benn.

Hibbs, Douglas. 1987. *The American Political Economy*. Cambridge, Mass.: Harvard University Press.

Hibbs, Douglas, and H. Fassbender, eds. 1981. *Contemporary Political Economy: Studies in the Interdependence of Politics and Economics*. Amsterdam: North Holland.

Holden, Matthew, Jr. 1966. "Imperialism in Bureaucracy." *American Political Science Review* 60, no. 4: 943–51.

Holme, Richard, and Michael Elliott. 1988. *1688–1988: Time for a New Constitution*. London: Macmillan.

Hood, Christopher. 1991. "Stabilization and Cutbacks: A Catastrophe for Government Growth Theory?" *Journal of Theoretical Politics* 3, no. 1: 37–63.

Hood, Christopher, and Andrew Dunsire. 1981. *Bureaumetrics*. Aldershot: Gower.

Ikenberry, G. John. 1988. *Reasons of State*. Ithaca: Cornell University Press.

Ippolito, Dennis. 1990. *Uncertain Legacies: Federal Budget Policy from Roosevelt through Reagan*. Charlottesville: University of Virginia Press.

Jordan, A. Grant. 1981. "Iron Triangles, Woolly Corporatism and Elastic Nets." *Journal of Public Policy*, 1,1, 95–123.

Kaldor, Nicholas. 1972. "The Irrelevance of Equilibrium Economics." *Economic Journal*, 82,4, 1237–55.

Kamlet, Mark S. and Mowery, David C. 1986. Influences on Executive and Congressional Budgetary Priorities. 1955–1981. *American Political Science Review*, 81, 1.

Kamlet, Mark S., Mowery, David C. and Su, Tsai-Tsu. 1988. Upsetting National Priorities? The Reagan Administration's Budgetary Strategy. *American Political Science Review*, 82,4, 2394–1307.

Katzmann, Robert. 1989. "The American Legislative Process as a Signal." *Journal of Public Policy*, 9,3, 287–306.

Kaufman, Herbert. 1976. *Are Government Organizations Immortal?* Washington, DC: Brookings Institution.

———. 1981. *The Administrative Behavior of Federal Bureau Chiefs*. Washington, D.C.: Brookings Institution.

Kingdon, John W. 1984. *Agendas, Alternatives and Public Policies*. Boston: Little Brown.

Kirman, Alan. 1989. The Intrinsic Limits of Modern Economic Theory: the Emperor Has No Clothes. *Economic Journal*, 99 (Conference 1989) 126–39.

Larkey, P., Stolp, C. and Winer, M. 1981. "Theorizing about the Growth of Government." *Journal of Public Policy*, 1,2, 157–220.

Laver, Michael and Schofield, Norman. 1990. *Multiparty Government: the Politics of Coalition in Europe*. Oxford: Oxford University Press.

Lazarsfeld, Paul, Berelson, Bernard, and Gaudet, Hazel. 1944. *The People's Choice*. New York: Duell, Sloan and Pearce.

Lee, J.M. 1980. *The Churchill Coalition. 1940–1945*. London: B.T. Batsford.

Levine, Charles, ed. 1978. Organizational Decline and Cutback Management: a Symposium, *Public Administration Review*, 38, 4, 316–25.

Lewis-Beck, Michael S. 1989. *Economics and Elections: the Major Western Democracies*. Ann Arbor: University of Michigan Press.

Light, Paul. 1982. *The President's Agenda*. Baltimore: Johns Hopkins University Press.

Likierman, Andrew. 1988. *Public Expenditure*. Harmondsworth: Penguin.

Little, I.M.D. 1963. *A Critique of Welfare Economics*. Oxford: Clarendon Press.

MacGregor, John. 1986. Unpublished letter of 6th February to Rt. Hon. Robert Sheldon MP, Chairman of Public Accounts Committee, on sources of public expenditure data. London: H.M. Treasury.

Mackenzie, W.J.M. 1976. "The Plowden Report: a Translation." In R. Rose, ed., *Policy-Making in British Government*. London: Macmillan, 273–81.

MacKuen, Michael B., Erickson, R.S. and Stimson, J.A. 1992. "Peasants or Bankers? The American Electorate and the U.S. Economy." *American Political Science Review*, 86, 3, 597–611.

Majone, Giandomenico. 1989. *Evidence, Argument and Persuasion in the Policy Process*. New Haven: Yale University Press.

Mayhew, David R. 1974. *Congress: The Electoral Connection*. New Haven: Yale University Press

———. 1991. *Divided Government*. New Haven: Yale University Press.

Mommsen, W. J., ed. 1981. *The Emergence of the Welfare State in Britain and Germany, 1850–1950*. London: Croom Helm.

Morishima, M. 1984. "The Good and Bad Uses of Mathematics." In P. Wiles and G. North, eds., *Economics in Disarray*. Oxford: Basil Blackwell.

Mosley, Paul. 1984a. *The Making of Economic Policy*. Brighton: Wheatsheaf Books.

———. 1984b. "Popularity Functions and the Role of the Media." *British Journal of Political Science* 14, no. 1: 117–28.

Mueller, Dennis C. 1989. *Public Choice II*. Rev. ed. Cambridge: Cambridge University Press.

Mufson, Steven. 1992. "Mortgage on America." *Washington Post Weekly Edition*, 5 October:6–7.

Muris, Timothy J. 1989. *The Uses and Abuses of Budget Baselines*. Hoover Institution Working Papers in Political Science P-89–3. Stanford, Calif.: Hoover Institution.

Neustadt, Richard E., and Ernest R. May. 1986. *Thinking in Time: The Uses of History for Decision Makers*. New York: Free Press.

Oakeshott, Michael. 1951. *Political Education*. Cambridge: Bowes and Bowes.

Organisation for Economic Co-Operation and Development [OECD]. 1985. *Social Expenditure, 1960–1990*. Paris: OECD.

———. 1988. *Why Economic Policies Change Course*. Paris: OECD.

Office of Management and Budget. 1990. *Budget of the United States Government: Fiscal Year 1991*. Washington, D.C.: GPO.

———. 1992. *Budget of the United States Government: Fiscal Year 1993*. Washington, D.C.: GPO.

———. 1993. *Budget of the United States Government: Fiscal Year 1994*. Washington, D.C.: GPO.

Olson, Mancur, Jr. 1968. "Economics, Sociology and the Best of All Possible Worlds." *Public Interest*, no. 12.

Page, Edward C. 1985. "Law as an Instrument of Policy." *Journal of Public Policy* 5, no. 2: 241–67.

Palma, Giuseppe di. 1977. *Surviving without Governing: Italian Parties in Parliament*. Berkeley and Los Angeles: University of California Press.

Parry, Geraint, and Peter Morriss. 1974. "When Is a Decision Not a Decision?" In Ivor Crewe, ed., *Elites in Western Democracies*. London: Croom Helm, 317–36.

Peacock, A., and J. Wiseman. 1961. *The Growth of Public Expenditure in the United Kingdom*. Princeton: Princeton University Press.

Pempel, T. J., ed. 1990. *Uncommon Democracies: The One-Party Dominant Regimes*. Ithaca: Cornell University Press.

Pfiffner, James P. 1988. *The Strategic Presidency: Hitting the Ground Running*. Chicago: Dorsey Press.

Poggi, Gianfranco. 1978. *The Development of the Modern State*. London: Hutchinson.

Pollitt, Christopher. 1984. *Manipulating the Machine: Changing the Pattern of Ministerial Departments, 1960–83*. London: Allen and Unwin.

Polsby, Nelson W. 1984. *Political Innovation in America: The Politics of Policy Initiation*. New Haven: Yale University Press.

Powell, G. Bingham, ed. 1991. "Symposium on Divided Government." *Governance* 4, no. 3: 231–94.

Pressman, Jeffrey L., and Aaron Wildavsky. 1973. *Implementation*. Berkeley and Los Angeles: University of California Press.

Prowse, Michael. 1993. "The Hallelujah Budget Plan." *Financial Times*, 19 July.

Rickets, Martin, and Edward Shoesmith. 1990. *British Economic Opinion: A Survey of a Thousand Economists*. London: Institute of Economic Affairs.

Ringen, Stein. 1987. *The Possibility of Politics: A Study in the Political Economy of the Welfare State*. Oxford: Clarendon Press.

Robbins, Lionel C. 1935. *An Essay on the Nature and Significance of Economic Science*. 2d ed. London: Macmillan.

Robinson, Joan. 1979. *Collected Economic Papers of Joan Robinson*. Oxford: Basil Blackwell.

Rose, Richard. 1965. "England: A Traditionally Modern Culture." In L. W. Pye and S. Verba, eds., *Political Culture and Political Development*. Princeton: Princeton University Press, 83–129.

———. 1972. "The Market for Policy Indicators." In A. Shonfield and S. Shaw, eds., *Social Indicators and Social Policy*. London: Heinemann, 119–41.

————. 1976. "On the Priorities of Government." *European Journal of Political Research* 4, no. 3: 247–89.

————. 1982. *Understanding the United Kingdom: The Territorial Dimension in Government.* London: Longmans.

————. 1984. *Do Parties Make a Difference?* 2d ed. London: Macmillan.

————. 1985a. "The Programme Approach to the Growth of Government." *British Journal of Political Science* 15, no. 1: 1–28.

————. 1985b. *Public Employment in Western Nations.* Cambridge: Cambridge University Press.

————. 1986a. "Law as a Resource of Public Policy." *Parliamentary Affairs* 39, no. 3: 297–314.

————. 1986b. "Common Goals but Different Roles: The State's Contribution to the Welfare Mix." In Richard Rose and Rei Shiratori, eds., *The Welfare State East and West.* New York: Oxford University Press, 13–39.

————. 1987a. *Ministers and Ministries: A Functional Analysis.* Oxford: Clarendon Press.

————. 1987b. "Steering the Ship of State: One Tiller but Two Pairs of Hands." *British Journal of Political Science* 17, no. 4: 409–33.

————. 1988. "The Growth of Government Organizations: Do We Count the Number or Weigh the Programs?" In C. Campbell and B. G. Peters, eds., *Organizing Governance, Governing Organizations.* Pittsburgh: University of Pittsburgh Press, 99–128.

————. 1989a. *Ordinary People in Public Policy: A Behavioural Analysis.* Newbury Park, Calif.: Sage Publications.

————. 1989b. "Political Economy and Public Policy: The Problem of Joint Appraisal." In Warren J. Samuels, ed., *Fundamentals of the Economic Role of Government.* Westport, Conn: Greenwood Press, 157–66.

————. 1990. "Inheritance before Choice in Public Policy," *Journal of Theoretical Politics* 2, no. 3: 263–91.

————. 1991a. "Is American Public Policy Exceptional?" In Byron E. Shafer, ed., *Is America Different? A New Look at American Exceptionalism.* Oxford: Clarendon Press, 187–221.

————. 1991b. "Prime Ministers in Parliamentary Systems." *West European Politics* 14, no. 2: 8–24.

————. 1991c. "Prospective Evaluation through Comparative Analysis." In Paul Ryan, ed., *International Comparisons of Vocational Education and Training.* London: Falmer Press, 68–92.

————. 1993. *Lesson-Drawing in Public Policy: A Guide to Learning across Time and Space*. Chatham, N.J.: Chatham House.

Rose, Richard, et al. 1992. "Periodisation in Post-War Britain: Transcript of a Witness Seminar." *Contemporary Record* 6, no. 2: 326–40.

Rose, Richard, and Terence Karran. 1987. *Taxation by Political Inertia*. London: Allen and Unwin.

Rose, Richard, and Ian McAllister. 1990. *The Loyalties of Voters*. Newbury Park, Calif.: Sage Publications.

————. 1992. "Expressive versus Instrumental Voting." In Dennis A. Kavanagh, ed., *Electoral Politics*. Oxford: Clarendon Press, 114–40.

Rose, Richard, and Edward C. Page. 1990. "Action in Adversity: Responses to Unemployment in Britain and Germany." *West European Politics* 13, no. 4: 66–81.

Rowen, Hobart. 1990. "In Deep Voodoo." *Washington Post National Weekly Edition,* 8 April.

Sartori, Giovanni, ed. 1984. *Social Science Concepts*. Beverly Hills, Calif.: Sage Publications.

Scheuch, Erwin K. 1966. "Cross-National Comparisons Using Aggregate Data." In Richard L. Merritt and Stein Rokkan, eds., *Comparing Nations: The Use of Quantitative Data in Cross-National Research*. New Haven: Yale University Press, 131–68.

Schumpeter, Joseph A. 1946. "The American Economy in the Interwar Period." *American Economic Review* 36, suppl.:1–10.

————. 1952. *Capitalism, Socialism and Democracy*. 4th ed. London: Allen and Unwin.

Sen, Amartya K. 1977. "Rational Fools: A Critique of the Behavioral Foundations of Economic Theory." *Philosophy and Public Affairs* 6, no. 4: 317–44.

Shackle, G. L. S. 1966. *The Nature of Economic Thought*. Cambridge: Cambridge University Press.

Sharkansky, Ira. 1970. *The Routines of Politics*. New York: Van Nostrand Reinhold.

Sharpe, L. J., and K. Newton. 1984. *Does Politics Matter?* Oxford: Clarendon Press.

Shklar, Judith. 1964. "Decisionism." In C. J. Friedrich, ed., *Rational Decision,* New York: Atherton. *Nomos,* volume 7, 3–17.

Simon, Herbert A. 1957. *Models of Man*. New York: John Wiley.

————. 1969. *The Sciences of the Artificial*. Cambridge, Mass.: MIT Press.

————. 1978. "Rationality as a Process and as Product of Thought." *American Economic Review* 68, no. 2: 1–16.

————. 1979. "Rational Decisionmaking in Business Organizations." *American Economic Review* 69, no. 4: 493–513.

Skocpol, Theda. 1987. "A Society without a State? Political Organization, Social Conflict, and Welfare Provision in the United States." *Journal of Public Policy* 7, no. 4: 349–72.

Skowronek, Stephen. 1988. "Presidential Leadership in Political Time." In Michael Nelson, ed., *The Presidency and the Political System*. Washington, D.C.: CQ Press, 117–62.

Solow, Robert M. 1985. "Economic History and Economics." *American Economic Review* 75, no. 2: 328–31.

Stanley, Harold W., and Richard G. Niemi. 1988. *Vital Statistics on American Politics*. Washington, D.C.: CQ Press.

Statutory Publications Office. 1982. *Index to the Statutes*. 2 vols. London: HMSO.

Stockman, David. 1986. *The Triumph of Politics*. New York: Harper and Row.

Stokes, Donald. 1963. "Spatial Models of Party Competition." *American Political Science Review* 57, no. 2: 368–77.

Tarschys, Daniel. 1975. "The Growth of Public Expenditure: Nine Modes of Explanation." *Scandinavian Political Studies Yearbook*, no. 10: 9–21.

————. 1985. "Curbing Public Expenditure: Current Trends." *Journal of Public Policy* 5, no. 1: 23–68.

Thurber, James A., ed. 1991. *Divided Democracy*. Washington, D.C.: CQ Press.

Titmuss, R.M. 1950. *Problems of Social Policy*. London: HMSO and Longmans.

Treasury. 1993. *Financial Statement and Budget Report, 1993–94*. London: HMSO House of Commons Paper 547.

Treasury and Civil Service Committee. 1991. *Memoranda on Official Economic Forecasting*. London: HMSO House of Commons 532-i.

Van Mechelen, Denis, and Richard Rose. 1986. *Patterns of Parliamentary Legislation*. Aldershot: Gower.

Weaver, R. Kent. 1986. "The Politics of Blame Avoidance." *Journal of Public Policy* 6, no. 4: 371–98.

———. 1988. *Automatic Government: the Politics of Indexation.* Washington, D.C.: Brookings Institution.

Webber, Carol, and Aaron Wildavsky. 1986. *A History of Taxation and Expenditure in the Western World.* New York: Simon and Schuster.

Weber, Max. 1922. *Economy and Society.* Edited by G. Roth and C. Wittich. New York: Bedminster Press, 1968.

White, Joseph, and Aaron Wildavsky. 1989. *The Deficit and the Public Interest: The Search for Responsible Budgeting in the 1980s.* Berkeley and Los Angeles: University of California Press.

Wildavsky, Aaron. 1975. *Budgeting: a Comparative Theory of Budgetary Processes.* Boston: Little, Brown.

———. 1980. *How to Limit Government Spending.* Berkeley and Los Angeles: University of California Press.

———. 1988. *The New Politics of the Budgetary Process.* Glenview, Ill.: Scott, Foresman.

Wilensky, Harold L. 1975. *The Welfare State and Equality.* Berkeley and Los Angeles: University of California Press.

Wood, David. 1971. "Birth of a Population Policy." *The Times* (London), 8 March.

Young, Hugo. 1982. "Wreckers or Obedient Servants? The Other Side of the Treasury Men." *The Times* (London), 25 February.

INDEX